DOORDARSHAN DAYS

Doordarshan Days

BHASKAR GHOSE

PENGUIN
VIKING
An imprint of Penguin Random House

VIKING

USA | Canada | UK | Ireland | Australia
New Zealand | India | South Africa | China | Singapore

Viking is part of the Penguin Random House group of companies
whose addresses can be found at global.penguinrandomhouse.com

Published by Penguin Random House India Pvt. Ltd
4th Floor, Capital Tower 1, MG Road,
Gurugram 122 002, Haryana, India

First published in Viking by Penguin Books India 2005

10 9 8 7 6 5 4 3

The views and opinions expressed in this book are the author's own and the facts are as reported by him which have been verified to the extent possible, and the publishers are not in any way liable for the same.

ISBN 9780670058341

Typeset in Sabon by Mantra Virtual Services, New Delhi
Printed at Replika Press Pvt. Ltd, India

www.penguin.co.in

To the memory of my mother and father,
Prafulla Devi and Nalini Mohan Ghose

Contents

Prologue

Summons from Delhi

I suppose the appropriate way to begin would be to recount my joining as director general (DG) of Doordarshan, and go on from there; but that seems a rather conventional way, too much the expected beginning. My days in Doordarshan were—if I were to use just one phrase—colourful and breathlessly exciting, and in recounting them I think it is fitting to set this seminal change in my career in a context that is vivid and detailed, if only to highlight just how great a transformation it was.

This, then, was the setting when it all began: the monsoon in north Bengal. The first weeks are savage; the rain comes down in near-opaque sheets, the hissing, roaring sound drowning out everything else. Blown about by the unruly wind it pours in through open windows and doors and gathers in large pools on the floors, leaving curtains, rugs and furniture dank, smelling of musty old clothes. There is a scurry to shut windows and doors against the onslaught, and each house retreats into the solitude brought by the insistent rain, cascading off the sloping roofs and the leaves of the trees. The outside world consists only of rain, grey, glistening and loud. Nearby houses appear as faint dark shadows and melt into the sheets of rain sluicing down, punctuated by the occasional rumble of thunder.

The palatial commissioner's bungalow in Jalpaiguri, a town huddled in the plains just below the mountains of the north, lessened the rain's menace and the isolation with which it enveloped smaller dwellings. From its deeply recessed large windows I could see the grey, hazy tangle of trees that lined the embankment in front of the big house, cutting it away from a wide expanse of grass that sloped into the giant Teesta river. Some years ago the Teesta, fiercely unruly, had begun tearing into the land in front of the house. Frightened engineers, and even more terrified commissioners, decided to raise the embankment, closing in the wide sunlit view from the house. That was all it did, actually; by the time the embankment was completed the restless river had eaten its fill in front of the large, gracious house, and turned its attention to the left bank more than half a mile away, leaving the embankment nothing more than an obstruction, serving no purpose except to block what must have been an enchanting view of a great green slope sweeping down to the turbulent, swirling river.

In the middle of the first lashing downpour of the monsoon of 1986, early in June, I had only just returned to that great bungalow I called home, being then the commissioner of north Bengal. In spite of the rain I was relieved to be back, and the tension coiled within me had begun to ease and ebb slowly out of my system. The past few days in Darjeeling had been a bit of a trial; the Gorkha National Liberation Front (GNLF) led by Subhas Ghising, a man once considered charismatic though eccentric, had just shown the enormous influence it enjoyed in the mountain regions of Darjeeling district. They had called a *bandh* of the district for the second time in less than a month, and, like the first one, it had been total. Every shop in every town and village in the mountains was shut. Darjeeling was a ghost town, with only policemen patrolling the streets on foot and by the odd police jeep. These, too, soon stopped, for the ingenious cadres of the GNLF devised a way of puncturing their tyres: they cut potatoes in half, embedded sharp nails in them, and then hid them in the myriad little potholes that the rains had filled with muddy water. It took a relatively short time to immobilize most of the jeeps.

I had been in Darjeeling trying to determine, with the deputy commissioner (as the district magistrate was then called), G. Balagopal, and the police authorities, what could be done to counter this virtual takeover of authority from the government. Attempts to talk to Subhas Ghising proved futile, as he insisted on talking only to the chief minister and only about the creation of a separate state called 'Gorkhaland'. This was just the beginning of an agitation that was to go on for a number of years till a compromise formula was worked out.

As messages were exchanged through intermediaries, the bandh continued, and the inevitable problems began to appear—shortages of food and essential supplies, marooned tourists unable to get down to Siliguri in the foothills, the railhead and also the town closest to the airport, Bagdogra, that linked Darjeeling to Calcutta and Delhi. We had asked for, and got, some units of the Central Reserve Police Force (CRPF), but patrolling on foot was all they and the local police could do. Without large vehicles to bring in supplies of food, and, more importantly, without shops opening to make all of this available to the people, the inhabitants of all the towns in the mountains where the GNLF writ ran—virtually the entire region—were confined to their homes, living on what little they had stored away.

Caught up in all this I was startled by a telephone call from Delhi. A call from the Prime Minister's Office, from a joint secretary who was not only a colleague but a friend, R. Vasudevan.

'The PM wants to know what the situation is like up there,' Vasu told me. 'You'll have to come to Delhi as quickly as you can.'

I was astonished and mystified. Why did they want me to go and brief them? I rang the chief secretary of West Bengal, S.V. Krishnan, at once and told him what Vasu had said. Krishnan too was surprised.

'Why you, I say?' he demanded. 'They could have spoken to me or the home secretary.'

I told him I had no idea why they wanted me to brief them.

'Have you been speaking to them?' he asked suspiciously.

The state was run by the CPI(M)-led Left Front, and the central government was run by the Congress under Rajiv Gandhi; relations between them were not exactly hostile, but wary. Neither trusted the other very much. In fact, a little later there were whispers among the Left Front leaders that the GNLF agitation could well have been inspired by agencies of the central government. Thus Krishnan's question seemed to me to insinuate that I was keeping some kind of clandestine contact with the Centre.

'I've no reason to do that,' I told him. 'The Centre has its Intelligence Bureau offices here and must be perfectly aware of what's going on.'

'Well, if they want you to brief them,' the chief secretary said with what seemed a distinct lack of grace, 'you'd better go. But come to Calcutta first and show me exactly what kind of report you're taking with you. And you must meet the chief minister before you go.'

This was the reason for my forced return to Jalpaiguri in the monsoon deluge. My car had a pilot jeep in front of it and one behind, and we had to inch our way down, behind policemen who cleared the road of the nail-embedded bits of potatoes that were liberally strewn about. By the time we reached the plains they had collected a sackful of these. We passed a CRPF truck standing on the road, a few of the CRPF men standing disconsolately around—all its tyres had been deflated by these improvised spikes. The policemen clearing the road ahead of my car advised them to do the same, if and when they got their spare tyres, for which they had sent a radio message to their camp.

'That we will do,' one of them said morosely, 'and we will get to Darjeeling tomorrow morning instead of this afternoon.' The GNLF had clearly got a firm grip on events, as well as on the people.

I arrived in Calcutta the next day and went straight to the chief secretary. He received me with little enthusiasm and a great deal of curiosity.

'Why the hell do they want you, I say?' he kept asking, as if to underscore the fact that a divisional commissioner in West Bengal is hardly the person to brief the prime minister's staff on anything. This was true—most commissioners have a limited role in the administration of the districts nominally under their charge; the district magistrates report directly to the state government. The more compassionate among them keep their commissioner informed; the rest don't bother. But north Bengal was different, something of which Krishnan was well aware. The divisional commissioner there was also the secretary, Department of Hill Affairs, of which the minister in charge was the chief minister himself, then Jyoti Basu. Therefore I met the chief minister regularly to dispose of official business, and, when that was over, he invariably asked about administrative matters in my division. Krishnan must have known only too well that I had a far closer working relationship with the chief minister than other commissioners, which was something he must not have fancied too much. There was little he could do about it, I suppose, except put in the odd snide remark. There was, as I am sure he knew, some justification in the Government of India wanting to hear about the GNLF agitation from me. Whether it merited a summons to the Prime Minister's Office was another matter; it mystified me as much as it must have exasperated Krishnan.

The chief minister, when I met him, was his usual calm, terse self.

'If they want to ask you about the GNLF,' Jyoti Basu said, 'it doesn't matter very much. But don't commit yourself to anything.'

Armed with this advice I set off for Delhi. On the way I kept wondering about the oddity of the whole business and I couldn't help feeling a little uneasy. Did they want me to work on behalf of the central government? Were they really thinking of carving out a separate state of Gorkhaland? That would put me in an awkward position. As a state government officer I couldn't very well act as an agent of the Centre if that meant going against the policy of the state, and the chief minister was absolutely firm that the mountain regions of Darjeeling could never be separated from the rest of West Bengal. But Indira Gandhi had turned Sikkim into a full-fledged state, even though in terms of size and population it was smaller than the Kalimpong subdivision of Darjeeling district. So why wouldn't her son try to make a much larger area, which was geographically, ethnically and in every other way quite different from the rest of West Bengal, a state? Assam had been broken up into six states, for reasons that were very similar. *But why ask me?*

We touched down at Palam, and the heat into which I came out from the cool interior of the plane was like stepping into a blast furnace. The monsoon was still a month or more away; Delhi lay scorched and shrivelled under the brazen sun, and hot winds blew thick dust from the desert of Rajasthan over it. The dust got into clothes and rooms and covered chairs, tables and floors; it hung like a dark hot shadow over the city. In June, Delhi is the nearest one can get to what we are made to believe is hell. Jalpaiguri, the torrential rains there and the closed, silent town of Darjeeling, seemed very far away.

I rang Vasudevan in the Prime Minister's Office and was asked to come over immediately. In his cool, darkened room Vasudevan, a tall, relaxed, handsome man, his thick dark hair tumbling over his forehead, smiled indulgently when I handed him my carefully prepared report on the separatist agitation in Darjeeling. He barely looked at it, and said, 'Ah yes, the Gorkhaland business. Never mind that for the moment. We haven't really called you for that. Do you know anything about television?'

I gaped at him. *Television?*

'Well,' I said, 'I mean, I watch it sometimes, and I've done a few interviews on Doordarshan some years ago, but . . .'

'Just get to know something about it,' Vasu said genially, and stood up. 'I think you'd better come and meet Gopi.' This was Gopi Arora, the one man in whom the prime minister had complete trust, and who was consequently a very formidable person in the corridors of power. He was also someone I had known before he had become the *eminence grise* he now was and we got along well.

Gopi—a small, thin man with a look of intense concentration on his face and an almost constant nervous manner of speaking, explaining an issue, or commenting on an incident—was one of the shrewdest officers in the government. Beneath that seemingly nervous exterior was an uncanny ability to size up people and situations. He looked at you only occasionally, but when he did his eyes were speculative, cool and appraising; you felt you were being assessed in the brief moment he looked at you before looking away.

'No, no, this Gorkhaland thing is quite serious,' he said nervously. 'But you needn't concern yourself with it. Not just now. The prime minister wants a good director general for Doordarshan. You'll have to meet him. That's why we called you here.'

'Meet the prime minister,' I repeated mechanically. 'When?'

'Oh, tomorrow, I think. We've slotted you into his schedule,' he said, looking through his papers. 'Yes, here. You'll see him at 3 p.m.'

'How do I—'

'Vasu will tell you,' Gopi said earnestly. 'Oh, Vasu. After that we must discuss the Gorkhaland situation with him. I mean we can't just . . .' he trailed off and was lost in a file.

I was not just astonished but aghast at having to see the prime minister in a shabby half-sleeved shirt, which was all I had brought as a change, thinking I would talk to the officers in the Prime Minister's Office and leave the following day. Years of training in the National Academy of Administration in Mussoorie and as a probationer in a district had conditioned me to dress 'properly' when meeting the Great and the Powerful—and whatever that was meant to be in summer, it wasn't a shabby half-sleeved shirt and creased trousers. But I had nothing else except that; however, I did manage to have the trousers pressed that evening. I was ushered into the prime minister's room the next afternoon by a disdainful orderly.

Rajiv Gandhi was immaculately dressed in a light cream button-up coat and trousers, looking cool and elegant. Seeing him made me acutely aware of how scruffy I must have looked. He smiled that very charming smile of his, though, and waved me to a chair. He did ask me, rather perfunctorily, about what was happening in Darjeeling, but soon got down to what he had brought me to Delhi to say.

'I'm very worried about Doordarshan,' he said. 'I think we need to do something drastic to make it show more attractive and meaningful programmes. Have you watched it? What do you think?'

'Well, sir,' said that sly improviser and sometime actor Bhaskar Ghose, looking earnest and concerned, 'I think we need to change the people, at least some of them, bring in fresh blood.' (I had prepared this beforehand, I need hardly add.)

Rajiv Gandhi brightened and smiled. 'Exactly!' he said. 'That's what I've been telling Gopi. Good, good. Who would you get?'

I searched hurriedly for a convincing answer. 'Perhaps we could bring in people from outside,' I said mendaciously, with no idea what that meant.

'That's it!' the prime minister said, nodding. 'I see you've got the right ideas.'

What ideas? I thought frantically.

He looked at his watch and said, 'Right, we'll get the paperwork done and send you your orders. Can you join in, say, a fortnight?'

Without thinking, I said I could.

'That's settled, then,' he said. 'And remember, you can always walk in or ring up if you need anything or if anyone gets in your hair. I think the government's got its fingers stuck too far inside Doordarshan. You'll have to pull them out.' He called his private secretary, George, into the room. 'George,' he said, 'put through any call Bhaskar Ghose may make to me once he takes over Doordarshan. And give him an appointment whenever he asks for it. Okay, I'll see you when you've joined.' He smiled at me and picked up a file. The interview was over.

Having been seen out by a much friendlier George, I went straight to Gopi's room, where both he and Vasu were waiting for me.

'What happened?' Gopi asked me in his nervous manner.

'He wants me to be DG of Doordarshan,' I told him.

Vasu smiled broadly and said, 'Great!'

Not surprisingly, Gopi looked worried. 'Yes, yes,' he said, almost to himself, 'I told him you would be suitable.' He paused, thinking about something, then looked up at Vasu. 'We'll need the UPSC's approval,' he said anxiously, meaning the Union Public Service Commission.

Vasu smiled comfortably and said, 'That's all right. We'll get it. Okay, then, Bhaskar, you just go back and wait for your orders.'

'No, no,' Gopi said in a worried tone. 'We must discuss the Gorkhaland thing with him. That's why he's here, officially. He has to discuss it . . . What's going on there, Bhaskar?'

I told him, in a few sentences, while he nodded distractedly.

'Yes, yes,' he said. 'I'm sure the home ministry's been in touch with Calcutta.'

The charade was over. As I turned to go, he suddenly called out, 'Oh Bhaskar,' he said, 'don't mention this to anyone just yet, all right? Just . . . just for a few days. We'll send the orders soon. You go back and tell them we discussed the Gorkhaland agitation.'

I did just that. I saw Gopi's shrewdness in actually having gone through the motions of a discussion on the Gorkhaland agitation, and was able to tell the suspicious Krishnan when I got to Calcutta, quite truthfully, that I had discussed Gorkhaland with the prime minister's officers. I added that Gopi had told me the home ministry would have been in touch with the state authorities. That seemed to satisfy him, and I returned to the dark skies and incessant rain of Jalpaiguri.

Why, I wondered over and over again, had I been chosen by Rajiv Gandhi as the new DG of Doordarshan? I couldn't find an answer that was entirely satisfactory, but I suspected that Rajiv and his aides had decided that none of the Doordarshan officers were suited to head the network—they wanted an Indian Administrative Service (IAS) officer. They needed to find someone in the IAS who had some sort of connection with either the medium or the performing arts. Both Gopi and Vasu knew that I had been involved with theatre for many years in my spare time, that I had acted in and directed a number of major plays in Delhi. They may have thought that my theatre experience would be of some help in managing an audio-visual medium like television, and suggested that Rajiv—who wanted to make the appointment himself—talk to me and decide if I would do.

Weeks passed, but I heard nothing. I stayed on in Jalpaiguri; returning to Darjeeling was not only going to mean a painfully slow journey back, but I wasn't really needed there. The able Balagopal had things well in hand. Also, I wanted to be in Jalpaiguri when the appointment orders came. In the meantime I watched Doordarshan avidly.

There was, in 1986, no other television network to watch. I watched even the profoundly boring programmes on development and the soap operas. There was an engaging serial called *Trishna* that was an adaptation of Jane Austen's *Pride and Prejudice*; the counterparts of the Bennet girls were all fashion models who couldn't act for toffee, except for one, who later made quite a name for herself as an actress on stage, in television and in films: Kittu Gidwani. While I watched *Trishna* and a lot of rubbish, hoping I would learn something about the thing called television, no orders came. Outside, the rain continued to fall from an iron-grey sky.

Just when I had begun telling myself that they must have found someone else, the chief secretary rang me up. 'You've been appointed DG of Doordarshan,' he said almost accusingly. 'I've been asked to relieve you immediately. But will you go?'

'Of course I will,' I said.

'All right,' Krishnan said without enthusiasm. Then he added, fretfully, 'It's most inconvenient for me. Who the hell do I send in your place? And with this damn Gorkhaland business starting to heat up. Anyway, the chief minister's agreed, God knows why. He wasn't even surprised. You'd better see him before you go.'

Jyoti Basu had a grim smile on his face when I went into his room. 'I knew that all that business about wanting to discuss the Gorkhaland agitation with you was nonsense,' he said. 'They were sounding you out for this Doordarshan post. Did Rajiv see you?'

'Yes, sir,' I said. 'He did.'

'I thought so. That's why they invented all this—,' waving his hand. 'It was unnecessary. If he'd asked me I'd have told him you could go.' His smile broadened, just a little. 'It's a thankless job. But go on, do the best you can.'

I kept quiet.

'You won't be able to do anything, you know,' he continued. 'They won't let you. Doordarshan is part of the Congress propaganda machine. But try. See what they let you do.'

It seemed a cynical view then, but, as I was to find out at my own cost, not incorrect.

It was still raining when I left Jalpaiguri. I couldn't help a slight melancholy as I passed through the gates of the great house I had lived in for some years, surrounded by giant trees and unruly bright green grass. One would have thought that living alone in a big house would have been a rather miserable business, but it wasn't. There was something about the house I cannot explain, a feeling of tranquillity and wholesomeness that surrounded me every time I came into it and climbed the big staircase that led to the large airy rooms on the first floor. It was as if the house was welcoming me back, and then enclosing me in an invisible cocoon of security and goodwill. I secretly revelled in the days when I was there on weekends, or on a day when everything was closed. That friendly, comforting envelope made me feel wonderfully at peace with myself and with everything else.

Now I left that behind me and headed towards Bagdogra. Would I ever come back, I wondered, and would I ever feel as tranquil as I did in that big house? Would I have changed my mind if I had known then that the answer to both was an emphatic 'No'? Probably not. Ambition lurks somewhere in the corners of the consciousness of every human being, except that some call it by other names. The sky was dark and low, rain-filled clouds scudding through the damp air. As I neared the airport the rain came down heavily, and the tall mountains were hidden behind it. I had to wait in the little airport restaurant for the rain to stop and the sky to clear, and through the banks of clouds the silver Boeing 737 came in, sinking to the ground, nose pointing enquiringly up, and then, as the wheels touched the runway, the roar of the reverse thrust drowned everything out. The plane slowed and turned towards the terminal building, now no longer graceful and fast, but clumsy and uncertain as it whined up to the apron. Finally the engines fell silent. Here was my passage to another world, one that seemed mysterious but vaguely exciting.

Delhi was oppressively humid when I got there. The sun was fierce and relentlessly bright, as it usually is in August. I was glad to get out of the burning heat of the car sent by the West Bengal government office in Delhi and into the flat in Defence Colony. As soon as I had put away my stuff I rang Suresh Mathur, an IAS officer a few years my senior who was DG of All India Radio (AIR), and temporarily holding charge of the post of DG of Doordarshan till I joined. I had met Suresh some years before, when he had come to Calcutta with Siddhartha Shankar Ray, who had been appointed chief minister of West Bengal by Indira Gandhi when the Congress party won its last election there in 1972, after Indira Gandhi had carved Bangladesh out of a livid but impotent Pakistan.

There was something about Suresh Mathur—our paths crossed a number of times and in ways that seemed strange to me. He was appointed secretary to the chief minister, having been Siddhartha Ray's special assistant when the latter was education minister and minister for West Bengal affairs during the period just before the elections, when the state was under President's Rule. He was perhaps one of the few officers Ray trusted then. I was another. I was formally director of census operations, a post under the home ministry, but also functioned part-time as a deputy secretary in the home ministry looking after matters that came up before the minister for West Bengal affairs. That brought me into contact with Suresh Mathur for the first time and I found him jovial and good-humoured.

However, there were some raised eyebrows when Suresh, who was from the Madhya Pradesh cadre, became secretary to the chief minister, a post earmarked for IAS officers of the state cadre. He began work in an atmosphere that was frosty, to say the least. This did not bother him at all.

'Listen, yaar,' he once said casually, 'I'll be here for as long as the boss wants me to stay and then I'll go back to Delhi. Who gives a fuck what these buggers think?'

But he had got it wrong. The officers, beginning with the chief secretary, began working on the chief minister, not really making things up, but with the odd remark here and there, which made him aware that they didn't much care to have an outsider working in what they saw as a very sensitive post. The ministers, no doubt primed by their secretaries, all West Bengal IAS officers, were more vocal. They complained to the chief minister that Suresh Mathur treated them in a cavalier fashion and that he was becoming a law unto himself. Siddhartha Ray gave in eventually. Within a few months Suresh found himself appointed to the post of West Bengal resident representative and secretary to the chief minister based in New Delhi. I was appointed joint secretary to the chief minister, since I was considered too junior to be the secretary. Inevitably, Suresh found that the rather strange post that he had been given had little or no work that would keep him occupied and got himself a posting in the Government of India. After some months, when I reached the necessary seniority, I was appointed secretary to the chief minister. Whenever I met Suresh afterwards, I got the feeling that he thought I had manoeuvred his exit, which was ridiculous. Even if one assumed that I had, in fact, wanted it to happen, I wouldn't have known how to go about it. Call it naivety or plain stupidity, I just didn't know how to manoeuvre for a post.

Now, years later, we met again as colleagues, and would have to work together. Suresh was his usual loud, good-humoured self on the phone.

'So you've got here,' he said. 'We've been expecting you. When do you want to join?'

'Tomorrow,' I said.

'That's damn quick,' Suresh said with a laugh. 'Don't you want to relax a bit?'

'No,' I told him, thinking of what the prime minister had told me and of all that needed to be done. 'I'd like to join tomorrow.'

'Suit yourself,' Suresh said. 'See you tomorrow, then.' And he hung up.

I went into Mandi House, where Doordarshan was housed then, promptly at 9 a.m. the next day. Mandi House had been the palace of the rajas of Mandi and I think the central government bought it off them years ago and used it for some office or the other till it became necessary to find Doordarshan a headquarters. Even today some of the old timers call the headquarters of Doordarshan Mandi House, though that old building has long been demolished. It wasn't a very attractive building, and had clearly never been one. It looked even worse when I first saw it because it hadn't been cleaned or painted in years. The reason for its neglect was an imposing modern building next to it, part of an unusual complex designed by Raj Rewal. The building, which had already been completed when I got there, was like an inverted pyramid, growing in size as it went higher. The second structure in the complex had not been built yet; it was to be much larger, straight up for several storeys, then growing outward like the smaller one. This larger building was to be Doordarshan Kendra, Delhi, and the smaller one the DG's office. Grouped around the larger building would be the studios.

As the DG's office building had already been completed no one saw any reason to clean or paint the old Mandi House. At the same time, however, there wasn't any plan to move into the new building because the fire department hadn't cleared it, and the power cables had to be laid and the transformers installed. Consequently the DG's office stayed in the dilapidated Mandi House, while the new building stood unused, except by some officers of the civil construction wing of AIR who had supervised its construction, and were now snugly ensconced in it.

I went into the DG's room, where Suresh Mathur was sprawled in a chair. He stood up, hand extended, and said, 'Welcome to your office, Bhaskar. Come, sit. *Chai ya coffee piyoge?*' Suresh had a way of extending his hand with all his fingers outstretched, making it difficult to shake hands; all you could do was a clumsy fumble. I never understood why he did it.

As I sat he said, 'I'll introduce you to your officers first. Then you might like to look round this office and the Delhi station in Akashvani Bhavan.' That was where Doordarshan's main station was, spread out in a haphazard manner in Akashvani Bhavan, which had been built next to Broadcasting House for AIR.

'I think I'll sign the joining report first, Suresh,' I told him.

He raised his eyebrows. 'Why? What's the hurry?' he asked casually.

'You can sign it at any time. In the afternoon, if you like.'

'No, I'd rather do it now.'

He looked a little discomposed, but said smoothly enough, 'Suit yourself. The papers are all ready.'

He summoned a private secretary who appeared with a folder, and looked at me with some apprehension, which I found odd. I signed the joining reports and Suresh signed the corresponding reports relinquishing his temporary charge. I had formally become DG of Doordarshan. There was the usual rather droll shaking of hands all round—the other officers having come in by then—and we sat down. There was an awkwardness I found difficult to explain. Not all the deputy DGs were there, but Shiv Sharma, the additional DG, and Shashi Kant Kapoor, deputy DG (news) were there. So was Madan Mohan, the engineer-in-chief of Doordarshan, who smiled warmly at me.

After exchanging some pleasantries Suresh got up and said, 'Well, it's all yours now. I'm off to AIR. I'll see you soon enough.'

After he left, I spoke to the officers, at a loss to say anything knowledgeable for the simple reason that I knew almost nothing at all about television. Shiv Sharma told me, helpfully, that he would give me a chart which would tell me which officer was doing what. He also suggested I might like to look at the Delhi Kendra; that was, after all, where the business of television was actually going on.

That afternoon I went to the Delhi Kendra and was taken into the studios, the control rooms and the Master Switching Room (MSR). All through, there was this tension; the station director, A.S. Grewal, was so nervous he could barely speak to me. Very mystifying, I thought. But what was the reason? That I was an IAS officer? Surely not—Suresh Mathur was DG of AIR and he was an IAS officer too. Then, while I was looking at some piece of equipment, I was told by the very agitated station director that the private secretary to the minister of information and broadcasting wanted to speak to me very urgently. There were no cellphones in those days, so off I went to the station director's room.

The private secretary, a young IAS officer called Johny Joseph, asked me if I was alone. I said I was.

'Tell me, sir,' he said urgently, 'have you taken over as DG?'

I said I had.

'That's a great relief,' Johny said. 'You see, some of these officers have filed a case against your appointment with the Central Administrative Tribunal. They've argued that you're not qualified to hold the post.'

'Because I'm an IAS officer?' I asked.

'Not really, though that's one of the issues. I'll explain when you come to the ministry. But their luck was out. The tribunal's only just heard their petition, at about four o'clock, and have said that if you've already joined then your joining stands, but if you haven't joined then your joining is stayed till they hear the case. And they've fixed the next hearing for next week.'

So that was it. That explained the tension and the nervousness. I wondered about Suresh Mathur's strange behaviour that morning. Why did he want me to delay signing my joining report? Did he know of the case, and did he think that if my appointment was stayed, he would continue? But why would he want that? Was I seeing conspiracies where there were none? Was he perhaps trying to get back at me for what he thought I was responsible—his removal, years earlier, as secretary to the chief minister of West Bengal? I didn't know, and still don't. But it did occur to me then, as I turned things over in my mind in the station director's room, that I didn't really care. I had not been prevented from joining as DG of Doordarshan; the real intention of those who had gone to the tribunal had been just that and they hadn't succeeded. That was all that mattered.

I went out where the officers were waiting rather tensely and told them, as airily as I could, 'That was about the case you've filed against my joining as DG. The tribunal has said that if I've joined then they will not issue a stay. If I had not joined then they would hear the case first and stay my joining. But as you know, I joined this morning. So that's that. Let's get on with what we're doing.'

Consternation, worry and open anxiety was writ large on all their faces, except that of Madan Mohan, the engineer-in-chief, who had a grim, rather satisfied smile on his face.

'Sir,' the station director said fearfully, 'I had nothing to do with it, sir. I was not one of those who signed the petition, sir. I thought it was very wrong.'

'Oh, don't worry,' I told him, with a heartiness I did not feel at all and which was ninety per cent bravado. 'I'm not bothered with such things.'

But I was bothered. I had to be bothered. When I got to the ministry to call on the minister, the secretary, Girish Mehra, looked very worried.

'These bastards have a point,' he said. 'If we want to avoid getting into deep shit we'll have to move very fast to set things right.'

He then explained to me what the 'deep shit' was. The post of DG of Doordarshan was equated with that of an additional secretary to the Government of India. I had been cleared earlier to be an additional secretary but the formal orders had not been issued. So, technically, I was still a joint secretary, and not qualified to hold an additional secretary's post. Therefore, I could not be appointed DG of Doordarshan.

As he was explaining this to me, Gopi Arora walked in. He knew what had happened and, not surprisingly, provided a way out. He spoke to the cabinet secretary, P.K. Kaul, and requested him to have fresh orders issued appointing me DG of Doordarshan and specifying that I was in the grade of additional secretary. He then explained to us, much in the way a teacher explains a point to students in a lecture room, that I had already been cleared for promotion as additional secretary the moment the decision to promote me had been made by the Appointments Committee of the Cabinet. The decision to appoint me DG of Doordarshan was therefore perfectly legal. The new orders arrived within half an hour and were put in place of the earlier orders that night itself. The officials who had petitioned the Central Administrative Tribunal against my appointment did not have a copy of the earlier orders, which were quickly destroyed. As he left, Gopi added, almost as an afterthought, that the case would fail.

So it did. Thus, late that afternoon in Augusr 1986, with an appropriate bit of drama, I began my eventful years as DG of Doordarshan.

1

The Early Years

I soon realized that if I wanted to be more than just a dummy, a sort of figurehead DG who had to depend completely on his officers because he knew nothing himself, I would have to learn something about the business of television. I got enough of the administrative side every day—more than I ever wanted—in files of all sizes, tidy and untidy. What I needed to know was just how the thing worked. How were programmes made? What happened in a studio?

It wasn't that I had absolutely no idea at all. I had done a few interviews for Doordarshan—or AIR-TV as it was called in 1979—and I had a vague notion of cameras and lights and sound booms. But I didn't know enough. I had never really seen what went on behind the camera, in the control rooms. Within a few days of joining I decided that I would spend every afternoon in the Delhi station, in the studios and in the control rooms, sitting in a corner with a programme executive and an assistant engineer to watch what went on, the two young officers explaining what seemed incomprehensible to me. I asked the other staff to continue doing whatever they were doing and not take any notice of me: I wasn't there to 'inspect' or anything, just to find out what television was about.

Madan Mohan, the quiet yet universally respected engineer-in-chief of Doordarshan, said that he would sit in with me. At first I thought he was doing it for the usual reason, because I was the DG and he wanted to make a good impression on the boss, but as the days passed I began to understand his real motive. He was doing it, wise man that he was, because he knew I was not only the DG but an ignorant DG, and it was important that I be taught about things in perspective, as they really were, something a raw assistant engineer might not have been able to do. There was another reason, something that helped me immensely. He had been with AIR-TV since its inception, as a junior engineer, and had actually worked as a cameraman for a number of years. That gave him a dimension in the field of production, where the cameraman is very much the key figure: he doesn't just shoot, but also has a major say in the composition of the shot and determines the nature of the lighting. Indeed, in film circles in Britain he was usually called the lighting-cameraman. Apart from briefing me about technical details, Madan Mohan would point out where a shot was poorly composed, when the lighting was not adequate or was excessive. I was convinced that had he not been the engineer-in-chief, he would have been a fine television director.

Madan Mohan was a remarkable man. Small, quiet, reserved and seemingly distant, he was in fact one of the most knowledgeable and decisive heads of engineering Doordarshan has had. His foresight set the new organization on an orderly way forward in terms of its technical ability. While overseeing the phenomenal proliferation of transmitters, for example, he was firmly unyielding on the quality of the units supplied by Bharat Electronics Limited (BEL), Hyderabad and by Gujarat Chemical and Electronics Corporation Limited (GCEL), Vadodara. He never concealed from me his feeling that the GCEL products were usually less than satisfactory, or the fact that he thought the company's staff were lackadaisical in their approach to their work; he preferred the greater professionalism of BEL, and made no bones about it. But as a man of principle he went by what measured up to his standards and the equipment which didn't, irrespective of which firm had supplied it, was rejected out of hand. This often led to major arguments and confrontations. Delegations of indignant, often furious officers (usually from GCEL) would come to see me to complain about what they said was Madan Mohan's arbitrariness. Soon after I had realized what a fine officer Madan Mohan was, I made it clear to all those who came that I would not interfere, or let the ministry interfere, with a decision taken by Madan Mohan on technical grounds. I was to thank myself for this later; my assessment of the man served the organization well for many years to come.

In those early days I sat in the darkness at the back of a studio or in a corner of a control room while Madan Mohan quietly explained the workings of the television system. I was initiated into some of the immense complexities of television broadcasting, from the generation of the signal in the camera to its transmission via a transmitter to a satellite or a television set. Listening to his quiet comments, invariably laced with dry humour, and listening to the other officers, often late into the evening after the office had fallen quiet and the clerks, peons, and importunate, expectant producers carrying sheaves of proposals had departed, a picture of how the organization had come into being slowly emerged.

Like Topsy—the little black girl in *Uncle Tom's Cabin* who had no parents and said 'I expec' I just growed'—Doordarshan just grew, but, unlike Topsy, Doordarshan had its growth hurried along by people who wanted either to use it to project themselves or to make the considerable amount of money it was soon able to provide, or both. There were exceptions, though, and two of them were prime ministers of India. Indira Gandhi saw television as a means of reaching out to the people and an effective instrument to sensitize them. Of course, she never thought of giving it any kind of autonomy and maintained quite openly that it was a government agency. She did, however, give it the impetus to become a national network by assigning it the necessary funds. Acting on the advice of her scientific adviser, Vikram Sarabhai, she instructed Doordarshan to use satellites to send its signal across the country. Her son, Rajiv Gandhi, was also fascinated by television. There was a television set on wherever he was, in the office or in his house, all the time. He not only gave it a good deal of attention, but spent time thinking of ways in which it could reach international standards. Many of the directions he gave were misunderstood by anxious bureaucrats over-eager to please, which sometimes led to bizarre results.

Doordarshan started as a tiny experimental operation in 1959 with some Philips equipment that had been brought in for a trade fair or exhibition and was left behind with AIR. The project was called the AIR Experimental Service (Television). Sadhan Mullick, one of the first AIR officers to be moved to this new set-up, recalls they had pathetically little to work with. Hardly any recording was done; all of the programmes were broadcast live right from the studio. Then the US Educational Foundation in India (USEFI) helped out and finally the West Germans provided some studio equipment. This was about the time when UNESCO asked the government if it was interested in using television for educational purposes, and fortunately the government was. Initially their broadcasts were on just four subjects: Road Sense, Adulteration, Care of Public Property and Manners.

Mullick recalls with fondness the spirit of high excitement with which they worked. 'We were like one big family. Nobody bothered with designations and rank.' Madan Mohan was a junior engineer then; so were many who, in the course of time, rose to senior positions in Doordarshan. They worked, Mullick told me wryly, in cut-and-paste fashion, making do with whatever they had.

In 1965 a daily one-hour service was started. It could be seen only in Delhi because it had a weak transmitter, and mostly by bureaucrats and politicians in whose bungalows television sets had been installed. The programmes ranged from the staid to the downright ludicrous. There were stony-faced people who read the news (only in Hindi) without expression, others who spoke in a stilted self-conscious manner that set one's teeth on edge. I once watched a song being telecast; throughout the song, only one image occupied the screen: a record playing on the turntable of a gramophone. I could only suppose that the person who made the programme thought he was reproducing what happened in real life when someone put a record on a player, which was daft, because no one spends his time watching a turntable with intense concentration.

Sadhan Mullick was a little defensive about these programmes. 'Consider our very great limitations,' he told me. 'We couldn't record anything, and yet we knew we had to have visuals, some kind of visuals. Sometimes we even used photographs.' As Dr Johnson told Boswell, 'Sir, a Frenchman speaking English is like a dog walking upon its hind legs. It is not done well; but the marvel is that it is done at all.'

As the years went by television began to grow, hesitantly at first. Delhi's programming went up from one hour to two in 1968; the Bombay Kendra began functioning in 1972; the Srinagar Kendra in 1973. In 1975 came a much-discussed television event, the Satellite Instructional TV Experiment, or SITE. For the first time a satellite, the

US ATS 6, was used to send programmes to remote areas in six states. Much has been written about this and I don't want to add to it. But what it did do was demonstrate the capability of satellites to send television signals across the country. A television signal sent from a land transmitter travels along the line of sight; that is, as the earth curves away, it travels straight on, so, relative to the earth, it heads upwards after about seventy-five kilometres and out into space, where it is lost. A television signal sent upwards to a satellite can be bounced off it and sent back to earth, where it comes down like a beam from a flashlight. That beam is called the 'footprint' of the signal. A signal from Delhi could be sent to a satellite with a footprint that covered the whole of India.

Then came the Emergency and the government's grip on television tightened. Nothing could be shown that didn't play up the virtues of Indira Gandhi's government. Sadly, many of the officers in the Delhi station not only accepted this complete control but became eager servitors of the rulers of the time. This destroyed whatever was left of the camaraderie and excitement that Sadhan Mullick and his colleagues—who by then were at the Film and Television Institute in Pune—had treasured so much. This was also the time when AIR and its television wing were formally separated into Akashvani and Doordarshan—a decision never fully implemented, leading to unending administrative and operational headaches. When the Emergency ended and Indira Gandhi was swept out of power, the new Janata government was eager to clear the electronic media of all those seen as collaborators. In the reshuffle that followed Sadhan Mullick was brought back as director of Delhi Doordarshan. Doordarshan had its first DG, too, in P.V. Krishnamoorthy, known to colleagues and subordinates alike as PVK.

Mullick speaks with bitterness of his days as director of Delhi Doordarshan. There was political interference from a variety of quarters, but most of all there was interference generated by the internal intrigues of his own staff.

'I can't blame the politicians alone,' he told me. 'Some of my own officers and staff used political connections to get things done.' The atmosphere in the station was vitiated by a couldn't-care-less attitude on the part of several of the staff who were political appointees.

The real damage done to Doordarshan, however, was the partial separation of AIR and Doordarshan effected during the Emergency. The officers all belonged to a common service, and the control of that service or services (there was an engineering service and a programme service) remained with the DG of AIR, who selected the best for television as long as he was responsible for both. As soon as he lost Doordarshan to another DG, however, he kept the most competent officers in AIR and sent the others to Doordarshan. Not that all those who came to Doordarshan were incompetent; many were fascinated by the new medium and soon mastered its intricacies. But there were certain habits picked up from their radio days that even some of the competent ones were not able to shed. The irritating use of excessive commentaries in programmes, for example, almost invariably employing language larded with hyperboles, or the constant music in the background—such practices were out of place in an audio-visual medium. You didn't have to hear talk of 'gorgeous, snow-clad peaks glittering in the dazzling sun against a sapphire blue sky' when you were seeing them for yourself.

Indeed, that was the basic cause of Doordarshan's programming problems. All the personnel brought in for the television operations started by AIR came from AIR itself. They were all radio people, who may have known how to make radio programmes but were clueless when it came to the use of images and sound together. They were put through six months of training at the Film and Television Institute in Pune, which was later reduced to three, and three months of television basics could hardly be expected to erase years of radio work that made some reactions and attitudes elemental, almost involuntary.

So when Doordarshan aired 'discussions', they were done in the only way the AIR staff knew: put four people behind a table, fix a camera so that they are all in the frame and then let them talk. The manner in which the discussion took place was again vintage AIR.

'Good evening.' Bright, patently artificial smile from the moderator. 'Tonight we have four eminent personalities with us to discuss the problem of trees that grow sideways.' Head down to read the rest of the script. Then, head up, artificial smile switched on. 'Dr Singh, what do you think is the problem?'

One panellist mumbles something while the moderator nods vacuously from time to time, artificial smile firmly in place. Then, turning to another panellist, 'Dr Khan, can you tell us something more?' The wretched man mumbles and waves his hands, and the moderator nods away, smiling brightly and fatuously. And so it went till either you switched off the set or the moderator said, 'That was a discussion on trees growing sideways. Thank you all,' smiling at the panellists, 'and,' turning to the camera, 'thank you for watching.' The moderator sat still, grinning in a fixed, strained way till the producer woke up and told the cameraman to switch off the camera. This kind of formula may have worked as a radio programme but was disastrous on television.

In a very real sense, the 1970s were perhaps the best time in the turbulent and increasingly unhappy progress of Doordarshan. For one thing, television was a new medium and had the goodwill of all viewers who were much more forgiving because of the sheer novelty of it. Calcutta Doordarshan, for example, was started in a ramshackle old film studio patched up to do television work. The new staff consisted of executives trained at the Film and Television Institute of India, bursting with new ideas and led by Mira Mozoomdar, a seasoned radio broadcaster who had headed AIR Bangalore and had then gone to the BBC for television training (she was one of the first to be sent there) before taking over the Doordarshan station in Calcutta.

'There was interest, tolerance, help and above all respect,' Mira recalls. 'And not only from people in general, but from artistes, film-makers, singers and most creative people in the city.'

They worked initially with 16mm film, then with tape, the old two-inch kind. This was, in a sense, the cause of a tragic loss. The supply of tape was limited, so it had to be used over and over again. This meant that some truly memorable programmes, such as a documentary on Mother Teresa made when she received the Nobel Peace Prize, were erased. After some time Calcutta received an Outside Broadcast van (an OB van, as it was called), which was used as a more modern control room for the studio. Later, when a second OB van arrived, a number of live telecasts were aired.

Moreover, the stations were not linked to each other, because at the time transmission was entirely terrestrial. This meant that each station had to function entirely on its own; there wasn't an imposed national transmission for them to contend with, because it wasn't possible to have one. Given this relative independence, at least in the production of most programmes except the news, the young producers were free to innovate, create new and interesting programmes, and viewers forgave them the obvious technical limitations within which they had to function. There were plays and stimulating discussions between actor/director Ajitesh Bandopadhyay and Shambhu Mitra, all of which the theatre-crazy Bengalis enjoyed. Mira Mozoomdar is modest about her contribution to the establishment of Calcutta Doordarshan and the traditions of quality and innovation that it developed. She merely says that there was a lot of camaraderie, enthusiasm and commitment. No one seemed to mind late hours, if it meant getting a programme right.

Mira mentions another problem that must have been formidable, even though she refers to it in a good-humoured way: Calcutta Doordarshan was started during the Emergency imposed by Indira Gandhi. One of the first effects, she recalls, was that she had to cancel what would have been the inaugural film for the station, a film by the celebrated film-maker Mrinal Sen. The film was *Chorus,* which had a clear Leftist slant and depicted Calcutta as it was then, buzzing with workers' rallies and demonstrations. The film-maker was livid with rage and didn't speak to her, nor have anything to do with Calcutta Doordarshan, for several years after that. But by and large the central office left the regional stations alone; they had a measure of independence that stations certainly don't have today. Mira Mozoomdar recalled that even in the news there was relatively little interference. Of course, in those years, the news consisted of little more than a transcript of what was called 'pool news' in the newsroom of AIR, which came already vetted and sanitized, and needed only to be read by attractive young men and women. The occasional visuals were always silent.

Those who worked in Calcutta Doordarshan, like Bibhas Chakravarty, recall with fondness the unique team spirit that kept them going in the seventies. Programme and engineering personnel worked as a team, with complete dedication to the work in hand. It was, he says, as if they had a mission: to create good television notwithstanding the primitive conditions in which they had to work. Sadly, he told me, that teamwork and dedication disappeared over the years. Abhijit Dasgupta, one of the finest producers Doordarshan had (he now runs a television company of his own), was a young, raw producer in those days, and recounts some incidents which must have been terrifying then but seem comic now. He was asked to do the first live broadcast using the special OB van provided to the station, but he had no idea how to do it. In sheer desperation he rang up none other than Satyajit Ray and asked him what to do. The great man listened to him patiently, then told him in precise, simple terms what he had to do. On another occasion, during a cricket match that he was covering, the tape got reversed and he watched in horror as Sunil Gavaskar was shown as a left-handed batsman, till he hastily corrected it.

Primitive equipment and studios notwithstanding, the programmes I watched in Calcutta in those early days were often well made and interesting. There were plays, music and dance programmes, shows of various kinds, and even live coverage of local sports matches and cultural events, like the celebration of Pochishe Boishakh (25th Baisakh), the birthday of Rabindranath Tagore. Calcutta Doordarshan covered this at Jorasanko and at the celebrated gathering of artistes outside Rabindra Sadan. The effects of the Emergency were not very noticeable and Mira confirms that by treading very cautiously they managed to produce a number of good programmes. 'It was more a question of doing non-political programmes—music, theatre, features, shows, and so on—and we pre-recorded a good deal of our programmes, which was a help.'

With a wry smile, however, Mira says that as the years passed viewers became more and more critical. It came to the point that when she had to attend any public function she frantically looked around to see if the managing director of the Calcutta Electric Supply Corporation and the general manager of Calcutta Telephones were present. She was third in the firing line, the other two attracting most of the ire of the people present, since in those days Calcutta suffered from terrible load-shedding and a chaotic telephone system that rarely worked. If either of the two wretched gentlemen was present, she got off lightly.

This rather special time came to an end in 1982, when India hosted the Asian Games in New Delhi. The most elaborate preparations ever to have been made for a sports event of this kind were taken up, with a high-powered organizing committee headed by Rajiv Gandhi, assisted by a number of his friends and an assortment of experts from different fields. A full-fledged secretariat came up with S.S. Gill—an officer of the rank of secretary to the Government of India—in charge. Crores were spent on the new Jawaharlal Nehru Stadium and on the biggest indoor stadium in India, fully air-conditioned and able to seat some 33,000 spectators. The swimming pool was a magnificent international-quality pool, though it was also a big disaster. It was meant to be an indoor pool but the design was found to be faulty. Something was wrong with the pillars that were meant to support the roof, so the pool had to remain open to the sky.

The city itself underwent major transformations. Flyovers—some, in retrospect, totally unnecessary, serving a very limited purpose even today—came up along roads leading to the stadium in anticipation of the organizing committee's visions of thousands streaming in to watch the events. Hotels were built to accommodate what the organizers thought would be a large number of international visitors. A residential complex was built along Khel Gaon Marg, past Jawaharlal Nehru Stadium, for the athletes, their coaches, managers, observers and other hangers-on. This was the Asiad Village, an assortment of flats and houses with two large dining halls for the athletes and all the other facilities they needed.

Doordarshan was central to these preparations because the events were to be televised live to all of Asia and other countries. Almost overnight it was decided that Doordarshan's black-and-white transmissions would be replaced by colour, and that satellites would be used to send the signals all over the country and to the rest of the world. Equipment poured in; squads of programme executives and engineers were sent for training and Doordarshan entered the era of modern television. On 15 August 1982, Doordarshan switched to colour and to a satellite-linked network called the National Programme.

While apparatus of all kinds arrived, some specialized equipment that was essential for the coverage of events like swimming—underwater cameras and their peripherals—weren't purchased. Consequently, the production teams had to improvise with whatever they could lay their hands on, guided only by their ingenuity. One of the stories that has become part of Doordarshan folklore is of a producer, Ananya Banerjee, who had been pulled in from the Calcutta Kendra and told to cover the swimming events. Ananya was a very young producer then, and looked even younger, rather like a schoolgirl, and it didn't help that she was small, tied her hair in pigtails, and wore very large spectacles. But beneath that childlike exterior was a steely determination. All she had by way of equipment was a camera, so she hunted around and got hold of a set of rails on which she placed a trolley that could carry the cameraman and the camera. This then was to be pulled slowly along the side of the pool by a few people. She spent a whole day or more laying rails alongside the pool. It wasn't very nice to look at but it was effective; in any case, it was the only way the swimming events could be covered, given that there were no underwater cameras. The day before the opening, the minister for information and broadcasting, Vasant Sathe, came to inspect the arrangements. When he saw the rails laid beside the swimming pool and the improvised trolley with a camera on it, he was astounded and indignant.

'Who put up this terrible thing?' he demanded. 'Get rid of it immediately!'

No one said a word. Then, suddenly, he was confronted by a very small, bespectacled girl in pigtails, who, frightened though she was, said firmly in a trembling voice, 'I put them there. And they're going to stay there.'

'Who are you?' Sathe asked, out of surprise more than anything else.

'I am the producer who's going to cover the swimming events,' the girl said, 'and I'm going to do it with that.' She pointed at the trolley on the rails.

The minister stared at her speculatively for some time. Finally, he spoke. 'I see. Well, do what you like.'

He left and Ananya was taken to task by senior officers for daring to speak to the minister in that fashion. But she refused to budge, and covered the swimming events with her trolley on rails. I understand the coverage was pretty good.

With the coverage of the 1982 Asiad in colour and satellite links, the era of black-and-white television and of kendras left to their own devices for prime-time programming came to an end. Sitting in Delhi, Doordarshan executives at the same time thought up what came to be known as the National Programme. This was seen as a means of using television to unite the people, of developing an awareness of the oneness of India. What it actually meant was that the local kendras broadcast their own programmes only from 5 p.m. to 8.30 p.m. At 8.30 p.m. all transmitters linked up to Delhi using the satellite links that had been provided for the coverage of the Asian Games. Using TVROs (Television Receive-Only dishes) the kendras received the signal sent from Delhi via the INSAT 1B satellite and transmitted it terrestrially, allowing the Delhi station to be seen all over the country. From 8.30 p.m. till 11 p.m., all viewers watched the National Programme, a series of programmes, including the news, transmitted from Delhi.

The trouble was that the programmes which formed the National Programme were mostly in Hindi—Hindi serials, Hindi shows and Hindi films. There was an English news bulletin and occasionally a current affairs programme (the inevitable discussion), also in English. English films were shown very rarely, although more often than not they were antiquated films made by Transtel, a German company. These programmes had very little by way of commentary; they were often recordings of grotesque games in which men ran a race while balancing six bottles of beer in each hand, or farcical stunts by clowns, or people doing the sort of ridiculous things we see these days in excruciating programmes like *Who Dares Wins*.

Since Doordarshan was the only television channel available, the preponderance of Hindi programmes in non-Hindi-speaking regions led to a considerable amount of resentment. In later years, when I was DG, I had to listen to an angry chief secretary of Tamil Nadu who lectured me on the way Doordarshan was dividing the country, and was at the receiving end of some sarcasm from the chief minister of Karnataka who thanked me for reducing the load-shedding in his state since, according to him, all television sets were switched off at 8.30 p.m. as soon as the National Programme started.

Another damaging result of this system was the erosion of enthusiasm among local producers in other cities where there were Doordarshan kendras but the state language was not Hindi. The time slots available for local programmes (serials or documentaries) were not popular: most viewers were too busy either at work or about the house to be able to watch television between 5 p.m. and 8.30 p.m. There was a terrible scramble for the 7.30 p.m. and 8.00 p.m. slots and the selection of programmes for these two slots from among the hundreds offered was a nightmare for most programme executives.

This may sound odd—television programmes were surely made in the kendras, so who would be scrambling for these time slots? A word of explanation. Someone in Delhi came up with the bright idea that private producers could be asked to make serials that were 'sponsored' by a commercial concern. This meant that the cost was met by that commercial concern, which then was awarded a certain number of minutes to advertise their products before, during and after each episode. This was called Free Commercial Time, or FCT. The sponsors paid Doordarshan the cost of airtime for each episode, which was not very high. In addition, Doordarshan could put in what were called spot ads, that is, advertisements for which Doordarshan charged about Rs 12,000 for ten seconds. There were many takers for this, and the sponsors, calculating on the basis of the rates for spot ads, realized that the FCT they got was equivalent to almost Rs 3 lakh for each episode. In other words, they were able to air ads for their products during the FCT virtually for free—all they paid was the modest airtime cost. There were, consequently, many commercial houses eager to sponsor serials, and a large number of producers wanting to make them because they could charge the sponsor almost three times what each episode of a serial actually cost. Hence the over-abundance of sponsored serials vying for slots during prime time, 7.30 p.m. and 8 p.m. for regional kendras and 8 p.m. to 9 p.m. in the National Programme.

The National Programme made Doordarshan headquarters the focal point, as decisions regarding programme format were taken there. The programme resulted in such a scramble for time slots that the Ministry of Information and Broadcasting virtually took over this aspect of decision making: the Fixed Point Chart became something determined by the ministry at meetings chaired by the secretary, Ministry of Information and Broadcasting. Of course, the ministry continued to strenuously deny any interference with Doordarshan.

I was told that the secretary who interfered the most was S.S. Gill, who suddenly reappeared, many years later, as the first CEO of Prasar Bharati and then disappeared almost as suddenly. He not only decided which programme would be telecast when, but selected the programmes himself and peremptorily told the DG to carry out his decisions. What seems to have made him a bit of an ogre was his predilection for coarse, sometimes obscene, language which he used very freely when berating producers if he saw something on the screen he did not like. Later secretaries may have used milder language but they didn't discontinue the practice of holding weekly Fixed Point Chart meetings, which the DG, all deputy DGs, the engineer-in-chief, all chief engineers and the director of the Delhi Kendra were expected to attend. Some of the secretaries flattered themselves, I think, by saying it was really a review of what Doordarshan was doing; to some extent it was true, because the secretaries did review the progress made by the engineers in setting up transmitters (then a vitally important aspect of Doordarshan's work) and in constructing new kendras.

When it came to programmes, however, they dropped the review bit and checked which serial was due to end when and what was to be broadcast after it. Instructions on the manner in which news bulletins were to be telecast were given in detail—so much detail that most of the news division people attending the meetings forgot most of it by the time they went back to their offices. How they chose which serial would be shown after one had ended is a matter I would rather not speculate on. There were pressures, at times from the minister, which often couldn't be resisted, urgings from friends, and so much else. Strangely, Doordarshan executives weren't too exercised by this; it was so much safer to follow orders given by someone else, carefully making a discreet note in a file, than taking a decision on their own that could land them into trouble later. And trouble could mean anything, from a CBI investigation to a transfer to a distant kendra.

Safe. This was a word used so often in Doordarshan that it became a sort of password. Is this programme safe? Is that news story safe? Is it safe to screen this particular film? I heard it so many times that it began to make me sick, but I couldn't really blame anyone for using it. It was amazing how hysterical the ministry got when something they thought inappropriate was shown—it could be a statement by a politician from an opposition party, or even a shot that seemed to linger on a particular opposition politician longer than was deemed necessary by the minister or a ruling party MP or by some over-eager flunkey in the bureaucracy. Summary transfers were ordered, entries made in annual confidential reports (passports to future promotions) or a 'memo' (a short note that conveyed the displeasure of a superior officer) was issued to the erring official.

That was Doordarshan in the mid-1980s—an organization that, being new and the sole television channel, was an obsession for the Ministry of Information and Broadcasting, for several members of Parliament, and above all for the press. Every paper had a journalist whose beat was Doordarshan, who hung around the corridors of Mandi House or the ministry to pick up little snippets of what they thought was juicy gossip to be written up as stories that appeared under large headlines. Mandi House was swarming with producers, some of them with links to powerful politicians, others ready with substantial sums of money, intent on getting their serials passed. The kind of programmes that Doordarshan had been set up to broadcast, programmes that informed and sensitized viewers, took a back seat, produced perfunctorily with very little intention of making them visually interesting or informative.

But there was also another side to Doordarshan during those years—the technical side. There was rapid expansion of the network of transmitters, the construction of new Doordarshan kendras and of additional studios in existing kendras, and the acquisition of ever more sophisticated and versatile equipment. Engineers had linked the four metropolitan cities—Delhi, Bombay, Calcutta and Madras—with a microwave link, which was meant to be a backup to the existing satellite link. Initially, the link was less than satisfactory—the signal quality was poor and consequently it was used only when there was a failure—but with better equipment the quality of the signal became more acceptable. This was later developed into the Metro channel.

2

Epic Serials and Serial Epics

Soap operas—serials in Doordarshan parlance—came to Doordarshan through a rather odd route. Early in the 1980s, David Poindexter, president of a US-based NGO called Population Communications International, brought to the Ministry of Information and Broadcasting the idea of using soap operas to communicate social messages subliminally. The then secretary, S.S. Gill, was interested and Poindexter was able to bring in Miguel Sabido, a pioneering producer of soap operas in Mexico who had used them successfully to carry messages about family planning. Why this started in Mexico isn't difficult to explain. In a predominantly Roman Catholic country like Mexico, family planning in any form is frowned upon; advocating it on television is out of the question. Nevertheless, concern over the high rate of population growth led to the idea of using soap operas to convey, very subtly, messages about the benefits of small families, the misery that afflicts large families living on a small income, the better quality of care received by children in small families, and so on. Nothing overt, just ideas woven into the storylines of what were otherwise turgid family dramas.

Miguel Sabido did this so well and his serials became so popular that he was seen as something of a genius by those concerned with using the media to propagate family planning. His visit to India was followed by visits to Mexico by officials from the I & B ministry and Doordarshan. In collaboration with script writer Manohar Shyam Joshi, who went on to become one of the most successful writers of scripts for serials, and financial backing from Nestlé, Doordarshan's first serial, *Hum Log*, was launched in 1984. The serial became a huge success—

thousands and thousands of viewers made it a point of following the fate of the various characters and eagerly awaited each new episode. Nestlé used the serial to launch Maggi noodles, which soon became a household name. Indeed, the serial was so successful financially that the producers gave up all pretensions of carrying any message, however subliminal or subtle. The script writer began to write plain soap opera episodes that lost none of the popularity of the original episodes; if anything, they were watched even more widely. This was only the beginning. *Hum Log* was followed by other serials, like *Buniyaad*; all of them brought in handsome profits to the producers.

I arrived as the craze for sponsored serials was building up. At first I was overwhelmed by it; every minute of my time during every working day (barring the afternoons, which I spent in the studios and control rooms of Delhi Doordarshan) was taken up with meeting producers frantic to get extensions for their serials or to obtain time slots for new ones. What a weird lot they were, these private producers! Among them were some very talented people (Shridhar Kshirsagar, for example), but there were also 'fixers'.

One serial which had a woman in the lead role was running when I joined Doordarshan. It was so bad that the sponsor, Hindustan Lever, called me up to say that the remaining episodes would be paid for by them, since they had already been made, but would I please remove all references to Hindustan Lever and its products from the serial.

When the serial was coming to a close in October 1986, the producer came calling. Preceded by a cloud of expensive French perfume, she drifted languidly into the room, a diaphanous sari barely covering her very generous frontage.

'The serial has had a very good response,' she said, smiling radiantly. 'I think you should extend it by another thirteen episodes.'

'I don't do these things,' I told her. 'There's a committee that decides.'

This was true; in order to insulate Doordarshan from pressures of this kind I had set up a committee of three deputy DGs to screen all proposals for serials. The deputy DGs evaluated each proposal separately and only I knew what their recommendations were.

'Oh,' she said, casually, 'do they?'

She swept out. A few minutes later I got a call from an agitated Shiv

Sharma, the additional DG.

'Did you approve an extension of the serial?' he asked.

I was astonished. 'Certainly not,' I told him. 'I told that woman it wasn't in my hands.'

'Well,' Shiv said, 'she's here, saying you have approved it.'

'Bring her down here,' I told him.

When they came in I asked the lady, who was still smiling radiantly, why she had told him I had approved the extension of her serial.

'Well,' she said demurely, 'I thought that was what you said. You didn't say no.'

'I said the committee would decide,' I told her. 'I made it clear that I don't make these decisions.'

I was rewarded with another beaming smile.

'I misunderstood what you said,' she said. 'I'm so sorry.'

She left in a mist of fragrance. I was hugely amused at the outrage on Shiv's face.

A few days later I was called up by the minister, Ajit Panja. 'There's a serial called *Nilima* or something,' he said.

'Yes, sir, there is. It's about to end,' I told him.

'Yes, well, do you think it could be given an extension?'

'No, sir,' I said. 'That has to be decided by the committee of deputy DGs, and they've rejected the request for an extension.'

'Well, you see,' the minister said, 'I have a little problem here. This serial is being strongly recommended by a party colleague. I really can't say no to him, he's a fairly influential man. The committee should be asked to reconsider their decision.'

'I'll tell them to do that, sir.' I knew by 'reconsider' he meant 'change'. I called up Shiv and told him to ask the committee to do just that. As I expected, the committee decided once again that the serial was not worth an extension.

I told the minister as much. He wasn't pleased but said nothing just then. After a week or so he sent for me. As soon as I entered his room he said, 'Mr Ghose, you've put me in a very awkward situation. My party colleague came to me and actually wept. He clung to my knees and wept. He pleaded for an extension for just one more time. Please get it done. I can't face him again.'

I told him I would urge the committee to take another look at the new episodes planned for the serial. They came back with the same decision: no extension.

Some days later the minister was conducting a meeting in his room on some matter related to Doordarshan. In the middle of the discussion he turned to me and said, 'Mr Ghose, what happened to the extension of that serial? You know the one I told you about. The man rings me every day.'

That's when I made a foolish mistake, allowing my rather exaggerated notion of the confidence I thought everyone had in me to get the better of my discretion.

'That extension isn't possible, sir,' I said loftily. 'I can't be responsible for every assurance given in a bedroom.'

The minister's face darkened. He didn't bring up the matter again, but it was undoubtedly the first of the black marks he put against my name. That tally was to grow as the years went by.

I mention this merely as an indication of the bizarre situations that I faced with some producers of serials. Another stemmed from my near-pathological reaction to what I thought was bribery. I had been told that Doordarshan was full of it. Many of the seasoned senior officers in Doordarshan had whispered to me dark stories of suit lengths (these seemed to be favourites with some of the Doordarshan officers) being handed over in the lobbies of hotels and of money being stashed away in lockers and bank vaults. As a result, I often found myself looking around to see if anyone was clutching a wad of notes and watching with some apprehension every time someone opened a briefcase in my presence. Then, one evening around Diwali, when I returned home after an exhausting day I found—horror of horrors—a packing case sent by an eager producer. On one side of it were the letters XXX.

'Booze!' I shouted in a frenzy of rage. 'The bounder's actually sent me booze!'

The next morning I had the case brought to the office and kept on the bit of patchy lawn that still existed in front of Mandi House. I told my private secretary to phone the man and tell him to come and take his property back. I also told the deputy DG looking after sponsored serials that the particular producer in question should never be considered for a serial again. The producer came to retrieve his packing case, and said to me tearfully from the door (I had told my staff not to let him in) that all the case contained was fruit.

'Fruit?' I said scornfully. 'You think I'd fall for that, do you? And what if it was fruit? You were trying to bribe me!'

The man took himself off; I never did find out whether the case contained fruit or booze. The incident, comic though it seems after all these years, did have one effect that I had not foreseen: I never again got a 'gift', in a packing case or in any other case. I discovered years later that I had gained a reputation for being fiercely upright. That amused me greatly. I had acted out of sheer fright, frankly, but the fallout was far better than I had expected.

Early in 1985 or thereabouts Rajiv Gandhi had written or spoken to the minister for information and broadcasting, V.N. Gadgil, about the kind of serials being shown on Doordarshan. The minister said that the PM had given him and the secretary, S.S. Gill, to understand that Doordarshan should broadcast serials that depicted the values enshrined in our ancient texts and philosophy, the kind of values that were contained in the Mahabharata and the Ramayana. Gadgil told me wryly that the secretary took this to mean that the PM wanted both the epics telecast on Doordarshan, and immediately shot off letters to two prominent film producers in Bombay, Ramanand Sagar and B.R. Chopra, asking them to produce these epics for Doordarshan. No shortlisting of producers who could be asked, no scrutiny of names and abilities, nothing. That, apparently, was Gill's style. He took pride in calling himself the chief producer of Doordarshan, despite knowing little of the way television worked. But then he was the secretary of the ministry and could bully and threaten anyone in Doordarshan to do what he wanted.

Both Ramanand Sagar and B.R. Chopra saw the immense possibilities of making a fortune from these serials. The former was asked by Gill to do the Ramayana, and the latter the Mahabharata. Both lost no time in getting hold of sponsors, who also recognized that these epics would draw large audiences. Within a short time, by early 1986, each had readied six or seven episodes of the respective epics.

I called on the minister when I joined as DG. He was an erudite, gentle and very civilized person who rarely put pressure to get something shown on Doordarshan. I don't know how he handled the pressures put on him by members of Parliament and others. What little pressure came down to me was put in a gentle manner and conveyed in the form of suggestions rather than peremptory orders.

After the initial niceties and his advice that I tread carefully in Doordarshan, he turned to a specific serial.

'Take a look at the pilot episodes of the *Ramayana*,' he told me. 'Personally, I think they are terrible, but you decide for yourself.' At that stage the first episodes of the *Mahabharata* had not come in.

I took a look at the episodes and found that the minister was right: they were dreadful. I called up Ramanand Sagar and asked him to meet me in Delhi.

'Ramanandji,' I said rather hesitantly, 'these episodes just won't do. Just look at the young Rama and Lakshman. They're thin and scrawny and totally disinterested. How can you use these children, and that too in episodes where nothing much happens except some wise precepts given to these children by various old men with flowing white beards?'

Sagar was indignant. 'These are trained child actors,' he asserted. 'And those old men are sages!'

When I insisted that the episodes wouldn't do he played his trump card. 'I've spent a lot of money on these episodes,' he said. 'And there's this letter from Gill sahib asking me to make the serial. I'm only doing it because the government wanted me to.'

I was trapped. The letter was there all right, and if I didn't let him go ahead he would probably make a big issue out of it. But I didn't let him get away with it completely.

'All right,' I said. 'But you simply must change those children. And put more of the story in the episodes.'

He agreed to do that and left. A few weeks later I got the revised episodes. The child actors had been changed, as he had promised, but there was still the endless sermonizing and nothing much happened in the episodes.

'I have to keep all that,' Sagar told me blandly on the phone. 'The philosophy of the Ramayana cannot be reduced at all.'

I was trapped again. I played for time; it was the one thing I could do. I said that a major serial like the *Ramayana* would have to be slotted after careful thought so I couldn't promise him a date. But Ramanand Sagar was on to me. Within a few days I was summoned by the minister.

'What did you think of Sagar's *Ramayana* serial?' he asked.

'What you did, sir,' I said. 'It's awful.'

Gadgil sighed and nodded. 'Yes, I know. Yes. But you see,' he said, looking away, 'I'm afraid we have to start screening it.'

I was incredulous. 'It's absolutely mediocre stuff, sir,' I protested. 'We simply can't . . .'

Gadgil held up his hand. 'Ghose,' he said in a melancholy tone, 'I have no choice. Some MPs have begun saying we are holding it back. I believe they mean to speak to the PM.'

'Has the PM himself said it should be shown?'

'No,' replied Gadgil. 'But it may become an issue. I don't want that. It may embarrass the PM.'

I couldn't help but admire the wily Ramanand Sagar. He had me by the short hairs.

'All right, sir,' I finally told the minister. 'I'll find a slot for it.'

'Do what you think is best,' the minister said quickly, indicating he was not taking the decision. He was, after all, a politician. He couldn't take the responsibility for showing the serial and what would inevitably follow. It had to be a decision taken by the DG or one of his officers.

When *Ramayana* started, in January 1987, there were the usual very critical comments. Many said I was responsible for a blatantly Bollywood presentation of the epic, that they expected I would bring in better programmes and just look at what I had started with, and so on. I kept quiet. I had been pinned down by Ramanand Sagar, who began to treat me like a wayward younger brother, and there was nothing I could do. The criticism was stilled after a few episodes had been telecast. The serial became so popular that the streets of all major cities were deserted when it was being shown as people gathered around television sets to watch. I had reports that large crowds watched it in Pakistan as well. The reaction is described in some detail by Nilanjana Gupta: 'The phenomenal success of these programmes [the *Ramayana* and the

Mahabharata] has often been recorded; streets were deserted, meetings of groups as diverse as the Sunday morning services in churches or of the CPI(M)'s propaganda meetings had to be rescheduled.'[1] To this Sevanti Ninan adds: 'There were reports from different parts of the country of people having a bath and doing puja before sitting down, almost prayerfully, to watch each Sunday's episode. Some accounts talked of the TV set at home being garlanded and anointed with sandalwood paste.'[2]

Some consequences were not very pleasant. An eye doctor in Bombay told me that he had a sharp increase in eye injury cases among boys; a few even lost their sight in one eye. All this was because of the craze that swept through cities and towns: children would make crude bows and arrows, tack on pieces of tin to their arrows and enact scenes they had seen in the latest episode of the epic. Inevitably, it led to some accidents.

Ramanand Sagar was undeterred. To make sure we couldn't raise any objections to an episode, he started sending them in just a day before they were due to be aired, leaving no time for the staff to examine each episode for quality. And he dragged out the story over hundreds of episodes. The entire episode in which Rama sees Sita for the first time, for example, consisted of the two of them looking into each other's eyes, with much devotional music in the background.

Unable to take this any longer, I rang up the old bandicoot. 'Ramanandji,' I said firmly, 'this simply has to stop. You cannot drag out episodes like this. I'm sorry, but whatever the consequences, if you do not finish the serial within the stipulated number of episodes, I'll just take it off.'

Sagar was unfazed. 'Ghoseji,' he said unctuously, 'you do not understand. When Lord Rama meets Sita Maiyya it is a celestial, divine moment, sacred to all of us who are true Hindus. How can you think of taking even a second out of that? That was why I had to keep it as long as I did. I was paying reverence to them. And if you want to stop

1. Nilanjana Gupta, *Switching Channels: Ideologies of Television in India* (Delhi: Oxford University Press, 1998), p. 47.
2. Sevanti Ninan, *Through the Magic Window* (Delhi: Penguin Books, 1995), p. 7.

the serial please stop it whenever you want. But just think of the consequences.'

'I have. They just will have to be faced.'

'Even if it comes up in Parliament?' the bandicoot asked me softly. 'What will the mantriji say then? You see how people are mad after the serial. Will they let you stop it?'

I kept quiet.

'You know it cannot be stopped now,' Sagar continued. I could sense his triumph. 'There will be chaos if it is stopped.'

He was right, of course. The serial continued.

Several scholars and analysts believe that it was this serial that gave the BJP and its organizations, the VHP and Bajrang Dal, a new lease on life. Suddenly, as millions began to watch the epic unfold on the television screen, the Hindu religion and its most revered figures became immediate. Put another way, the rather comic acts and statements of Hindu fundamentalist groups seemed to become relevant and meaningful and their ranting about Ayodhya took on a new and dark meaning which evoked a response among a large number of those who watched the serial. In a sense, the destruction of the Babri Masjid can be traced to the telecasting of this serial and of the *Mahabharata* that followed. Both Gupta and Ninan refer to such analyses in their books.

Meanwhile, Ramanand Sagar was going from strength to strength. He took to appearing at the end of each episode, dressed like a sadhu, and delivered smarmy sermons while smiling urbanely. I watched in impotent fury; I felt he ws doing it to bait me more than anything else. Fortunately, no one really took him seriously, and today many people remember the telecasting of the *Ramayana*, but no one remembers the sermonizing of Ramanand Sagar.

During this time, early 1987 to early 1988, Doordarshan enjoyed its highest audience ratings ever. The demand for spot advertisements during the telecast of these episodes was phenomenal and difficult to keep in check. Sagar made a killing, naturally, but the sponsors weren't complaining. They were getting audiences of a size they couldn't otherwise dream of. And it wasn't just the sponsors of the *Ramayana*. Serials coming in immediately before and after an episode of the epic got a sort of spin-off benefit from its immense popularity. In their eagerness not to miss even a second of an episode, viewers would switch on their sets well before it began, and the fascination they felt, the reverence and awe and even devotion, kept them watching for a good while afterwards.

Finally, the *Ramayana* ended in 1988. Ramanand Sagar did his utmost to extend the epic but subsequently lost interest I think, because he was inundated with requests from foreign channels in countries with large numbers of people of Indian origin. These channels wanted to buy rights to broadcast the *Ramayana* on very generous terms. Sadly, Doordarshan merely rented out airtime for serials but never acquired any rights to them, so they had no rights to the *Ramayana*. In fact, if Doordarshan wanted to re-broadcast a programme they had to pay the producer. Besides, being the shrewd customer that he was, Sagar had ensured that all other rights (video and everything else) remained with him. And on those, too, he is said to have made a tidy sum.

Shortly after the first epic ended, the *Mahabharata* began. It, too, lost no time in picking up a very large audience, though it was never quite as big as the audience for the *Ramayana*. It was relatively better made; B.R. Chopra had spent more money on the battle scenes, on the lavish interiors of the palaces and on costumes. Nonetheless some of the special effects—particularly in the opening sequences of each episode—were rather crude, even comical. For example, the representation of the cosmic wheel of time looked suspiciously like a ceiling fan. The arrows shot by warriors never seemed to hit anyone; they were seen flying through the air and then a number of enemy soldiers were seen falling down. The images of gods and goddesses were so obviously superimposed that it caused a good deal of laughter among the less credulous. The overall impression was, however, that it was made with more care than the *Ramayana*.

Chopra once said to me, only half in jest, 'You see, Gill sahib made a mistake. Ramanand is a staunch Sanatan Dharma man. He should have been asked to make the Mahabharata, which is not really religious, except for the portion where the Gita comes in. Now, I am an Arya Samaji; I would have done the Ramayana with a little more realism, and less of the religion.'

The one serial that I am still glad I arranged to telecast was Govind

Nihalani's *Tamas*. I remember he asked me to see it in Bombay one day, on the condition that I see it all, not just one episode. He told me I simply would have to find the time—four or five hours—and if I couldn't he would arrange for me to see it later. But he was anxious that I see it right then because the sponsors, Godrej, were becoming nervous as they had put in a good amount of money into the serial.

I managed to find one afternoon when I could see it. To say that I was overwhelmed by it is to put it very mildly indeed. After months of watching pilots of all kinds of serials, mostly awful stuff, I was suddenly watching a brilliant film unfold, poignant, powerful, with the menace of violence looming over every episode like a dark, swaying snake. Govind had literally built a small village in Bombay where he shot the serial, and it was authentic in every way. Even the litter on the streets, the dogs sniffing through it, everything about it was real and utterly convincing. Om Puri played the bewildered, frightened labourer superbly, and everyone else put in convincing performances, in particular Deepa Sahi as Om Puri's wife, heavily pregnant and apprehensive for his safety. After it ended I sat there quite overcome and decided right then that it had to be screened. True, it had a distinctly Leftist touch and it also suggested, never directly yet unmistakably, that the violence that engulfed the little town was started by the RSS. There was, I felt, nothing wrong with that; they may well have done so in the town Bhisham Sahni remembered and used for his novel, which Govind had made into this fine, compelling serial. There must have been other towns where Muslims had started the violence. *Tamas* was certainly not implying that all the violence during Partition had been started by the RSS.

I had a slight reservation about the end. The heroine died and her baby with her. I pleaded with Govind to alter it so that the baby lived; amidst all that terror and violence I felt it would be a faint ray of hope, of life continuing despite all the grief, death and suffering of Partition. Govind was not convinced initially but he finally agreed to make the change. I like to think it altered the nature of the serial so that it became a saga not only of death and misery, but also of the affirmation of life.

I took the master cassettes back with me and told the minister, Ajit Panja, and the secretary, Girish Mehra, about the serial. The serial starts with a very powerful scene in which Om Puri is trying to slaughter a pig. I was worried about the effect that might have on the audience and shared my concern with them. Girish Mehra was sympathetic, as always, but said that it was best that the decision be made by Doordarshan's staff. He felt that any arbitrary decision from him would be inappropriate. Panja was much more direct: he said he would have nothing to do with the decision. It was for me to decide and he simply did not want to hear about it.

So it was left to me. I must confess that I was very uneasy the night before the serial started. What if it caused a riot? Press coverage had already ignited controversy about the serial's potentially objectionable nature and this had whetted the appetite of the television audience. Thus we expected a large number of viewers for the first episode. Would it result in a conflagration, an avoidable orgy of violence?

By the next morning I had made up my mind. *Tamas* was going to be shown and we would face whatever the consequences. I relied on the exceptionally fine nature of the serial, which is still, in my mind, one of Govind Nihalani's greatest works. The first episode of *Tamas* was broadcast at 9 p.m. To my great relief there was no reaction at all. I suspect the audience was too stunned by the sheer power and forthright quality of the episode. Whatever the reason, nothing happened. And the viewership for the first episode was, from the reports I received, over 70 per cent of those who had access to television and it stayed around that figure for all the other episodes.

We didn't get away totally unscathed, however. The Hyderabad Kendra was attacked by some vandals after the serial had been telecast for some time, when the RSS's role in the violence became evident. Fortunately no one was hurt, but we lost a number of valuable archival tapes of the earliest programmes telecast from that kendra. A few weeks later a large mob tried to attack Delhi Kendra at Akashvani Bhavan. This was a major incident—the police had to use teargas and lathis to clear the mob, who managed to damage the wall and a gate leading to the building. Mercifully, they couldn't get in.

I must say that right through all this neither the minister nor the secretary ever asked me to stop the serial. In fact, they never spoke to me about it at all. The press acclaimed the serial as one of the finest to have been broadcast and Govind Nihalani became a celebrity. He was fêted in Calcutta and elsewhere as a courageous and exceptionally good film-maker. As far as I was concerned, the telecasting of this serial did much to wash away the memories of Ramanand Sagar's serial. I should add, however, that after the *Ramayana* was telecast Ramanand and I became good friends, recognizing that we had played a game together that he had won.

*

Most of my working days were spent in meetings and fending off eager, anxious, angry and sorrowful producers of serials. It left me little time to think of what to do to improve matters in Doordarshan's unwieldy organization. One thing did become clear: Doordarshan was becoming, at least as far as entertainment was concerned, a mere renter of airtime. The days when it produced serials of its own seemed to be over. When I had first joined Doordarshan I was quite bewildered by the absence of serials made by Doordarshan's own producers. I remembered with some fondness having watched *Trishna*, done with an admirable degree of smoothness. Where were those producers? Well, they were there all right, a rather demoralized lot, because the craze for sponsored serials had pushed their work and the possibility of their making new serials right off the stage. There was a good reason for that happening: Doordarshan was after all a government office (in bureaucratic terms, an 'attached' office) and subject to all the financial procedures that any other government office has to follow. That Doordarshan dealt with material of a special kind—information in the form of documentaries and features, entertainment in the form of short and long films and serials—meant nothing to the financial powers of the time.

The direct consequence of this was that the making of serials by Doordarshan producers was an excruciating ordeal. Every little item had to be justified, sometimes more than once. One producer bitterly recounted an incident during the making of a film by her in which a character broke a doll in a fit of rage. The producer bought two dolls, in case she had to reshoot the scene. This led to a major run-in with the financial adviser. Why had the second doll been purchased, he demanded. When it was explained to him that it was necessary in case the scene had to be reshot, he countered by saying that since it hadn't been necessary to reshoot the scene, the expenditure was infructuous. The second doll should have been bought only when the scene actually had to be reshot. The poor producer, Saba Zaidi, a very talented film-maker who had come to Doordarshan dreaming of making good films and programmes, explained again that that would have taken time, that the whole cast and crew would have had to be kept waiting till the doll was bought. But the finance adviser was adamant. The tussle went on for three months, until the finance man grudgingly approved the expenditure with a stern warning to the producer.

Small wonder, then, that fewer and fewer serials were produced in-house. It was simpler to let outside producers make serials and then show them. The problem was that Doordarshan never commissioned serials. They asked producers to find sponsors who would put up the money for the serial and charged the producer only for the airtime. The result was that the copyright stayed with the producer and Doordarshan never had an opportunity to show a popular serial a second time. If they did, the producer charged Doordarshan a hefty fee and didn't bother with the marketing of the free commercial time provided with each episode. Of course, Doordarshan's own commercial unit was never a place where any actual marketing was conducted.

In this virtual no-win situation I thought I saw a way out. Why not form a society with all the senior staff as members, and register it? It could be given an initial grant of Rs 1 crore. The society could take some producers, film-makers and other staff on loan from Doordarshan and make serials and films without getting into the morass of financial procedures of a government office. As a society, they could frame their own practical rules of business. The serials could be offered to Doordarshan, which would screen them and sell the free commercial time provided with every episode in the market. A substantial portion of that money would go back to the society. A reasonably popular serial could fetch around Rs 18 lakh an episode; the cost of making an episode was, in those modest days, about Rs 3 or 4 lakh. This meant that some Rs 15 lakh per episode could be shared by Doordarshan and the society. A serial normally ran for thirteen episodes, i.e., a quarter of a year at one episode per week. That meant a revenue of almost Rs 2 crore for every serial! The society could use its share of the money to make more programmes and keep augmenting its revenues, while Doordarshan could keep adding a fair amount to its advertising revenues.

I called all the senior officers together and put forward this plan to them. Their initial surprise and hesitation was gradually replaced by smiles of approval, and their reaction gave me a huge amount of enthusiasm. I sat with some of my colleagues and drafted a proposal that would have to be sent to the ministry, since it meant creating a society made up of officers of Doordarshan, in other words, government officers. I took the proposal to the ministry's financial adviser, P.K. Sarkar, a wise and shrewd man whose caustic tongue concealed a generous, friendly nature, and explained it to him. He thought about it, then said I should leave it with him as he needed to study it more carefully.

'Don't be in such a hurry,' he told me. 'The heavens won't fall if you wait a little. And judging by the way you're setting about all this, a little waiting will do you good.'

Sarkar called me up after a few days and asked me to see him. In his room he looked at me speculatively and said, 'That scheme of yours is a little hare-brained but it might work. I'll support it.'

I was relieved and excited.

'But,' Sarkar went on, 'I'll have to get it okayed by the Ministry of Finance. It'll have to go to S.P. Singh, the additional secretary in the Department of Expenditure. This is a major redeployment of revenue and I would like him to clear it.'

'Wasn't he the financial adviser of this ministry a few years ago?'

'He was,' Sarkar said, then added acidly, 'but don't depend on it. It might actually go against you.'

He was right. Singh turned down the proposal.

But I wasn't going to give up so easily. I went to the secretary, Girish Mehra, who listened to the proposal and was very supportive. He took me down to the minister, Ajit Panja, and told him I had a proposal that might change things at Doordarshan. Panja heard me out and then asked me what I wanted him to do. I asked if he would speak to the minister of state for finance, and to my surprise he agreed. He spoke to the minister straightaway and a meeting was fixed to discuss the proposal.

At the meeting, Singh, a portly man with a hard face, repeated his objections. The minister asked him why he was objecting to Doordarshan using its own budgeted money to make more. Then Singh revealed his real objection.

'The scheme is a backdoor method of giving Doordarshan autonomy,' he said harshly. 'And I will never clear it. I am sorry, sir,' he said to his minister, 'but if I have to, I will take this up with the finance minister himself. I will never clear it.'

The minister of state for finance laughed uneasily and told Panja that since Singh had such strong objections, perhaps the proposal could wait. Panja agreed. And that was the end of it. I left the finance ministry seething with rage. I had come up against the worst kind of bureaucratic bigotry and found it difficult to accept.

In my own office I raged against all the secretariat officials, till one of the internal finance people said, 'But, sir, you needn't have gone to the ministry at all.'

I looked at him blankly, and he produced the Doordarshan Code, which was a manual of regulations approved by the government, based on the AIR Code.

'Here,' he said. 'Just look at the first provision set down under "Financial Powers".'

I looked at it. It said, simply, 'The Director General shall have all the financial powers of a Central Ministry except with regard to the creation of posts carrying a salary of over Rs 1800 per month, and of writing off any amount in excess of Rs 1 crore.'

I stared at him. This was late 1986, early on in my tenure, and I hadn't read the huge volume very carefully. The powers of a central ministry! I rang Sarkar and told him that I needn't have gone to the government at all and that I could act on my own in exercise of my own powers.

'You could have,' he said, 'but now that it has been seen and turned down by the government, you can't. That would amount to disobeying the government's orders.'

'Why didn't you tell me I had these powers?' I demanded.

'I'm not the DG,' Sarkar said dryly. 'You are. You are expected to know what your own powers are. I suggest you do some reading. It might do you good.'

To say I felt foolish would be to put it very mildly indeed. My haste, my carelessness, my inexcusable ignorance of my powers as DG was the real reason why the proposal never took off. All I can say in my defence was that my hectic schedule hadn't left me any time to read up on these essential rules and regulations. But I was, after all, a civil servant, and a basic requirement of any good officer is that he know what he can and cannot do under whatever rules are in force. I had not done so and paid the price.

I took home the enormously fat code, which came in a number of equally fat volumes. I would simply have to read through it, as any officer would have done, before I came up with other bright ideas.

*

The world of serials wasn't an altogether bad experience. I met some very talented film-makers and, of course, some not so talented ones, some who were shrewd, greedy and arrogant about their political connections, and condescending producers very taken with their own abilities, which impressed few other than themselves. One of those whom I met and who became a friend was the distinguished film-maker Shyam Benegal. One of the projects to which Doordarshan had been committed was the making of a serial based on Jawaharlal Nehru's *The Discovery of India*. We felt that Shyam Benegal was the best man to make the serial, and spoke to him about it. He agreed, and in the many meetings we had to finalize the agreement with him, I got to know him as a warm, sincere person who had not allowed the eminence and fame he had acquired as a film-maker to change him; he remained as friendly and sincere as he had always been.

The agreement with Shyam Benegal was perhaps the most unique that Doordarshan had entered into till that time. To begin with, the serial was a commissioned serial, the expenses for which were being borne fully by Doordarshan. In addition, we decided that there would be no short cuts and no compromises. The serial would be shot on

35mm film and in the actual locations Nehru mentioned in his book. Shyam chose Roshan Seth to play the role of Nehru; he had done it in Attenborough's *Gandhi* and Seth did it so well that he was asked to play Nehru in a number of other television programmes. Even though the costs were borne by Doordarshan, we agreed that Shyam Benegal would keep a portion of the rights to the serial. There was a good reason for this. Doordarshan was not renowned for its marketing skills, to put it mildly; Shyam, on the other hand, could, through the many contacts he had in the film world, have the serial sold to a number of international television networks. That would bring in a certain amount of revenue to Doordarshan, but, more importantly, it meant that the serial would be seen in parts of the world where it would otherwise never have been shown.

It was a gigantic affair. The total cost was upwards of Rs 11 crore. This may sound like a modest sum in today's world when a two-hour feature film costs three times that much, but in 1987 it was a huge amount. We were determined that it would be a spectacular and finely made serial. To be sure, it never got the kind of viewership enjoyed by the *Ramayana* and the *Mahabharata*, but it got a pretty good viewership, all things considered. Perhaps it was too long; it could have been a few episodes shorter. But Shyam was hesitant to edit out pieces from the book, and the fact that Jawaharlal Nehru's grandson was prime minister was not irrelevant to the decision to keep the serial scrupulously faithful to the book.

I suppose I did, in the end, enjoy selecting serials that were attractive and had some substance. The actual selection of serials was done by a committee of senior Doordarshan officers, it is true, but they insisted I give the final clearance. Perhaps they did not want the responsibility and I couldn't blame them. The ministry could get very nasty with someone who displeased a person of consequence, and it was surprising how many such persons were involved with the production of serials. I was discreet about the fact that the final clearance came from me. Had it become generally known, my life would have become a nightmare. It was bad enough as it was. I used my power of veto quite ruthlessly and the results weren't altogether unsatisfactory.

Some serials bring back pleasant memories. One such is *Ek Kahani*, produced by Manju Singh. Each episode was one complete story and Manju, who never compromised on quality, shot each one on location where the story took place and used local people to play different roles. There was something special about these stories; they were absorbing and very interesting to watch without descending into the usual stereotypes that we usually couldn't avoid in other programmes.

A serial that won the hearts of many was of course *Rajni,* started before my time and which made the actress playing the lead role, the late Priya Tendulkar, a star. The idea developed by the producer, Basu Chatterji, was clever and appealed to many because it identified some of the unsavoury aspects of our society—offensive, callous behaviour, demanding bribes from helpless, poor citizens and the like. Having Rajni come in to set things right gave viewers much surrogate satisfaction since they often believed that there was indeed someone called Rajni who could do what they would have loved to do themselves. Other good serials included *Nukkad* by Saeed Mirza, and the serials by Shridhar Kshirsagar, which had storylines not very different from some good US serials but were well executed and always worth watching.

At the end of the day, these are the kinds of serials that one remembers. They were good and they were popular. In making them the producers didn't pander to what marketing people now swear by, the preferences of the 'masses'. Producers like Manju Singh and Basu Chatterji had a very clear notion of what they wanted to present and were skilful enough to do it in a manner that attracted large audiences. These may be just two instances, but they were enough to make the world of serials less overtly commercial and stereotypical.

3

Newsworthy Efforts

News broadcasts on Doordarshan started out in the 1970s as not much more than a reading out of the pool news—news put together in the general newsroom of AIR. It had little by way of visuals, except the occasional shot of the odd photograph and of newspapers. Gradually, however, 16mm Arriflex cameras were acquired and the major stations started to get photo laboratories where film could be developed and then used on the tele-cine machines, which ran the films directly through as television signals. It was clumsy and time-consuming, so visual coverage was used mainly for 'soft' stories, not for breaking news.

Then came the Electronic News Gathering (ENG) cameras—lightweight shoulder-carried cameras that made the old 16mm film cameras obsolete almost overnight. They shot on tape, which eliminated the need to process film, so that events could be covered and then shown quickly during the bulletin. It also meant that, with the help of what were called Electronic Field Processing (EFP) vans, footage could be edited right in the van and sent as a microwave signal to the control rooms at the station.

While all this was exciting, it didn't quite match up with the facilities and the space provided to news crews in the stations. They were crowded into one or two shabby, dirty rooms, littered with paper and lined with rows of typewriters on which the scripts were written. They had to share the editing facilities with producers of other programmes, which was a source of frequent arguments and friction. Above all, there were certain conventions that for some reason were considered sacrosanct. For example, even though the new cameras could record sound together with the pictures, the footage shown was always silent; the only exception was when the prime minister said something. The main source of news remained the pool news from AIR. News or 'agency feed' that came in from the Press Trust of India (PTI) and United News of India (UNI) was also used, but it was invariably cross-checked with the AIR newsroom. Doordarshan had, I discovered, just one television journalist, whose stories were used selectively and erratically.

This then was the news set-up when I joined Doordarshan. The central newsroom, where the national bulletins in Hindi and English were prepared, was housed in dingy quarters in some squalid barracks at the back of Akashvani Bhavan. From there the newsreader had to cross the compound between the barracks and Akashvani Bhavan and take the lift up to the fifth floor, where the news studio was located. The editing of visual footage was done quite separately using editing suites located in another part of the barracks. There were hardly any archives, and tapes of events were kept in stacks all over the floor in one particular room. Only the person in charge of this 'library' knew what was where, and if he wasn't around (which was not infrequent), no one, literally no one, knew where to find the footage that was needed to make up a news item.

Presiding over this newsroom was C.V. Raman; not the celebrated Nobel laureate but a thin, grey-haired and very shrewd newsperson whose cynical smile spoke volumes for what he had witnessed or been a part of. He also had a short temper and was not impressed by eager DGs from the IAS; however, as time passed he became more relaxed and informal. At times he even seemed pleased to see me, which, knowing Raman as I did by then, was quite something. He had to get his bulletins ready despite not only the constraints I have mentioned but also another exasperating bureaucratic problem—he had virtually no financial or administrative authority.

Under the rules framed by our wise men in the finance, personnel and home ministries, an office can have only one head. As a proposition this makes sense. That head exercises the powers given to him by government order. Consequently, all that went on in Delhi Doordarshan was under the supervision of the director of the television centre, or DTC. He had all the equipment and he decided what equipment would be made available to which unit. To him the news unit was just another unit of his station. Raman never considered himself a part of Doordarshan Delhi; he was preparing national news bulletins that were part of the National Programme. The fact that the National Programme was broadcast from the Delhi station was merely coincidental. In a proper set-up the central news unit would have had its own studios, cameras, editing equipment and other facilities; its news bulletins would have been transmitted directly from the MSR to the earth station that sent the signal to the satellite, from where all transmitters would receive the signal, boost it and retransmit it terrestrially. But as things were, Raman had to ask the DTC Delhi for everything, even a car to take a news team to cover an event. I suspect this state of affairs was what made him as testy as he was, and, of course, the fact that news always makes those dealing with it testy and irritable. Eventually I persuaded the DTC Delhi to let Raman have some cars at his disposal and to ensure that priority was given to news coverages when camera teams were sent out. The DTC didn't like it, but agreed when I pointed out that Raman was a very senior man. Seniority was a big thing with all government officers then, as it is now.

News reading, the kind which was a visual version of the AIR news, was how news reading had evolved at the BBC, from where Doordarshan got all its ideas—hardly surprising when you consider that the first lot of people who were trained for news on television were sent to the BBC. That fascinating series called *Television* made by the British TV channel Granada, now sadly unavailable, had two episodes on news. In one there is an amusing account of how, in the first years, the newsreaders were not shown on screen; the news was read while the BBC logo was displayed on the screen because the news producers were afraid that the readers might show some expression on their faces that would compromise the BBC's reputation for impartial, objective news, read in measured tones shorn of all emotional nuances. They gave up that silly practice soon enough, but newsreaders continued to read the news with wooden expressions until the coming of celebrated news anchors like David Frost and Chris Chataway.

There was little chance of showing any expression when the news was read on Doordarshan, because the readers (or newscasters, as they liked to call themselves) read from scripts kept on a table in front of them, looking up briefly and then down again at the script. They had made quite an art of it, this ability to look up and then look down without losing their place on the page. Perhaps they marked out where they would look up—I don't know and never found out. But it meant that the viewers saw, for the most part, the glossy hair of the newscaster, all done up very carefully, in certain instances to cover receding hairlines and balding pates.

After I had watched some news bulletins and the glossy heads of the newsreaders bent over their scripts, looking up occasionally and then down again into their papers, I asked Shashi Kapoor, the deputy DG in charge of news and current affairs, why they didn't use teleprompters.

'We have a set of new ones,' he told me. 'Digiprompters, they're called. The trouble is they can only use the Roman alphabet. If we use them for the English news and not for Hindi, there'll be trouble.'

It was Madan Mohan who sorted that one out for me: 'Get the old models. They're nothing more than small cameras on a boom that shoot the script and project it onto a mirror, which then reflects the image onto a darkened screen in front of the lens of the camera. Since it's shooting a page it can shoot whatever is on that page—Devnagari, Bengali, English, anything.'

We acquired the old teleprompters, called Autocue, long discarded by other television networks, and got the newsreaders to rehearse with them for a few days. Then, one night, I watched with a certain amount of pleasure and satisfaction as the newsreader looked at the viewer and began reading the news. For verisimilitude they had been told to glance down occasionally at their papers to give the impression that they were refreshing their memory; otherwise they read the news straight from the teleprompter.

From that night onwards reading from a text on the table ended. Newsreaders looked at the audiences, and the audiences got to see who was reading the news. Tejeshwar Singh, Neethi Ravindran, Renee Simon, J.B. Raman, Salma Sultan and others became familiar faces. This led to another one of those silly tussles that kept occurring. Some news producers felt that these newsreaders were becoming prima donnas and needed to be put in their place, so they had to be taken off from reading the news from time to time. The newsreaders were furious, because they thought this most arbitrary. I had to tell the producers firmly that the task of a television network was, in fact, to build up newsreaders or newscasters, because that helped increase viewership. They would have to keep the newsreaders on as scheduled, irrespective of their airs and graces.

One night, in late 1986, I was in my office when Raman rang up. Shashi Kapoor was on leave or on tour and Raman said he was facing a major problem. The newsreader for the English bulletin, Neethi Ravindran, hadn't shown up, and there was just an hour to go before the news was broadcast.

'Have you tried calling her up?' I asked. Newsreaders had to leave their contact numbers with the station precisely for contingencies such as this.

'Of course,' Raman said irritably. 'There's no response. From any of the numbers.'

'Hold on,' I said. 'I'm coming down.'

I went to the central newsroom to find a tense Raman pacing up and down. I asked him if he had tried the standby newsreader. There was always a standby waiting at his or her house or at the end of a telephone line.

'Yes. The standby's not there either.'

'This is all wrong,' I said. 'What's happened to the system? They've become a law unto themselves.'

'I told you they were becoming prima donnas,' Raman said.

'Anyway, we have to do something,' I said. 'Try the AIR newsroom. Do they have a newsreader there?'

They did. I asked the AIR people to send him down to the Doordarshan newsroom immediately. Since AIR was in the next building, or rather, the Doordarshan newsroom was in those derelict hutments behind Broadcasting House, the home of AIR, he was there within minutes.

'Have you ever read the news for television?' I asked.

'No, I haven't,' he replied. 'But I'd like to try.'

'There you are, Raman. Problem solved.'

Raman looked gloomy and called in the news producer. The news producer flatly refused to let the AIR reader do it.

'Why not, for God's sake?' I asked.

'He's never done news on television, sir,' the producer said earnestly. 'I can't take the risk. Suppose he simply dries up halfway through?'

I saw that the objection was valid. Years on the stage had made me realize that novices can do just that when they come on for the first time. It obviously was the same for the news, even though the script was there in front of you; unless you had had some practice you could just freeze. And that would be the end of the bulletin.

'Is there any presenter in the kendra?' I asked desperately. 'Someone making some announcements?'

The news producer rang up the duty officer and looked up at me. 'There is,' he said. 'Amita Kohli's there, waiting to make the final announcements for the night.'

'The news bulletin will be over long before that,' I said. 'Get her down here.'

A very nervous Amita was brought in.

'I've never done a news bulletin,' she said. 'I don't think I can do it.'

'You've done announcements in Hindi,' the news producer told her. 'This isn't so different. Come on, Amita. Your English is pretty good and you've done plenty of television work.'

'No, I don't know,' Amita said, becoming increasingly frightened. 'I'll make a hash of it. I know I will.'

'No you won't,' the producer said. 'Go on, get made up.'

Amita was taken to the make-up room.

Raman still looked gloomy. 'She's so nervous, I don't know if she can do it.'

'She's a pro,' the news producer said. 'She'll do it all right. We just need to persuade her that she can.'

Raman still looked uncertain. By now there was just half an hour left for the bulletin to go on the air.

'Why don't *you* do it?' Raman suddenly said to me.

I gaped at him.

'You've been on stage. You know what it takes. Just do it like a part.'

'Good idea,' the news producer said. 'And you did a few interviews on Doordarshan some years ago, didn't you? So it's not your first time before a camera.'

'It'll be the first time I'm looking at a camera,' I replied. 'And it's nonsense, anyway. Amita can do it very well. We'll work on her.'

'No,' Raman said firmly. 'You've got to do it. I can depend on you. Go on. Read through the script. Quickly!'

It began to feel a little unreal. Was the DG of Doordarshan going to read the news? And yet, I felt a tingle of excitement. It might be fun, I thought. I began rolling down the sleeves of my shirt. Could I do it, say, once a month?

All of a sudden the problem resolved itself. Fifteen minutes before the bulletin went on the air, Preet Bedi, one of the regular newsreaders, came in casually for a chat. It wasn't his day for the news; he had just dropped by. The moment he came in Raman grabbed him by the arm, gave him the script and virtually frog-marched him to the make-up room from where a thoroughly frightened Amita Kohli had just come out.

'It's on the prompter,' he said to Preet curtly. 'Just go in and read it.'

Poor Preet. He read the news that night, very smoothly, without a hitch, but it seemed to me he had a sort of stunned look about him, a look, as I kept telling him, he never lost after that.

The crisis was averted, but I have to admit I left the newsroom feeling a little forlorn. I had come so near to reading the news—and perhaps making a regular feature of it—and it had all faded away. Raman came with me to the gate and smiled grimly.

'You really wanted to do it, didn't you?' he said. 'Well, give up your job and come and audition. I might just take you on.'

'Oh, get out,' I said grumpily and slammed the car door shut.

A contrite Neethi Ravindran later explained that she had got the dates mixed up, and so had the standby newsreader. Which was all very well; the fact was I missed a chance of becoming the first DG to have read the news on television. And I bet I would have been pretty good.

There was another area where I felt that things needed to change immediately. The signature tune for the news was, in the words of a newspaper critic, like a galloping donkey with a broken back. It verged on the ludicrous and infected the bulletin that followed with the same foolishness. This, I felt, had to be set right. We got in touch with the very talented Louis Banks, who composed a bright, brisk, catchy signature tune. It was played over a visual of a revolving earth around which the title words appeared, which replaced the earlier mish-mash of images of various dull events. The earth then changed into the Doordarshan logo just as the music ended. We had a slightly different one for the regional news bulletins used by the kendras, with similar visuals but different music. It provoked a fair amount of comment when it was first used (just about everything Doordarshan did then was commented on), but on the whole the new logo and signature tune got general approval and stayed with the news as long as I was in the organization.

*

Raman would smile his cynical smile when asked about pressures brought on him to carry a particular story. Those pressures were at times intense, ranging from peremptory orders from the minister's office to messages from other ministers, secretaries and powerful people in the Congress. I told him he could refer all these to me.

'Not necessary,' he said. 'I'll handle them. I've been doing that for some time now. If it gets too much I'll speak to you. But I doubt if I'll need to.'

He had spoken too soon. Not too long after that he rang me one night. The I & B minister's private secretary—the same Johny Joseph—had phoned him and ordered him to carry a story about some inauguration or other by the home minister. Raman had said that it was hardly a news item and in any case there simply wasn't space in the bulletin. But Joseph was adamant, apparently, and told Raman he had better drop one of the stories to make room for the home minister's story.

'This is going too far,' Raman said angrily. 'He's actually telling me what I should and shouldn't carry!'

I assured him I would do something and get back to him. I rang Joseph up and said, 'Johnny, if you have something to tell the newsroom, tell me, not them, okay? I'll decide if they need to change the bulletin. Don't speak to them directly.'

I then rang Raman and told him to put out the bulletin as it was.

The next day I was asked to see the minister. Gadgil was agitated, which was not like him.

'Look here,' he told me abruptly. 'If I say something has to go in the news it has to go. It should never be contradicted.'

'It wouldn't have been, sir,' I replied, 'if you'd told me yourself in the first place. When your private secretary rings up the newsroom it upsets everything there. We mustn't devalue the authority of the chief editor.'

'But I am the minister,' said Gadgil. 'I must be obeyed.'

'That's just what I'm saying, sir. All you need to do is tell me, not your secretary. After all,' I added ingenuously, 'I'm one of your officers too.'

'But you didn't carry that news item about the home minister,' he said, still annoyed.

'Very true, sir,' I replied. 'There was no space for it. In fact, if you tell me whenever there is a request for coverage, I can discuss it with you. If it can't be carried for good reasons we can always say so. And you know, sir,' I added craftily, 'the PM very clearly told me to carry only what was considered newsworthy.'

The minister was quiet, sullen. Finally he said, 'All right. You may go.'

I left the room quietly. Never again did that good man or his secretary ring me or the newsroom.

Pressure to put stories into the bulletins was only one of the problems afflicting the news. The basic predicament was its identity. Was the news unit part of each kendra or part of a distinct news division located in each kendra but answerable ultimately to the chief editor and to the news editor in each kendra, not to the DTC? If it wasn't, then how would it function in terms of studio time and editing equipment, get facilities like camera teams, vehicles to take news teams to different locations, find office space in which to operate, and so on? Whenever we met, every DTC explained to me that whether one liked it or not he was the person on whom the maximum pressure was put to carry certain stories. He was also the one targeted by local government leaders or power groups of one sort or another if a particular story was not well received. If the news was to be treated as a unit distinct from the kendra, he would be in the unhappy position of being considered responsible for the news and yet not a part of the news unit.

I felt the answer lay in a nice mix of the two: the DTC had to be involved, to the extent that the news editor should keep him informed of the content of each news bulletin, but he should allow the news unit to put together the bulletins independently, making available whatever facilities he had. There was no equipment earmarked for the news—whatever the kendra had was shared between the news unit and other producers. That seemed wrong—the news unit needed to have its own equipment, including cameras, editing suites, transport, computers, its own direct links, satellite or microwave, with other kendras and the central unit, and its own funds for the expenses it incurred. There was a good reason for this: news stories waited for no one. When they happened they simply had to be covered as fast as possible, in as much depth as possible, and sent to all kendras, or at least to the central news unit in Delhi, where the chief editor would decide which kendras would receive the stories.

There was another matter that seemed to be a major problem: human resources. The newsrooms had mainly officers from the then Central Information Service (CIS), which later became the Indian Information Service (IIS). These people were recruited through the UPSC, the Indian Police Service (IPS) and other services, and were all government officers. They were sent to Doordarshan on deputation and they manned all the posts of editors at different levels and even of correspondents, although there were a few news correspondents recruited directly by AIR and sent on to Doordarshan. One of the ways, in fact, of 'punishing' a news editor for a story considered to be inappropriate was to post him somewhere in the units manned by the IIS, such as the Research and Reference Division or the Directorate of Field Publicity.

This was not right at all. Doordarshan news needed to have its own professional news staff—journalists, editors and newsreaders. The last was necessary because, while many of the existing newsreaders read well and looked attractive, they were not professional newspersons: they had full-time jobs and read the news as a sort of hobby, because they were good at reading aloud. Some of them were good theatre people; this must have helped them develop presence, voice modulation and other qualities which enhanced their reading. There were a few who were full-time newsreaders, like Minu and Salma Sultan, but they had no exposure at all to flesh-and-blood news reporting. They just read the news. I was convinced that newsreaders had to be journalists first. Only when they spent time in the field, putting a story together, reporting as others did and then came back to the newsroom to write up the text and edit the footage, would they become genuine newsreaders.

This led me to the idea of a professional news service for Doordarshan hired directly from among those who had some idea of journalism or a background suitable for it. They would be trained as television people first, then as journalists over a period of two years, and finally they would take over the newsrooms. We would begin with the central news first, that is, the news bulletins that went out nationally, in Hindi and in English. Later, a second lot would be recruited to work in the regional languages in each kendra.

These journalists would function as teams, each journalist with a cameraperson and a sound recordist, and a Maruti Gypsy (no Qualises then!) specially adapted for coverage of all kinds of events. The cameraperson and reporter would be able to climb through a hatch in the roof to record an event and there would be wire mesh around the roof to protect them from stones and other objects that might be thrown at them, as they often were. Each Gypsy would be in radio contact with the newsroom so the editors would know what was coming. In each city there would be special points—preferably in an AIR building or any other office—with microwave links to the newsrooms. This would ensure that footage was sent back to the newsrooms in time if the Gypsies were caught in traffic jams. Ideally, each Gypsy ought to have its own microwave unit, but that was financially and physically impossible. Not only would it cost the earth, but we also couldn't fit the link into a Gypsy.

I worked on this idea and put together a complete proposal after discussions that went on long into the night with C.V. Raman, Shashi Kapoor and the finance officers in Doordarshan. We felt we needed four kinds of newspeople: news correspondents, assistant news correspondents, news editors and assistant news editors. News correspondents and news editors would have some background in journalism, either in a newspaper or in another news organization; the younger ones would have had some exposure to news, or a degree in journalism or something similar. Side by side we put in requirements for more camerapersons, sound recordists and junior engineers. They would come from the ranks of those already being taken in by Doordarshan; the numbers would just be increased to allow for the secondment of some to the news units on a full-time basis.

We also provided for a good number of Gypsies, to be modified to suit our needs. The biggest breakthrough was the cameras. The wise and very supportive Madan Mohan, retired but still working as a valued adviser, suggested we look at the new Sony Betacam cameras then coming out of Japan. The Betacam was far more advanced than the heavy shoulder-carried U-matic camera. It was smaller and lighter, it needed no sound recordist since it recorded directly into a video cassette, and it could shoot in any situation the cameraperson might encounter. It could be used, for example, to shoot into the sun, or for a pan shot without the jerkiness typical of such a shot on a U-matic camera. It needed no extra lights unless it was extremely dark, and then all one needed to do was mount a light on the camera.

These were news cameras, real news cameras. In the market there were models from Sony, Ikegami, Hitachi and the German company Bosch, which used Sony recording cassettes. All of them claimed to have unique features but ultimately it came down to Bosch and Sony. We watched both companies demonstrate the virtues of their cameras, and I asked Madan Mohan and the new engineer-in-chief, O.P. Khushu, what they thought.

'There's not much to choose between them,' Madan Mohan said after a while. By that time he was stricken with what became a fatal illness and was constantly in pain. But being the man he was, he never let it show. 'Unnecessary fuss' was what he put it down to, but it had slowed him down. And he walked with an effort, using a stick.

'But surely,' I asked him, 'it's better to have a camera made by one company rather than a hybrid which uses one part from one company and makes only the camera? There's bound to be some complication and there'll be the usual blame game. Bosch will blame Sony and Sony will blame Bosch.'

He smiled and said, 'You've become a little more practical I see. Yes, it's always preferable to take something made entirely by one company.'

We chose the Sony Betacam for the news units. That the decision was right became evident soon enough: within a few years the other models had all disappeared.

Having addressed all our equipment needs, I finally trotted down to the ministry with my proposal for a professional news service. Sarkar raised his eyebrows when I told him about it.

'Another hare-brained scheme?' he asked, smiling wryly. 'You enjoy creating work for me. Avoidable work.'

'What do you mean hare-brained?' I asked him full of righteous indignation. 'You supported the idea of the Doordarshan Society . . .'

Sarkar held up his hand. 'All right, all right. Now what have you started up?'

I began to explain the scheme eagerly to him. He closed his eyes and said, 'Bhaskar Ghose, just leave the proposal here. Let me read it. You go home and sleep. Or say your prayers. Or do something that will calm you down.' I knew it was no use talking to him then, and left.

A few days later he called me up. 'That news scheme of yours, it's good. You'd better come and discuss it with the secretary.'

I dashed across. Girish Mehra had always been not just supportive, but affectionate. We spent a good deal of time exchanging odd pieces of gossip, and he was never anything but kind and considerate to whatever I took him by way of proposal, complaint or comment. He listened to my exposition of the scheme and then heard Sarkar on the financial aspects. Suman Dubey was also there; Suman was information adviser and a very close friend of the PM's. In fact he had given up his career in journalism and had taken this assignment on mainly to help Rajiv Gandhi. Suman thought the scheme was very good and needed to be taken up immediately. Girish Mehra gave it his approval. We had to go through further procedures, just to make sure there wasn't some mess-up at a later stage. We spent hours discussing the project in the Ministry of Finance and the Ministry of Information and Broadcasting, and, finally, the papers were placed before the minister, Ajit Panja, who signed them. It was done: the proposal was no longer a proposal but a project. I was elated, overjoyed and excited all at once.

The next few months went by in feverish activity. Several administrative problems had to be overcome. How, for example, could we, a government agency, recruit people except through the UPSC? We found the answer in one of the many powers given to the DG in the code: the power to appoint 'staff artists' on contract. The DG of AIR had been appointing musicians regularly on that basis, and we saw no reason why we couldn't do so for people in the newsroom. In all this I had the constant and wise support of Shakuntala, deputy DG in charge of administration. She had risen from the Central Secretariat Service, which gave her a deep and wide-ranging knowledge of governmental rules and procedures, and she added to it a sense of vision, with which she was able to see the end of a project, foresee the pitfalls and take steps to avoid them. She was, above all, frank and totally averse to negotiation on what she felt was ill-advised or incorrect. This led to many occasions when I was short, even harsh, in my comments on her advice. She never let it ruffle her, but patiently explained why she felt I was being too hasty, or why a particular matter needed to be referred to the ministry or to the financial authorities. It was much later that I realized what a fine officer she was; were it not for her the recruitment and appointment of the television newspersons would never have happened.

Shashi Kapoor, C.V. Raman and some others sat down and devised a question paper that candidates would have to answer. Meanwhile, an advertisement for these posts came out in all major newspapers, and a large number of applications came in. Those eligible were asked to take the written test and the ones with the highest marks were called for an interview. I had put together a fine board to interview the prospective television journalists: Jamal Kidwai, former I & B secretary and at that time founder and moving spirit of the Mass Communications Research Centre at Jamia Milia University, a centre now named after him; S.S. Gill, another former I & B secretary; M.V. Kamath, seasoned, urbane journalist and mediaperson, who unfortunately couldn't attend all the interviews; Suman Dubey, who made it clear that he was not to be on the official selection committee; and a veteran of the AIR newsroom and of the early years of Doordarshan, N.L. Chowla.

At the initial meeting of this board, some of the members pointed out that the kind of person we needed couldn't be found on the basis of his or her performance in a written examination. Much would depend on the ability of the candidate to think on his or her feet, to speak coherently, and not to be overwhelmed by events or people. This meant that their assessment by the board had to be of greater importance than the marks they had received in the examination, which was really more a means of testing their fluency in Hindi or English. So we decided that we would in fact make their performance at the interview the deciding factor, the marks in the written examination determining their *inter se* ranking.

The interviews went on, and meanwhile the engineering department began preparations to acquire the cameras and other equipment, including the Gypsies. I flew to Pune and tied up arrangements for the training of the journalists in the Film and Television Institute of India. They were to be trained as television people first, I had decided, because they needed to think of news in images rather than as something written in notebooks. It was therefore essential that their first reactions to an event be in the language of television and not that of print journalism. After three months at the institute, they would be given regular training as journalists in the field.

One of the most gratifying aspects of this process was the enthusiastic support I got from all those I went to for help: everyone, including Reuters, the *Times* correspondent and several newspaper editors, agreed to take on one or two of the trainees and put them through their paces as journalists. Thanks to the generosity of Friedrich-Ebert-Stiftung (FES), a German NGO that helped media organizations in developing countries in a variety of ways, I also got two English-speaking television journalists to come down to train the recruits for a month on how to cover a story as a television journalist, how to edit footage and write to the images they were going to use.

Finally, when the interviews were over, we looked at the list of those who had been recommended by the board and were very satisfied. A full list was prepared and sent to the ministry for approval by the minister, which was necessary because we were appointing a large number of staff artists. And that was when the balloon went up.

Girish Mehra sent the file to the minister recommending that the appointments be approved. Ajit Panja took his own time, and nine days later returned the file, which was sent to me by the secretary without comment. Panja had rejected the appointments completely. He also said that 'the entire matter should be looked into *de novo*', whatever that meant. I was utterly astonished. Girish Mehra and I had discussed the project in the minister's room on a number of occasions, and he had raised no objection to it then. In fact, I had mentioned to him that the recruitment of television journalists was one of the recommendations of the Joshi Committee, a committee set up by the ministry some years earlier under the aegis of P.C. Joshi, which laid down the guidelines on the way Doordarshan should function. This particular recommendation, I had pointed out to the minister, had been accepted by the government.

I explained all this in a longish note to the ministry and sent it to the secretary. It had no effect. The file was returned with the directions that the minister's orders had to be followed. I then discovered why there was such strong objection by Panja to the appointment of these journalists. The minister's private secretary had, by mistake, sent two papers along with the file, that were obviously not meant to be seen by me; they were part of the internal notes made in the minister's office. One was a note from the private secretary to the minister mentioning that the minister was right in saying (obviously to the private secretary) that he was seeing the file for the first time. What the private secretary had not clarified to the minister was that the matter had been discussed verbally on earlier occasions. The second paper was another note from the private secretary to the minister forwarding a letter from a certain candidate who had applied for the post of news correspondent.

The candidate, a woman whom I shall call Nandini Sharma, was a rather colourful character. I had first met her soon after I had joined as DG. She had come wreathed in smiles and informed me that she was from my college (St Stephen's) and that her husband had been in the IAS but had died rather suddenly. She didn't sound or look very disturbed by it, and I remember thinking that she was probably putting on a brave front. She had told me that she had been doing programmes for Doordarshan 'since she was a child' and was very keen to read the English news. Hearing her speak I knew she would never be able to. She spoke in that comic way some people do when they try to put on what they think is a very British accent to cover their natural, Indian accent; occasionally the accent would slip and her Indian English would come through. At the time, I had told her in my usual diplomatic manner that I would refer her request to the committee that auditioned people who wanted to read the news, and she had gone away, her smile intact. When I mentioned her request to Shashi Kapoor later, he hit the roof.

'Nandini Sharma read the news?' he shouted. 'It's absolutely out of the question!' He followed that with some other remarks that I will discreetly pass over. But I persuaded him to get the committee to audition her, and he agreed to do so, very reluctantly. As he and I had expected, the committee rejected her out of hand. A few days later she came to see me again and asked me what the decision was. I told her.

'But they don't know anything,' she said. 'They themselves cannot speak good English.' This of a committee that had, among others, Joy Michael, director of Yatrik Theatre, who had trained in the London Academy of Music and Dramatic Art, and spoke faultless English, her mother tongue.

'That's nonsense,' I said sharply. 'And besides, what they've said is true.'

'What?'

'You do speak very funny English,' I said. 'You'll never be able to read the news.'

On hearing this, the lady went berserk. She started screaming at me at the top of her voice, '*You* speak funny English! Who are you? I'll see how you keep your job!' and more to that effect.

Hearing the commotion, Shiv Sharma and Shashi Kapoor came into my room. They got hold of her and firmly took her away. I could hear her screaming outside, and then, mercifully, the door shut.

I didn't see her after that for a good while; the next time I encountered her was when she came for the news correspondents' interview, looking demure and quiet. She fumbled with most of her answers, and after she left, the board was in no doubt about her unsuitability for the post. However, because she had received reasonably good marks in the written examination, she made it to the list of those selected as assistant news correspondents.

But Ms Sharma hadn't been making programmes at Doordarshan 'since she was a child' for nothing. She had obviously built up extensive contacts, and knew of their decisions even before the file went to the ministry. She then used some of her other contacts—I can only guess who they were—to get an appointment with the minister, whom she obviously regaled with a tearful account of how badly she was being treated. Her note, marked prominently 'to be shred when read', was a half-literate account of why she should actually be a news correspondent and not be offered a lower post. In his covering note the private secretary had said, to his credit, 'It may be pointed out that her note is motivated—if the original plan is implemented then she would get the higher post of news correspondent. Now she has been selected as ANC only.'

The private secretary's note was completely disregarded by Panja, for reasons best known to him. I was then told by someone on his staff that if Nandini Sharma were to be made a news correspondent the minister would approve the scheme in its entirety. I called the dependable, clear-headed Shakuntala and told her all this. She thought for a while, and then said, 'We are taking fourteen news correspondents, is that not so? If this woman is taken in as one of fourteen, will it destroy the news set-up you want?'

'But how can we do it?' I asked her. 'On what logic, on what rationale?'

'That you leave to me. But do you agree to take her as a news correspondent to save the whole project?'

'Yes, dammit,' I said with exasperation. 'I'll just have to suffer the creature's presence in a newsroom. I can't abandon the project.'

Shakuntala went away with the papers and came into my room the next morning. 'I have worked it out,' she said to me wearily. 'Here is the new list.'

Nandini Sharma's name was on it.

'How on earth . . .' I began.

'I had to rework the cut-off marks, but I've done it, and ensured that the others still stay on the list. Only, you now have fifteen news correspondents, not fourteen. This will stand up to scrutiny in any forum. And now, if you don't mind, I will go home and sleep.' I could see she needed to.

I sent the file with the new list back to the ministry and waited. I didn't have to wait long. Back it came, duly approved. All Panja's objections appeared to have vanished.

Perhaps this was compromise, an instance of craven acceptance of pressure of the worst kind, but I can only plead that I was desperate to save the new scheme for Doordarshan news, and felt that the price I paid was relatively small. It was, after all, in Panja's power to have stopped the scheme. Those were days when one had to tread carefully through the minefield of political requirements of different kinds, encounter obstacles raised by financial mandarins and deal with the ambitions of the unqualified and mediocre. I got the project going and to me, that was what mattered.

In August 1988, all the newly hired correspondents reported to the Film and Television Institute in Pune, and I went there to meet them. There were some minor complaints about accommodation, but the bunch was, on the whole, cheerful and eager to get going. Nandini Sharma arrived accompanied by Desh Raj Singh, a joint secretary in the Ministry of Urban Development. He seemed to be a special friend; in her joining report she had put down his address as her permanent residential address. While all the recruits had arrived by second class AC—it was all we could afford—Nandini and her companion had flown. I knew this because they were on the same flight as I was. Desh Raj Singh took me aside and asked me to make sure that Nandini was 'properly looked after' and 'given a good room' in the hostel, and so on. I told him as coldly as I could that she would get exactly what the others got; no more, no less.

I spoke to the recruits on the first day of their training, and they, naturally, were concerned about their future in Doordarshan. I told them they had a bright future; they would be ushering in a new era of television journalism in Doordarshan. Their worry was that they had been hired on contract; what would happen when the initial period expired?

'Don't worry,' I assured them heartily. 'I'm here, and you have nothing to worry about.' I said it as if I was going to be DG of Doordarshan forever. As it happened I had just a short time left in the organization, but I didn't know that then.

Meanwhile, the news bulletins continued to be made with newsreaders who actually had faces instead of glossy heads of hair or shining bald pates. And with them came the pressures. 'Carry this' or 'carry that' were not really very common; what was usual was hysterical rage on the phone at a story which showed the government, or the ruling party, 'in a bad light', or was 'pro-opposition', or just didn't give someone the publicity they were desperate to get. Initially rather gently, then with a little more confidence, I persuaded the newsrooms that they should refer any such requests or reactions to me, and just get on with their work.

Often the angry reactions were comic. One member of Parliament, livid with rage, railed at me because of what he perceived as Doordarshan's deliberate, malicious omission to cover him. Apparently at some event or the other he was on the dais with the prime minister and other dignitaries.

'The camera was focused on PM sahib,' he bellowed, 'which we of course all wanted, then it moved slo-ow-ly to the right, covered the honourable HM [home minister] and then kept going towards the right. I was *just three* seats from the HM and saw the camera moving in my direction. I pushed my chair in that direction, leaned towards the person next to me, and do you know what happened, Mr DG Doordarshan? The camera stopped *just* before it came to me. *Just before!* This was deliberate! They are trying to eliminate me! I demand that the cameraman be sacked!'

I looked very concerned and told him I would take stern action, and reassured him that all of us admired him greatly. After shouting for another ten or fifteen minutes, he finally left.

We commissioned a number of current affairs programmes. One of these was called *Focus* and was anchored by M.J. Akbar. It was rather cleverly done. Akbar knew how to get the mileage that he wanted and yet did it in a way that would leave the ruling party and the protectors of the governmental image clueless. I let him have his way, and *Focus* rapidly became one of the most widely watched English current affairs programmes. There were also some very interesting programmes done by Ramesh Sharma, who was young, eager to make hard-hitting programmes, impatient with the procedures and the precautions that the news unit took. He came to me in exasperation fairly frequently, and I made it a point to let him do his programmes his way. These, too, got large audiences. Ramesh's programmes were not so much news as issue-based—lack of amenities somewhere, or some problem elsewhere. In one, however, we came pretty near the bone. This was a programme on the Gorkhaland agitation, which Ramesh knew a great deal about, having grown up in Kalimpong, one of the major towns in Darjeeling district and a centre of the Gorkhaland activity. He brought in the programme for me to watch; it had Priyaranjan Das Munshi, then minister of state for commerce, saying on camera, 'You can't believe anything the CPI(M) says. They are all liars.'

Ramesh cut from that to the chief minister of West Bengal, Jyoti Basu, saying, 'Why should I tell lies? I am not a Congressman.'

This was too delicious to pass up, so we kept it that way in the programme.

The next day Girish Mehra called me up.

'What the hell did you show last night?' he asked. 'There's a huge *hulla-gulla* going on about it. You had better come over. The minister wants to see you.'

I went to the minister's room with a tape of the programme. Panja was looking grim and asked me if I had seen the programme before it was telecast.

I told him I had.

He then asked me why I had let pass that remark by Jyoti Basu calling Congressmen liars.

'Well, sir,' I began, 'it wasn't exactly like that . . .'

He interrupted me and told me it had become a serious affair, and officers from the Prime Minister's Office were coming over to find out what had happened. Within a short time, Gopi and H.Y. Sharada Prasad, information adviser to the prime minister, came in.

'Well,' Sharada Prasad said, 'let us see what the programme has.'

They watched the offending bit of the programme in silence.

'There's nothing so very terrible,' Sharada Prasad said. 'Das Munshi said the CPI(M) were liars and Jyoti Basu said what amounted to the same thing about Congressmen.'

'I thought it was pretty clever,' Gopi said. 'Definitely witty.'

'Anyway,' Sharada Prasad said in his unruffled way, 'the fact is, both said much the same thing. There's nothing wrong with giving both versions together.'

Panja looked as if he was going to cry.

Sharada Prasad and Gopi got up. 'It's all right, sir,' Sharada Prasad said to Panja. 'No harm's been done. We'll brief the PM about this.'

As they were going out, Gopi took me aside. 'It was really a clever exchange,' he said. 'But just be a little careful. You see how hypersensitive these people are.'

After they left, Girish Mehra grinned at me and said, '*Sala,* you got away with it this time. But don't push your luck.'

There were other, more gratifying moments, too. One was the coverage of what was called Operation Black Thunder: terrorists had holed up in the Golden Temple, and the the Black Cat commandos of the National Security Guard (NSG) were given the task of flushing them out. Coordinating the efforts of all the paramilitary forces was K.P.S. Gill, then director general of police in Punjab. It had been decided, right in the beginning, that they were not going to repeat Operation Blue Star—no tanks, no troops. The entire area was surrounded by the NSG and for some time it looked like a stalemate. But the terrorists had no access to food and the only water they could get was from the waters surrounding the Harimandir.

The NSG and police did not allow the media near the Harimandir but I felt we could at least get some 'live' footage of what was going on and use it with the footage shot by the NSG's cameramen. But how could this be done? There was an EFP van in Jalandhar and it could be moved to Amritsar; the signal from the van could be relayed by Jalandhar to Delhi using the telecom microwave link. But the staff manning the van refused to move. They were certain they would be shot, either by the terrorists or by the security forces. With a great deal of persuasion we were able to get them to agree, and having got the van to Amritsar, they moved it inch by inch as close as they could, pushing it for the last bit, lest the sound of the engine be heard by the terrorists. They finally got into a position from where the cameras had a clear view of the temple.

While all this was going on, we were looking around for someone to report from the scene. I asked Ritu Sarin, a journalist with the *Indian Express*, if she would do it. I had found her stories objective and rational, and thought she would do a good job reporting from Amritsar. She agreed on condition that she could do other stories—not for Doordarshan—from there. I saw nothing wrong with that, and Ritu was sent to Amritsar. She covered not only the frequent firing from the temple and the carefully targeted firing by NSG snipers at the terrorists—one remarkable sequence showed a terrorist furtively inching forward to fill a vessel with water and the NSG firing at him, not to hit him but to make him drop his *lota* and scurry back—but also the daily briefings given to the media by K.P.S. Gill. She often did some pieces flattened against the side of the EFP van, to avoid being shot at by the terrorists. This was a brave series of stories, done by a brave young journalist, someone who never got, nor sought, the kind of media coverage others have received decades later. She had woefully inadequate equipment: no satellite phones (they didn't exist then), no video phones (they didn't exist either), no mobile satellite news-gathering units (also non-existent); just an equally brave camera crew and a great deal of courage to go physically as near the action as she was allowed to, entirely on her own. And, fortunately, we managed to get access to footage shot by the NSG themselves. Doordarshan was, in fact, the only television team that covered the event.

The terrorists were eventually flushed out. They surrendered meekly and there was no damage whatsoever done to the sacred precincts. It was a triumph for the NSG, for it was a far more intelligent and carefully planned operation than the tragic Operation Blue Star. Black Thunder was also a triumph for Doordarshan news. Not only had a news team operated from the danger zone for the first time, it had done so for days together. For the first time, a journalist had reported live from a danger zone, with a calmness and clarity that belied the tension and fear that must have been all around. Doordarshan's coverage was taken by the BBC and other television networks and later won a prize in

Australia for the best news story of the year. This was something that more than made up for the usual pressures to carry all kinds of non-news items in the news.

One of the truly unedifying instances of pressure came from Krishnakumar, who had been made minister of state for information and broadcasting when H.K.L. Bhagat was appointed the Cabinet minister in the ministry. This was in May 1988. Krishnakumar was apparently rung up by Defence Minister K.C. Pant, who was going by helicopter to open a girls' school at some place in the Garhwal mountains.

'Let's see who really runs Doordarshan,' he is supposed to have taunted Krishnakumar. 'You get the news unit to cover the opening ceremony, if you really are the minister of state for I & B. I'll take the camera team in my helicopter.'

Krishnakumar took this on as a challenge. He rang up the newsroom and told them that as minister of state he was giving orders that the function which K.C. Pant was attending be covered. A team should accompany him.

A distraught news editor rang me up. He probably couldn't get anyone else. 'The trouble is,' he said, 'there is no team available. All we have is a stringer with a 16mm camera and very old film in Pathankot.'

'Tell the minister's office that,' I said. He did, but the minister was adamant. Send that stringer, then, he ordered. He had arranged it with K.C. Pant: the man would be picked up by helicopter and brought back to Delhi. The news editor, poor man, did as he was told. When the stringer came back they found his footage totally unusable. It was mostly too dark, with only occasional flashes of some face or the other. Once again, I got a call. What was to be done?

I called up Krishnakumar. 'Sir,' I said, 'you've asked the newsroom to send a cameraman to cover the opening of a school by the defence minister.'

'Yes,' he said truculently. 'What of it? See that they use the footage.'

'That's the trouble, sir,' I said. 'It can't be used. It's useless. The film was old and nothing has come out. It's all in virtual darkness.'

'I don't care,' the minister said shrilly. 'It has to be shown. I've given the defence minister my word.'

'And what will he think when he sees these worthless pictures, sir?'

I asked. 'He'll think it's some kind of joke. He will not be amused.'

'Never mind,' Krishnakumar said. 'I'll tell Pantji.'

'And show these useless shots, sir?' I asked him softly. 'After he's taken the trouble to fly the cameraman there? What will he think of your instructions?'

'Just show them,' Krishnakumar said, but sounded less certain.

'Sir,' I said, earnestly, making it sound like an appeal for help, 'you're our minister. We look to you for protection, for support. No other minister's really interested. Not even Mr Pant. And if you make us broadcast footage that's absolutely worthless what will people say, sir? What will they think of Doordarshan news? I depend so much on you helping us to improve the quality of news, sir. And it has. You must have noticed. Soon we'll have our own professional teams out there. And if we show this, just to please a minister . . . Sir, I seek your protection. We're your staff; to whom will we turn in times like this?'

There was a long silence. 'All right,' Krishnakumar said finally. 'Do whatever you think is best.' Then, after a pause he said with a half-laugh, 'K.C. Pant was right about who ran Doordarshan.'

'Good night, sir,' I said deferentially, much as if I were reading an elegy over a grave. 'Thank you, sir,' and hung up, too sickened by the whole business to tell him he didn't have a clue about who really ran the wretched network.

*

Meanwhile, Girish Mehra's prophetic words were about to come true. I was pushing my luck, pushing it too far. In 1988, Girish Mehra had been succeeded by Gopi Arora, and while he gave me just as much support as Girish Mehra had, Gopi had his own ideas about how things ought to be run in Doordarshan. I had just come back after a longish trip, first to London for a set of discussions with the BBC and then on to a meeting of the Commonwealth Broadcasting Association (CBA) in Nassau, where I had been elected president after the DG of the BBC completed his term. I came back and found things in the newsroom in an uproar.

It had to do with the coverage of the unfortunate Right to Privacy

Bill, which Rajiv Gandhi had sought to introduce in the Lok Sabha. The press was up in arms, saying the bill was an attempt to abridge their freedom of speech and expression. Doordarshan had been covering the issue fairly extensively. They were, of course, giving the official viewpoint, but also including the views of the press, giving both sides of the story as they had by now become accustomed to doing. This infuriated some Congress MPs and ministers. By the time I came back, anger at Doordarshan's coverage had begun to boil over within the ranks of Congressmen, and for some odd reason they put the blame on me.

Shortly after I came back, one particular incident convinced them that I was the villain who was secretly trying to subvert the bill (as if Doordarshan could do that, but some people will believe anything they want to) in cahoots with the press. To counter the widespread criticism of the bill in the media, some Congress leaders and ministers close to the PM had worked out what they thought a clever little plan. At a Youth Congress function in Vigyan Bhavan, the PM was to make a speech, and a selected Youth Congress member would ask him a prepared question about the bill. The PM would then make a carefully drafted reply, ridiculing opposition to it in some very witty sentences. This would be covered by Doordarshan and prominently featured in the English and Hindi news bulletins.

Unfortunately, it all went wrong. The Doordarshan team arrived at Vigyan Bhavan late—not an unusual occurrence—and by the time they and their equipment had got past the security checks, the PM was due to arrive within minutes. As a result, the security cordon around the dais refused to allow the team to place a microphone on the table where the PM would sit. Frantically, the sound recordist tried to patch the sound system in Vigyan Bhavan into his recording unit, but couldn't do it. Then the PM arrived. All that the camera team could then do was use a boom mike (a mike on a long rod) held up towards the PM, and hope they would pick up what he said. As luck would have it, the person asking the question was standing right next to the camera team, so, when he asked his question it was recorded loudly and clearly. Rajiv Gandhi's reply, recorded by the boom mike from some distance, came through a little faintly and was muffled.

Shortly after the team returned to the newsroom and the editing of the footage began, no less than six ministers barged in to supervise the editing. Once they saw and heard what had been recorded they got up and left in a rage, convinced that this had all been done deliberately. To make matters worse, the terrified video editor—he had never had six ministers in his dingy little cabin—pressed the 'record' button on the VTR in which the cassette with the footage was, purely by mistake, and the first part of the PM's reply disappeared. This was seen as absolutely irrefutable proof that Doordarshan was subverting the government's policies and projecting the government 'in a bad light'. And the villain of the piece was, I discovered with some astonishment, none other than the DG himself.

Gopi Arora spoke to me a few days later, sounding worried. 'There's a lot of talk going on about your being pro-Left,' he said. 'Particularly by the Congress MPs from Bengal, Priyaranjan Das Munshi, Ajit Panja and the rest. A sort of committee has been set up by the PM to find out what's going on.'

'What are they going to do?' I asked. 'Sit in the newsroom and supervise the news bulletins?'

'No,' he said. 'They will examine you.'

And they did. For three days, starting in the evening and going on late into the night. The committee was headed by the then I & B minister, H.K.L. Bhagat, the first of the I & B ministers I had served under (and the last), who had Cabinet rank. The other members of the committee were Ajit Panja, then minister of state for finance, Priyaranjan Das Munshi, minister of state for commerce, and Santosh Mohan Dev, minister for steel and mines. There may have been a few more, but I remember these in particular. The meetings were in Bhagat's house, in a large room where a row of chairs had been arranged in a straight line facing one single chair. That single chair was for me; the inquisitors sat in the row facing me.

I was asked all kinds of questions. Why was I giving so much attention to the opposition in the news bulletins; how did Doordarshan mess up the coverage of the Right to Privacy Bill; why were certain 'important' events not covered, and so on. I answered as best as I could, pleading that all I was trying to do was present facts objectively, but not in a manner that would embarrass the government.

'What about your coverage of the Allahabad by-election?' I was asked.

My interrogators were referring to Doordarshan's pioneering live coverage of the by-election in 1987 held after V.P. Singh had resigned as finance minister and from the Congress over the Bofors issue, and had fought the by-election against the Congress candidate Anil Shastri, Lal Bahadur Shastri's son. The Congress had put all its resources into that contest; Ghulam Nabi Azad had been put in charge of the campaign and had spent close to a month in Allahabad marshalling fleets of cars and mobilizing thousands of workers to ensure Anil Shastri's victory.

As we all know, V.P. Singh won and the trend was evident almost from the first round of counting. Dismay was writ large on Ghulam Nabi Azad's face and on the faces of other Congress personages who sat throughout the day and late into the night on the commentators' panel in the Delhi studio. All this was telecast live—Ghulam Nabi Azad was in Allahabad being questioned by the two anchors from Delhi via the links set up by Doordarshan's engineers. During one session, one of the anchors asked Azad whether he agreed that it had been a mistake for the Congress to use a fleet of cars during their campaign while V.P. Singh's campaigners had used bicycles.

'But you must remember,' Ghulam Nabi Azad said in all seriousness, 'the Congress is a very, very established party. Therefore we were using cars.'

Since this was live it went out to all viewers, no doubt to their great amusement. The ministers and power brokers in Delhi, on the other hand, were not amused. Hence the question during my inquisition. I explained the nature of live coverage to the committee. I also told them that our surveys were showing a slightly better level of credibility for Doordarshan news and pleaded that they should not allow individual instances to cloud their assessment of the effort being made to present the news as fairly as possible. But it soon became clear that some members of the committee—in particular Panja and Das Munshi—were not interested in what was good or bad for Doordarshan. They wanted to establish that I was anti-Congress, pro-Left and therefore a 'subversive element' who had no place in a 'sensitive' medium like television.

This was underlined by the fact that halfway through this seemingly endless interrogation Santosh Mohan Dev, who clearly didn't share this view, got up and said to Bhagat, 'You are making a big mistake. This will have a very bad effect on the party. I don't wish to be associated with it.' Then he left, and did not attend any other session.

Bhagat, who had stayed rather quiet throughout, took this opportunity to bring the interrogation to a close as quickly as he could. The next evening when I prepared for another round of gruelling questioning he said that it had gone on long enough, that they had sufficient material to place before the prime minister.

'It's all right,' he told me. 'You can go.' I could see the impotent rage on Panja's face as I left, but I didn't care; I was just glad that the inquisition had come to an end.

Later, on my way home, I suddenly remembered what Rajiv Gandhi had said to me when he had interviewed me for the job: 'Try to get the government to take its fingers out.' I knew now what he had been referring to. As I looked back, I knew that I hadn't really achieved very much. The newsrooms were messy places, their equipment antiquated; there weren't yet any properly trained television journalists in the field or in the newsrooms, just the officers from the IIS who had spent a number of years on the job but remained primarily government officers, not journalists.

And yet, there were things I could look back on with satisfaction. It was the move we had indeed made towards a more independent news policy, with more real news and less of those dull-as-ditchwater coverages of book releases and ministers opening or closing events. Inevitably there had to be compromises and the refusals lost me a great deal of goodwill among, of all people, officers in the ministries. It was they who egged their ministers on to complain that Doordarshan wasn't 'cooperating', meaning it wasn't covering some footling ceremony which would have earned the officer a pat on the back from his minister. That, alas, was the price I had had to pay.

One of the most invigorating things that happened to the news units—something that helped give the newsrooms an idea of what independent news reporting was like—was the workshops conducted by three news editors from three different private US television stations owned by Westinghouse in Pittsburgh, Cleveland and Boston. I had arranged this because I thought that the US model of television news was the one the world had more or less been following, and it would be valuable to get some American newspeople to interact with. I had been warned not to expect too much; in fact, to be prepared for the workshops to fail. C.V. Raman in particular was very cynical about the whole business.

I knew why. There had been some workshops conducted by the Thomson Foundation, UK that had been arranged before I joined but were held during my tenure. These had gone terribly wrong for whatever reason—the trainers thought the participants were bored and unreceptive, and lost interest in them, and the participants found the trainers superior, rather cold and condescending. The result was that in the last training session there was just one participant. I was briefed about some of this by the icily angry Thomson team when they came to see me before they left, and I heard the other side of the sad business from some of the newsroom staff who had attended the sessions.

'We're going to put all this in our report, naturally,' one of the Thomson team told me.

'Naturally,' I said. 'The participants don't seem to have found the course very interesting, or useful.'

'Then there's no use in our continuing with them, is there?' they asked frostily.

'No,' I told them. 'There isn't.'

And that was the end of Doordarshan's collaboration with the Thomson Foundation. It was a pity, in some ways. Many of those who started television news at Doordarshan had been trained by Thomson experts in the UK. But it was clear that the present lot of newspeople simply weren't responding to the way they were being handled.

In spite of this, I went ahead with the US trainers, hoping this time all would be well. Besides, I was determined to expose our people to international news-gathering techniques and presentations of news. Our staff tended, I found, to become rather insular and assume the world of news ended with what they had set up. Nonetheless, I was more than a little apprehensive. If our newspeople couldn't get along with the British television journalists, how would they be able to learn anything from television people who obviously were used to the very latest equipment? When the three American editors arrived I took them over to the building where they were going to conduct the workshops and introduced them to the news staff who had come from different kendras and from the central newsroom. There was complete silence when I left the room.

Two days later I happened to pass by, and was astonished to hear a great deal of noise—arguments, raised voices, groups gathered out on the lawn around a camera, others arguing volubly in another part of the building. Fearing this was the beginning of a messy end to the workshops I ventured into the groups and asked what was happening.

'We're doing a story,' said one of the participants happily. 'We've all got different ideas on how to do it and he,' pointing at one of the American trainers, 'says we've got it all wrong.'

'Of course you have,' the American shouted. 'You haven't got the key part . . .'

'Just let's do it, why don't we just do it,' some of the newspeople shouted back.

'Is everything all right?' I asked the American nervously.

He grinned. 'Of course,' he said. 'We're having a ball.'

They were. The trainers and participants took to one another very warmly and when the two-week workshop came to an end all of them were very downcast. I saw the final session: the room was so full of people that there wasn't space for anyone to sit. Some had to perch on the open widows.

'We must have more such sessions,' our newspersons told me later, with much excitement. 'And with *them*, no one else.'

A few days later I took the three Americans out for dinner. 'What exactly did you do to them?' I asked. I told them about the Thomson disaster and they laughed.

'We started off by telling your guys that we worked in the same conditions they did,' the young woman from Boston said. 'No equipment, having to make do with patched-up stuff, and so on. That really got them warmed up.'

'And we also told them they knew zilch about pressure,' the editor from Pittsburgh added, and laughed. 'We told them to come and see the dirty pressures *we* have to cope with.'

In other words, they spoke the same language. No condescension, no superiority. They spoke as newsmen to newsmen; it was all of them against the rest of the world. No wonder the workshop had gone off as well as it had.

The sad thing was that I never got these three to come again. The following year was election year in the US and the directors of the three stations flatly refused to let them go. Nevertheless, this one workshop proved to be invaluable in many ways. It showed our newspeople how stories could be built up, how they needed to be structured, and they learnt this from trainers who worked with them without talking down to them. It was enough to set Doordarshan on the road to a regime free of direct interference. The most heart-warming confirmation of this was pointed out to me by a journalist: the main stories on Doordarshan news, he said, are now no different than the main stories in the next morning's papers. He couldn't have paid me a greater compliment.

4

The Many Faces of Television

When I joined Doordarshan, films could be screened by paying a royalty to the copyright holder. This was a disastrous way of showing films because the royalty paid by Doordarshan was pathetically small—about Rs 20,000 or less—and as a result all we could acquire were old, mediocre films. The prints were bad and the equipment we had then, called the tele-cine chain, which actually ran the film and converted it into television signals, broke down fairly often. Either the machine itself would stop functioning or it would tear the film. (No one had yet thought of recording films on videotape, let alone DVDs.) This meant frequent use of that board for which Doordarshan became notorious: *Rukawat ke liye khed hai.* Given the shoddy quality of the film, the bad sound and the frequent breakdowns, we got very few advertisements and earned extremely small amounts, which made it even more difficult to justify laying out substantial sums as royalty.

It was much later that we switched over to sponsorships and the rental of airtime for films, which brought in newer films and more revenue. Till then we kept mindlessly airing third-rate films offered by indifferent producers who submitted them despite the tiny sums we paid because their films weren't accepted by distributors for public screening or had been screened before and were now of little commercial value. Even within the limitations of this system, however, we tried out some new genres of films that we felt would develop their own audiences. One of these was the airing of 'adult' films at 11.30 p.m. The idea came, to be honest, from Rajiv Gandhi himself, who felt that we ought to cater to more mature viewers and not restrict ourselves to the bland films shown earlier in the evening. We picked up only acknowledged classics like Fassbinder's *The Marriage of Maria Braun,* but there were always problems with screening rights that made for a great deal of extra labour. I felt it was worth it if we did show good films just once a month; but a number of people, including some very vocal MPs, thought otherwise. They accused Doordarshan of screening pornographic films that went against the great cultural traditions of Bharat Mata, of deliberately corrupting the tender minds of our children and other similar allegations. 'This is shameful,' they bawled in different forums. 'A disgrace. It must be stopped.'

When they got really hysterical, Rajiv Gandhi spoke out in favour of the films being shown. These films were indeed not meant for children, he said, as television was not intended solely for children. It had to cater to a wide variety of tastes, including those who enjoyed watching films made by some of the world's finest film-makers. It was for the parents of young children to ensure that their offspring were asleep—11.30 p.m. seemed an appropriate time for that—or prevented from seeing these films. It was not possible, he said firmly, for the government to act as nursemaid.

This stopped most of the criticism. However, some critics—leftovers from Victorian times to whom names like Fassbinder, Truffaut, Kurasawa, Ray, Buñuel and others meant nothing—were obsessed with sanitizing Doordarshan. They wrote in various magazines and newspapers, held meetings and gave press conferences accusing Doordarshan of perverting the minds of children. One such bigot told me, outrage writ large on her face, that I should know that parents usually came home exhausted and were asleep by 11.30 p.m. while the children sat up and watched these films because they knew they weren't supposed to see them. I couldn't help wondering just how many houses she had peeked into to make sure that parents were asleep (did she tiptoe into their bedrooms?) and then observed children watching a film like Kurasawa's *Kagemusha.* Did she think all foreign films were pornographic or sadistically violent? The nights must have been alive with the rustle of her clothes as she slipped furtively from one house to another, lips compressed in self-righteous rage, eyes narrowed, while she searched for porn on television, evidence that Doordarshan was corrupting our youth.

The need to screen better films in general kept bothering me. We weren't getting very many of them even for the late-night slot. I thought then of making our own films, of getting good film-makers to make full-length feature films for Doordarshan with modest budgets. It seemed like an interesting idea, but it certainly wasn't new. I remembered, like an old refrain from a familiar song, something a broadcaster had once told me about television: 'If you've thought of something absolutely new and radical, remember, it's been done before.' But even if this wasn't a new idea, I thought we could give it a try.

At this time—it must have been 1987—Pradip Krishen came to see me with his wife, Arundhati Roy. Pradip had just finished making *Massey Sahib* and the film had been much appreciated. They came to tell me of an idea they had for a film set in a school of architecture. I thought it an unusual and interesting concept and decided Doordarshan would commission them to make it. Arundhati wrote the screenplay and Pradip directed it. This was, of course, *In Which Annie Gives It Those Ones*. The film, at that time, didn't get the kind of acclaim and notice that *Massey Sahib* had received, but I thought it was a very clever and perceptive film. Arundhati had based some (not all, she hastened to tell me) characters on students and teachers she had met at the School of Planning and Architecture in Delhi, and she wove the story together in a satirical but ultimately good-natured way. The dialogue was in the sort of language students used then (and probably do now, too). 'Those ones', for example, meant serious, pontifical statements or thoughts, the sort of things teachers sometimes tell their students—such as 'you should pay more attention to your studies and less to gossiping with friends' or 'this is the time for you to learn, to improve yourself, prepare for the outside world'. Perhaps it was this rather special language that mystified many viewers; it was more a question of understanding the language than of liking or not liking the film.

Pradip and Arundhati told me of an amusing sequel to the making of this film. They had taken it to Channel Four in London, where the executives liked it and wanted to screen it. They had one stipulation, however. 'We will, of course, have to put in English subtitles.'

Arundhati was quite astonished. 'But the film *is* in English.'

'Well,' the Channel 4 man said, 'it's not the English that anyone here would understand.' Small pointers to the emergence of our very own version of the English language!

We needed a place, though, in which the films could be made. Soon after I joined Doordarshan we were given, by prime ministerial decree, the dining halls built for the Asian Games village. There were two, one presumably for vegetarian fare and the other for non-vegetarian; whatever their use during the Asian Games, we now had a building with two very large halls. We decided that this would become the Central Production Centre (CPC) for in-house programmes. The engineers felt the roof was too low but devised an ingenious way of lighting the studio in spite of the inadequate height. For once the very latest equipment was purchased—computer-assisted cameras and computerized editing units were among the many new items installed, including the digital Quantel Paintbox, which could produce a bewildering array of graphic images. Today it's probably no different than MS Paint on a PC; far more sophisticated software and equipment are now being used to produce the kind of effects one sees in movies such as *Star Wars* and *Jurassic Park*. But in 1987, Quantel Paintbox was something straight out of the space age.

I had decided right from the start that these studios would be used to make programmes by Doordarshan—films, serials, everything. It would give us a new dimension in terms of programming. I couldn't wait, so I would visit the site once a week and throw regular tantrums if work was not going as scheduled. We had a number of problems, not the least of which was the obstructive attitude of the occupants of the apartments in Asiad Village. They threatened court action and used pressure of various kinds to get us to stop the work. It took all our persuasive skills to make them understand that, once the complex was ready, it would be very quiet indeed. This was true: television stations don't make the kind of noise that, say, a powerhouse or a manufacturing unit does. Whatever goes on inside happens behind sound-proofed doors. I think the residents were apprehensive that something very noisy would come up, with loud music and all kinds of sounds emanating from the studios. Once they saw that nothing of the sort was happening after the centre was constructed—there were just the odd car, taxi or autorickshaw going in and out—their antagonism died down.

The work was complex and the engineers were not used to working with a structure already in place. Thus, despite their best efforts and my weekly goading, the CPC took a long time to finish. It was completed just a few months before I left Doordarshan. Work had informally started in it though, with films being made by a talented lot of producers and directors. The formal opening took place later, after my departure in late 1988; I wasn't asked to attend. Nevertheless, the CPC became a reality because of the hard work done by the engineers and it was functioning because of the enthusiasm and dedication of talented producers. That I had helped develop it—the only production centre Doordarshan has ever had—and acquire the very best equipment that money could buy, and that I had got our best talents to start it working was satisfaction enough.

Sometime in 1987 another very exciting event occurred: I met Peter Brook. He was a legend in the world of theatre. As a student in St Stephen's and in later years I had pored over issues of *Plays and Players,* reading about his magnificent production of *A Midsummer Night's Dream*, the production of *King Lear* that even today is regarded as one of the greatest ever to have been staged, and about the radically new experimental plays he had done using a language that was completely incomprehensible. To someone like me, who considers theatre to be the most intense form of communication and a source of endless pleasure, he was more than just a legend—he was a giant figure, something out of a Greek myth. Peter Brook was in India to look for a place where he could stage his production of the Mahabharata.

One always expects great men to be physically imposing as well. It's not necessarily true, I know, but reputation does sometimes create physical definitions in a person's mind. And when they turn out to be incorrect, there's a sense of shock, even though it doesn't lessen the respect and wonder one feels. It was so for me with Peter Brook. I don't really know what I had expected—possibly a tall man with a deep, commanding voice. I met, instead, a smallish, gentle man who smiled timidly and spoke in a voice that trembled, it seemed, with anxiety. I was to discover later that these were no indications of what the man really was, but at first I thought he looked like a mild country vicar.

We got on very well indeed and I spent some breathless hours talking to him about theatre, about the plays he had done, about the Mahabharata in particular. He told me that people had criticized him for casting a black actor as Karna.

'I told them,' he said gently, 'that he's Indian. An Indian from a family settled in Trinidad. But it didn't help, I'm afraid. Oh dear. It didn't at all.'

'What did you tell them then?' I asked.

'Oh, I didn't *tell* them anything more,' he said and smiled. 'I took the whole cast to the Shankaracharya of Kanchipuram and asked him to bless them.'

Then his face lit up. 'And do you know, he came out and identified every actor by the role he was playing? Including Karna. *That* put a stop to any further comments on my casting.'

Theatre aside, there was a time when Doordarshan came close to working with him when he was looking for a studio in which to shoot his film version of the Mahabharata. He wanted a thousand-square-foot, air-conditioned, sound-proofed studio. We went out scouring the cities for likely studios, but none of them suited him. There was only one so large and air-conditioned, in Film City, Bombay, but it wasn't sound-proofed.

Peter wanted to use natural sound. 'Nothing else sounds real, you see. It must come from here,' he said, putting his fingers to his mouth and moving them away, expanding his hand as if sound was flowing out of his mouth. 'Otherwise it distracts, it's not authentic.'

But why such a huge studio?

'Well,' he said in that diffident manner of his, 'the sets will be in the *centre* . . . and beyond them, stretching away,' he waved his hands outwards, 'will be mists . . . and the river . . . the reeds . . . that sort of thing . . . and they'll be part of some scenes, but it'll all recede, you know, go away into the mists . . .'

I wasn't sure what he meant then; it was only after I saw the film that it made sense. In the end he shot the film in Paris, but I saw to it that Doordarshan was involved in the production, even though it was in a minor way. We provided the material for the costumes, and two of our people accompanied Peter's very temperamental costume designer all over the country to select reams and reams of cloth. She would send some of it to France, only to return and once again look at yards of material in a bewildering variety of shops. But we gave her all that she wanted and as a result Doordarshan holds the rights to the film in certain territories. It may not sound like much, but this was Peter Brook. Just being part of his wonderful film was, I felt, the sort of tribute a person could pay to one of the greatest dramatic minds of our time.

Feature films apart, we tried to encourage the making of documentary films as well. The bright young people in the CPC produced some good ones and we got others from freelance film-makers. Among them was Nilita Vachani, who made a remarkable documentary called *Eyes of Stone* in 1987 about women who were seemingly possessed by a goddess or spirit and had to be taken to a temple and subjected to a sort of exorcism that involved some very bizarre rituals, like carrying old shoes on their heads. This was a documentary I commissioned Nilita to make and I must confess that in the discussions I had with her I engaged in a little deception to help keep the costs as low as possible, given the fact that I had a very small budget for commissioned films. I had clearance from the financial people to give her a certain amount to make the film but I thought that if I could cut her budget a little more, I would have enough to commission another film. I called her in and said with much melancholy that I simply couldn't find the funds to make the film.

'But I've cut the costs to the bone,' Nilita wailed. 'I just can't cut it down further. I've even made Vangelis shoot it for free.' Vangelis was her husband, a professional cameraman; he was Greek and looked like one of the gods, with fine features and golden hair.

I sighed deeply. 'I know, I know,' I said despondently. 'But the finance people aren't willing to spend anything more than what I'd told you we can pay.'

She kept quiet for a while, then said, 'All right, I'll see if I can cut the costs a little more.'

She met me a week later and said, 'I've cut out some costs. It will mean we'll be using virtually every foot of raw stock, with very little room for wastage. But Vangelis says he'll manage.'

'Well, let me see if I can persuade the finance people,' I said, even though they had, in fact, already agreed to her original budget.

I let a day or two pass, then I rang her up. 'It was a great struggle, Nilita,' I told her, 'but I've finally got them to agree. The film's cleared.'

'Oh, thank god,' Nilita said. 'Oh, Bhaskar, how wonderful. Thank you, thank you.'

The film was a great success. Nilita spent three months with a family where the wife was 'possessed' from time to time. She did nothing for the better part of the time she spent with them except to get to know them, so they came to accept her and the cameraman and the rest of the crew as fixtures in their house. Their initial curiosity and resultant awkwardness disappeared and they went about their daily work as usual. That's when Nilita and her crew began shooting.

What emerged in the film is remarkable. The woman was—subconsciously, to be sure—using the 'possession' to empower herself, to be able to talk to her husband on equal terms. She was not aware of what she was doing; in fact, she really believed the goddess came upon her from time to time. But Nilita's film caught the moments when the 'possession' occurred: they were always after the husband had directed his wife to do something she didn't want to, or something she felt was humiliating. One sequence in particular was very significant.

'I'm going to Bombay,' the husband told his wife. 'I'll be away for some time.'

'For how long?' the wife asked.

'Oh, I don't know.' Then he added teasingly, 'Maybe I'll get myself another wife. Someone who looks after me better.'

'You do what you want to,' the wife said in a low voice. 'Maybe I'll go to my father's house.'

'And who will look after this place?'

'You ask your new wife to do it,' she replied sullenly.

'No, you have to stay here and look after this house,' the husband said, now thoroughly enjoying his wife's obvious jealousy and hurt. 'The new wife shouldn't have to do all that. She'll be here for my enjoyment.'

The wife said nothing; she just got up and went inside. The husband continued to smoke outside in the courtyard. A little later the wife came out, now 'possessed' by the goddess.

'I hear and see everything,' she said in a stentorian voice. 'You neglect your wife.'

The husband became very apprehensive. 'No, no, Mother,' he pleaded. 'I look after her, I promise.'

It was clear just what had brought the 'possession' on.

The film won Nilita and Doordarshan a number of awards, including one at a festival in Paris. While Doordarshan bureaucrats had otherwise been singularly unhelpful when Nilita's proposal for the film had first come in, they were very prompt in flying out to Paris to receive the award as the producers of the film. Worse, Nilita's share of royalty paid to Doordarshan when it was telecast on TF1, the French national channel, was not paid to her for years, even though she threatened to take the matter to court. Then, when I became secretary for information and broadcasting, she was suddenly paid with almost unseemly haste.

After she had made the film I told her about my little bit of play-acting about the finance people and the budget. She was speechless with outrage and indignation, and I think she would have thrown something at me if there had been something handy. Then she began to laugh.

'And to think of the days and nights I spent sick with worry about cutting the budget,' she said. 'You're quite awful.'

'But look at it this way, Nilita,' I said. 'You've made a great film on a very modest budget. It means you can bring costs down if you think it out carefully.'

She agreed. 'Yes, I know. But the cost of doing it on a miserably small budget also means tensions and near nervous breakdowns. And poor Vangelis wasn't paid a paisa.'

'That, I agree, was a little too much,' I said. 'But it was the only thing.'

'Well. What about my near nervous breakdowns?' she demanded.

'*Near* breakdowns don't count,' I told her. 'Now, if you'd really had a nervous breakdown I might just have revised the budget . . .'

'All right,' she said, the light of battle glinting in her eyes. 'You'll get your breakdown. Next time.'

Another excellent documentary was made by Sanjay Kak on the life of common people in terror-ridden Punjab. The voices, expressions and body language of the persons he filmed were so eloquent that Sanjay kept his commentary down to a minimum. The film as a whole made a vivid and disturbing impression on the viewer. Sanjay told me that while making the film he had asked an elderly Sikh ice-cream vendor what he thought of terrorism and the terrorists.

'It's a difficult life,' the man said. 'I have three daughters to get married.'

'Yes, but what do you think of the demands the terrorists are making?' Sanjay persisted.

'Sales are also going down,' the man said. 'I used to make about twice what I make now every day. These new shops and new brands are not good for us.'

'I know,' Sanjay said. 'But I am asking you how you feel about the terrorists.'

'I know what you are asking!' the old man shouted angrily. 'Do you think I can't hear? But I have a family to feed and how can I do that if my earnings are going down?'

Sanjay said he could not have asked for a more telling sign of the numbing effect that terror has on the minds of ordinary people.

Other fine films were made. After the tremendous success of *Tamas*, Govind Nihalani made three films based on classic European plays: *Pita* was based on Strindberg's *The Father*, *Jazeere* on Ibsen's *Little Eyolf* and *Rukmati ki Haveli* on Lorca's *The House of Bernarda Alba.* Each of these was powerful and starkly beautiful, both visually and in the manner in which Govind scripted them. Then there was Aparna Sen's gem of a film called *Picnic*, which revolved round the jealousies of two sisters attracted to the same man, and a beautiful film by Girish Karnad, *Cheluvi,* based on an old folk tale about a girl who was able to produce exquisitely scented flowers by becoming the tree that bore those flowers.

This folk tale was told to Girish by A.K. Ramanujam and he was so taken with it that he burst into my office one day and told me that a film he was then planning to make for Doordarshan needed to be shelved because he simply had to make a film on this folk tale. He felt, and rightly, that it was in fact very relevant to our times because of what was happening to the environment. I thought it was a very good idea and when he came back with the completed film it was clear that my faith in Girish's talent as a film-maker and his own fascination with the story had translated into one of the most moving films that I have seen. It was shown on Doordarshan a number of times and remains one of the strongest statements made on what is happening to the environment today—all from an old Kannada folk tale!

Apart from these films made by celebrated film-makers, there were others made by directors whose talents are no less admirable. In the CPC, Saba Zaidi and Ved Sinha made some excellent telefilms, that is, films made to fit into the time slots of the kind of programming we did. All of these were made on very modest budgets, and if their quality did not suffer on that account it was entirely due to the ingenuity and imagination of the directors. I like to think that these little changes added something to the quality of the programmes Doordarshan was broadcasting.

Besides the committees I had set up to screen the many proposals for serials that were pouring in, we also had a committee to select films and programmes for children. It consisted of some twenty-odd children from different schools and age groups. To assist us we had a child psychologist, because we soon found out that getting a clear answer from the children wasn't as easy as we had thought. It was the psychologist who helped us out by asking the children first which films they liked. The children said, not unexpectedly, that they liked all of them. Then she asked them about each film one by one.

'Was this one good?'

'Yes,' the children said in chorus.

'Would you like to see it again?'

'No,' was the answer.

She turned to us and said, 'Now you've got a true critical assessment of the film.'

We selected only those films that the children said they wanted to see again, though some of these were, I thought, quite awful. We screened them nonetheless, and the feedback we got from our audience survey units was that they were extremely popular. I realized that as adults we are often unable to identify what children like in a film or programme. Thereafter we began to go by what our young critics thought was good, rather than by our own assessments. It paid off—the popularity of the children's programmes we showed increased considerably.

*

By the end of 1986 we had moved into what is now the headquarters of Doordarshan. When I had joined we were still in the old palace of the rajas of Mandi and the new building, though complete, was unoccupied because some essential clearances had not come in from the municipal corporation and the fire department. I put the engineers on the job of getting these clearances within six months, which they thought was utterly unrealistic because they simply couldn't make the municipal corporation or the fire department move that fast. Both these august bodies had their own pace of working, which was, to put it mildly, leisurely. Again, it was Madan Mohan who set things in motion.

'We can persuade them to come and inspect the buildings if we go ourselves,' he said in his quiet, imperturbable manner. He despatched two senior engineers to go and sit in the offices of both the corporation and the fire department. 'Go every day,' he told them. 'Every day till they come.'

This persistence worked and the inspections were completed. While the municipal corporation's clearance came through fairly quickly, the fire department raised a major objection. The air conditioning plants had been placed in the basement; this, they said, was a hazard. The plants had to be removed and put at some distance from the main building. The same thing had to be done with the transformers.

'There's no money,' the civil engineers said despondently. 'We can't do all this.'

'Come on, Madan Mohan,' I pleaded. 'Think of something.'

He laughed and said, 'Well, I'll probably end up answering endless audit objections, but I'll find a way out.'

While a solution was being found we had the partitions for officers and staff put in place, and began the dreadfully messy business of shifting files and documents, making sure nothing got lost. Not that losing files was something unusual in Doordarshan; files were routinely lost, usually proposals for new serials from independent producers. They were asked to submit fresh copies of documents, fresh pilots, fresh everything. I often wondered where the lost files went; like the mythical elephants' graveyard, was there some sort of separate dimension into which these files were transported? There had to be—so many were lost that we would have been swamped if the lost files were physically somewhere in the building.

When all was ready, we moved in with no fuss, no solemn ceremony, nothing. I felt it was totally unnecessary. We should have moved long ago, and now having done so, we simply got down to work. The building is hexagonal in shape, with the lift shafts in the centre. This made one literally go round and round, often ending up where one started. It took me a few months to get my bearings. I think most of the officers who had rooms on the fifth floor where I had my office, especially the secretaries and peons, got used to the DG wandering about aimlessly on the floor looking for the lift. They would point out the way to the lift the moment they saw me. Then one of my staff took to escorting me to the lift. That made life simpler for everyone.

It seemed to me that the move to the new building brought a new enthusiasm. A few staff on each floor were made responsible for the cleanliness of the corridors and the toilets. Once a week I went round all the toilets with our housekeeping staff to see for myself how clean they were. This may seem a little comical, but anyone who has been to a government office will know why this is actually a serious matter. If there is one special hallmark most government offices have, it's the stench emanating from the toilets. I was determined that the new building would be different, and the only way to ensure it was to inspect the lavatories myself.

What with inspecting toilets, coming out of the lift on the fourth floor and going into other officers' rooms instead of my own, and the unending flow of visitors (mainly producers of serials), I got used to spending twelve to fourteen hours every day in the office—from nine in the morning to ten or eleven at night—partly in the studios during my six months as an apprentice, so to speak, partly in the spanking, modern office I had, and only occasionally in the ministry, where the rooms were airy and spacious but the corridors stank. I don't think I was terribly popular in the ministry; there was a coldness I sensed in most officers, except in the secretary and the financial adviser.

One particular incident made me even less popular with the ministry. It was winter, late 1987 or early 1988. The chairman of the board of governors of the BBC, Marmaduke Hussey, known to be very close to the then prime minister of the UK, Mrs Margaret Thatcher, was visiting Delhi. Several engagements had been scheduled for him: he was to lunch with the minister for external affairs, meet the prime minister, attend a dinner hosted by the minister for information and broadcasting, and visit AIR and Doordarshan. I was also hosting a dinner for him. We had worked all this out with Mark Tully, the BBC's representative and bureau chief for India. Then all hell broke loose.

Two days before Mr Hussey was to arrive, the BBC showed a programme called *Rajiv Gandhi: India's Pilot Prime Minister* as part of their *Panorama* series. A team from the BBC had come to Delhi and been in touch with the Prime Minister's Office. I think they gave officials there the impression that they were going to make a film showing how Rajiv Gandhi ran the country, visiting distant places, meeting people, etc. In other words, a film that would be appreciative of the way in which he functioned. Thus the team was taken along on several of the prime minister's visits to different places; they even accompanied him on his journeys within Delhi from his residence to Parliament and South Block. They also spoke to a few people, but they did not give much importance, as I was to learn later, to the advice given to them by Mark Tully, who knew far more than they did about the ways of the government and the Prime Minister's Office. This was a terrible mistake; had they done so, the complications that followed might well have been avoided.

The film they showed was anything but complimentary to Rajiv Gandhi. It made him out to be a prime minister who knew little of how his people actually lived. They conveyed this by juxtaposing images of his convoy speeding down roads kept clear by the police, shot from within one of the cars in which the team travelled with the prime minister's entourage, with those of dense traffic on Asaf Ali Road—trucks, cars, autorickshaws, even tongas, all enmeshed in one of the usual traffic snarls.

'This is what Rajiv Gandhi sees on the way to his office.' The pleasant voice of the narrator contained more than a hint of mockery as the shots of empty roads taken from the convoy were shown. 'But does he know what the real India is like?' Then followed shots of Asaf Ali Road.

The whole film consisted of variations on this theme: shots taken from the prime minister's aircraft, placed next to shots of villages, tube wells that weren't working, and so on. 'India looks attractive from up in the air,' the same pleasantly mocking narration continued. 'But it's a little different on the ground. The ground India's pilot prime minister doesn't get to see.' They placed shots of poverty-stricken villages and slums next to a smiling, immaculately dressed Rajiv Gandhi explaining all that was being done to increase the pace of development, but admitting it was difficult to get the bureaucracy to work.

When it was telecast in London, the Indian high commission recorded the programme and then sent it to the Prime Minister's Office where the reaction was, understandably, furious. They felt they had been deceived, taken for a ride by the smooth-talking *Panorama* team. And the anger focused, quite wrongly, on Marmaduke Hussey, who happened to be coming to India after a longish visit to Australia and who had absolutely no idea of the violent reaction that had set in after the tapes had been seen by senior ministers and party leaders. All Hussey's engagements were called off—no meeting with the prime minister or with any other minister, not even the minister for information and broadcasting. No lunches, no dinners. He could go ahead and visit AIR and Doordarshan, but that was all.

I was called in by the secretary, Gopi Arora, and told I would have to cancel my dinner for the BBC chairman. I protested. I explained that the government's anger had been expressed more than explicitly. Further, I was, strictly speaking, not a part of the government, in the sense that I was not an officer in a ministry. I was the head of a television network. It would be odd for me to cancel the dinner, so I was going ahead with it.

'You decide what's best,' Gopi said. 'But you're taking a risk.'

'No,' I said. 'I'm not. In fact, you'll have to come.'

'Certainly not!' Gopi said, horrified.

'You must,' I insisted. 'As my guest, as a friend.'

'Well,' he said doubtfully, 'I'll come, but only for a drink. I can't stay for dinner.'

'That's okay,' I told him. 'But please come.'

He did attend, and I took him and Marmaduke Hussey to a quiet corner and sat them down with a bottle of Black Label whisky, ice and water, and turned to attend to the other guests. Every now and then I stole a look at them; they were deep in conversation. An hour later Gopi had still not left. I was about to ask that dinner be served when he came up to me and took me aside.

'Bhaskar,' he said, that familiar thoughtful look on his face, 'I think we got it all wrong. This poor man knew nothing about the programme. He was very upset when I told him about it. He said he would go back and put an end to this practice of teams flying in, making programmes and flying out, without really learning anything at all about what's going on.'

'Now you see why I went ahead with the dinner,' I said.

'Yes,' Gopi replied. 'I'm glad you did. Look after him. Poor fellow. He's really been treated badly. Anyway, let's see what we can do. But I have to go.' He left, and I escorted a rather relieved-looking Marmaduke Hussey to the dining table.

'Your secretary's a rather nice fellow,' he told me. 'Very understanding.'

The next day some of the engagements that had been fixed for Hussey were restored. He didn't meet the prime minister, as far as I remember, but he did see the minister for external affairs and the minister for information and broadcasting. The night before he left India, Mark Tully had an informal dinner for him at his house, to which I was invited. Marmaduke Hussey, or 'Duke' as he was called, told me that it seemed to him positively absurd to have people who knew next to nothing about a country fly in and make a programme when the BBC had someone as knowledgeable as Mark right there. He said rather grimly that he was going to get to the bottom of it all.

He obviously did. In a letter to the high commissioner of India, the BBC formally expressed regret at the 'pain' the programme might have caused. The producer of the programme was reprimanded and a little later he was asked to leave the BBC. His dismissal was perhaps not entirely due to this programme, but it may have been a part of the reason.

Oddly enough it was that dinner, and the meeting I had set up between Gopi Arora and Marmaduke Hussey, that actually resulted in something being done about that *Panorama* programme. Had the ministry done what it had wanted to—send cold aides-memoire to the BBC and then humiliate the chairman of the board by refusing to see him or offer him any hospitality—the government would have gained little. The BBC would have, as they had often done in the past, stood by their programme and left the Prime Minister's Office and the government to stew in futile rage. This time the BBC actually did something about a programme that had caused the Government of India a considerable amount of offence.

That, however, was not how the ministry saw the incident. What mattered to them was that I had brazenly refused to follow the directions given to cold-shoulder Duke Hussey, thereby demonstrating once again that I was getting a little more uppity than an obedient DG should be. Nothing happened immediately afterwards, but it all added up to the final denouement.

There were other bizarre, often comic, and at times dark incidents that occurred in those hectic times. One of these was my being summoned to appear in 1987 before the Public Accounts Committee (PAC) of Parliament during its examination of the working of the Ministry of Health and Family Welfare. I was quite bewildered. *Health and family welfare?* What did I have to do with the functioning of that ministry? But if you're summoned by the PAC you simply have to appear; so I did, wondering what it was all about.

It didn't take me long to figure it out. The media adviser to the ministry, Rami Chhabra, was testifying before the committee, telling them about all that she had done to project the need to limit the size of the family. She said that she could have done much more, had Doordarshan been more cooperative. I was astounded. Soon after I had joined, Rami had come to see me and told me she wanted to prepare 'quickies'—short two-minute messages using a song and some selected visuals—that would convey the message of family planning. She wanted a producer from Doordarshan to be sent on deputation to the Ministry of Health and Family Welfare to do this. Being new to the organization, I first consulted my colleagues, and on their advice sent a producer from the Delhi Kendra, Suman Bajaj Kalra. Rami then said she wanted a two-minute slot before and after the Hindi news for these quickies. I agreed, and once the quickies began to arrive we started showing them before and after the news. This was prime time, because the Hindi news did have a very wide viewership in the states where the issue of family planning was the most critical: Rajasthan, Uttar Pradesh, Bihar and the north-eastern part of Madhya Pradesh.

Almost at once there were protests from public figures in those regions. They complained that the quickies were unsuitable for children and that they needed to be shown later at night. I discussed this with Rami and we decided that we would continue showing them as we had planned. The argument that children would be exposed to these 'embarrassing' messages was, we felt, specious, because children never watched the news. Then Rami said she wanted the quickies to be shown before and after the English news bulletins as well. I pointed out that the target audience did not watch the English news bulletin, so quickies just before and after it in Hindi would have little effect. But she was adamant that they be telecast.

Some time before this, Sanjoy, my nephew who worked with villagers near Bikaner, had visited me. He ran an NGO that had been encouraging villagers to form dairy cooperatives to supply milk to the new Mother Dairy project, and to form societies to make various handicrafts and to help with prenatal care for mothers.

'What do you think you're doing, Kaku?' he asked me. 'These messages have caused havoc in various parts of Rajasthan. The primary health centres are being flooded by people wanting contraceptives and vasectomies. The health centres simply can't cope. They don't have the supplies or the facilities for vasectomies.'

I was disconcerted. If we persisted with the messages, I felt it might result in a sort of backlash, and the credibility of all such messages would be compromised. Sanjoy said as much.

'If you go on showing these messages, people will just switch off,' he warned. 'They'll dismiss it as the usual government propaganda.'

I told Rami this but she refused to have them taken off. 'My job is to make people aware,' she said firmly. 'If the services aren't in place, that's not my problem.'

I let the quickies linked to the Hindi news bulletins stay but refused to start any with the English news. This is what Rami referred to as my 'non-cooperation' before the PAC. After she finished, I was asked to face the committee. I explained what we were doing; the quickies were only a part of it, there were also other programmes done in regional languages from the kendras. But why, the committee asked, was I not broadcasting the messages before and after the English news?

Again, I explained that the viewers watching the English news were perfectly aware of the need to practise family planning and were not the target audience for the campaign.

'That's not for you to judge,' one member said. 'If Mrs Chhabra wants it before the English news bulletin then you should put it there.'

I explained, yet again, that the audiences were altogether different, but was told by one member, 'Yes, yes, we know that. But you show it anyway.'

'Sir,' I said, 'showing these messages before and after the Hindi news is costing us over Rs 14 crore a year. If we now put them before and after the English news, when we're showing commercial advertisements that earn us that kind of money . . .'

'This is a top national priority!' a member shouted suddenly. 'And you talk about money! Do you understand how important this campaign is?'

At this point, I must confess, I lost my temper. Perhaps it was the tension that had been accumulating for over a year, perhaps it was the bare-faced manner in which Rami Chhabra had put all the blame on me, I don't know.

'I am an Indian, sir,' I said angrily, 'and I'm as concerned about the welfare of my country as you are. But what we earn is public money and it is to be used for the public good. Each of us has to do our work as best as we can, and I have to try to earn revenue in the best way I can for the public good.'

'How dare you tell me you know what is for the public good?' the incensed member shouted.

The chairman, L.K. Advani, intervened. 'I have been minister for information and broadcasting,' he said calmly. 'I know the pressures the DG of Doordarshan is under. Let us now leave it at that and pass on to the next item.'

His measured yet firm comment silenced the irate member and I could not help being very grateful to him. Later, after the hearing, when we were having a cup of tea, I went up to him and thanked him.

He smiled benignly. 'You mustn't take all that is said to heart,' he told me gently. 'It's nothing personal. I'm sorry you were spoken to in that manner and on behalf of the committee I apologize.'

All I could do was mumble my thanks and make myself scarce. But it was some months before I could bring myself to forgive Rami Chhabra for having so cold-bloodedly thrown me to the wolves.

There were pleasant moments too, of course. I noticed a current affairs programme produced in-house by the Delhi Kendra where various persons were interviewed. The interviewer always had her back to the camera; all we could see was her long, silky hair. I asked the director of the Delhi Kendra, A.S. Grewal, why he kept her studiously turned away from the camera. He gave me a rather long explanation of how the person being interviewed was the real focus of the programme, and how the interviewers could become prima donnas if they were allowed to face the camera and began to be recognized by viewers.

This was all nonsense in my opinion, and I told him so. If people watch programmes because of a particular anchor or presenter, then it's all for the best; viewership increases. Get her to face the camera, I told him, introduce the personality being interviewed and then do the interview without her back to the camera. An occasional shot over her shoulder was acceptable, but you had to have reaction shots from her, 'noddies' as they were called.

He agreed reluctantly, and so the young lady with the silky, long hair was allowed to face the camera. The power of expression is a great factor in television, and Nalini Singh has that. She was relaxed, natural and came across as very sincere, not to mention that she was, and still is, very beautiful. These have made her one of the most celebrated and respected television anchors in the country. And all because, I flatter myself, I managed to persuade the DTC Delhi to let her face the camera when conducting interviews!

*

In August 1988 the CBA was to meet in Nassau, in the Bahamas. A.R. Shinde, DG AIR, and I attended as members. I had a particular reason for doing so: some months earlier I had been asked by the vice-president of the Canadian Broadcasting Corporation to support an initiative that the Canadian government was taking to prepare a package of good programmes that would be made available to member broadcasters at a very nominal fee. This would not only mean that many television networks, particularly the Caribbean networks which were financially in bad shape, would have access to some good English-language programmes, it would also become a kind of Commonwealth link, which is why the Canadian government was so keen to push it through.

There was opposition from the BBC and from the Canadian and Australian Broadcasting Corporations, because they usually made a fair amount of money from selling such programmes. We felt it was a good thing, although in India English-language programmes had a rather limited appeal (this was 1988, remember; we've moved a long way since then). The Canadian Broadcasting Corporation was piloting this at the explicit request of their government, even though, as I have mentioned, they weren't too keen on it themselves. They wanted me to go to the meeting and push for its acceptance.

At the meeting I spoke about the benefits of such a package: broadcasters in developed countries could give others a helping hand, and that surely was what the CBA was all about. There were the usual arguments against it from the Australians and the BBC; the Canadians, having put it on the table, kept a discreet silence. It looked like a stalemate, but the next day Alva Clarke, secretary general of the CBA, told me there had been a change of heart in the BBC. They were all in favour of it. Possibly some message had come from some quarter; I never found out. But Michael Checkland, DG of BBC, made a very supportive speech that swung the tide, and the Canadian proposal went through. Alva Clarke was elated and showed it. He was a shrewd, street-smart Jamaican who had worked for the BBC for many years before becoming secretary general of the CBA. There were no flies on Alva; he always knew which way the wind was blowing, and he never hesitated to take just that direction.

Alva sought me out later in the day. 'You know,' he said, 'the current president of the CBA, the DG of BBC, well, his term's over. We have to elect a new president.'

'Yes, I know,' I told him. 'Anyone in the running?'

'Would you like to be the next president?' he asked.

'Me?' I was astonished. 'Look, Alva, I'm not really a broadcaster, you know, I'm a civil servant.'

'We know that,' Alva said. 'But to us you're a broadcaster because you head a broadcasting network. Simple.'

'But why me?' I asked.

'Well, it seems word has got around about what you've been doing with Doordarshan. And you're the one most members think should succeed Checkland.'

'Which members?' I asked. 'I haven't spoken to anyone about this and no one's spoken to me.'

'That's not how it works, my friend,' Alva said and smiled his broad smile. 'They may not speak to you. But everyone speaks to me.'

'And they want me as president?' I asked incredulously.

'That's what they say,' Alva said.

I thought about it for a moment. Not bad for an IAS bureaucrat, I mused, to head a body of professionals, after being *elected*, without even trying. I told him I would think about it and let him know. Then I rang up Gopi in New Delhi.

'Accept immediately,' Gopi said. 'Don't waste time.'

I sought Alva out. 'Okay, Alva. I'll toss my hat into the ring.'

He shook my hand.

The evening before the election I bumped into Michael Checkland. He seemed a little ill at ease.

'You know,' he said, 'I'm actually doing the balance of Alastair Milne's term as president.' Milne had been DG of BBC but had been summarily dismissed by the chairman of the board of governors, Duke Hussey, acting on the instructions of Margaret Thatcher.

I kept quiet.

'Yes,' Checkland said. 'Now wouldn't you say that I could do a full term in my own right?'

I wasn't sure whether he could or not but told him, 'Look, if you want to do a term as president, I'll propose your name.'

'But I gather it's more or less settled that you'll be the next president.'

'It doesn't matter,' I told him. 'I'm not really interested either way.'

He thought about it and then said, 'No. We'll let it go. I'll be voting for you.'

'That's up to you.'

'No, no,' he said more firmly. 'You'll be the next president.'

I felt he was reluctant to let go of the post, but something stopped him from trying to keep it. What was it? I wondered. It took me a little while to figure it out: Marmaduke Hussey, the person I had made an effort to welcome in India because I felt he deserved it. He must have told Checkland and Alva Clarke that he wanted me to be the next president. This had to be the explanation; I really couldn't think of anything else.

The next day the election took place and I was duly elected president. That evening Alva Clarke took Michael Checkland and me out for a celebratory drink.

'You know,' Alva said to me with a crafty smile, 'it wasn't a unanimous election.'

'No?' I was a little disconcerted. 'I thought it was.'

'Oh, everyone voted for you,' he said. 'Except one member.'

I knew what was coming.

'Your compatriot, Shinde,' Alva said, and laughed out loud. 'He voted against you, man.'

Both he and Checkland laughed a great deal. I felt a little sick and humiliated. *The only other Indian member voted against me.* What a way to start.

'Well, if he wanted to be elected he only had to say so,' I said. 'After all, they probably wanted someone from India . . .'

'No,' Alva said. 'They didn't want him. They wanted you. If he'd stood, he'd have lost.'

After a few polite noises I left. Shinde had been one of those who had filed the case against my appointment as DG of Doordarshan. Now, even though he knew his would have been the only vote against me, vote against me he did. Pure malice. But then, I thought, how very ironic. He files a case to stop me becoming DG of Doordarshan. He loses. He votes against my becoming president of the CBA, once again to no avail. Eventually the droll side of the whole thing got to me and I had a good laugh in my room, by myself.

In spite of my doubts about the manner in which I got the post, it was exhilarating being asked to head an association of broadcasters when I was just a civil servant. And I must say I enjoyed the new friendliness and warmth that I got from all the delegates at the meeting. The only embarrassment was when we were leaving. A number of delegations, including the BBC delegation, a rather fetching young lady from Hong Kong television and some others, were leaving by the same British Airways flight as I was. At the airport, I discovered to my chagrin that they were all flying business class. Thanks to the miserly ways of the finance ministry, I was flying economy. I managed to check in very furtively, hoping they wouldn't notice the president of the CBA travelling cattle class, and I think I managed to get in without being seen. Or perhaps they did see and pretended they hadn't.

Tempestuous days, when time seemed to fly, every morning bringing some new event, problem or celebration—these were what made my tenure as DG so memorable, colourful and rewarding. Perhaps they were not always pleasant, but they engaged me fully. They made up a world in which I lived practically all the time. That was why, after I left Doordarshan, my world suddenly seemed so empty and grey.

5

Going Live

If there was one area of television in which Doordarshan could claim to be as good as any other network, it was live broadcasts. Not of all events, but a few, particularly the Independence Day function at the Red Fort and the Republic Day parade. The camera positions were carefully and sensibly chosen and the picture quality was excellent. Doordarshan used professional and competent commentators and the whole effect was as if the viewer was actually there. They 'established' the locations extremely well and used some very imaginative angles, such as shots from the top of India Gate for the Republic Day parade. The Independence Day function was covered just as well, the producers cutting deftly from the organized crowds to the prime minister, to the minarets of the Red Fort and the cluster of domes and rooftops that have come up beside Chandni Chowk. The producers had some fine Canon cameras fitted with Angenieux lenses, which, according to Madan Mohan, were the best available then. They also had state-of-the-art OB vans that made it possible for the producer to replay the events or superimpose images on what was being shown.

These were events in the capital, where the best equipment was available and where it was relatively easy to establish microwave links from Rajpath and the Red Fort to the control room in Akashvani Bhavan. Things weren't quite as good outside Delhi as far as equipment went, but there were some very talented production staff in the kendras who managed near miracles with primitive equipment.

The problem was with the coverage of sports events, particularly cricket. It was, to be honest, quite awful most of the time. The cameras would wander all over the grounds, showing infuriated viewers everything except what they wanted to see—the action on the field. When it was shown, the producers would at times be crass enough to cut to an advertisement just when a batsman was declared out. I got virtually skinned for the poor quality of our cricket coverage, not to mention the coverage of other games. It seemed as if all that Doordarshan had learnt during the Asian Games had been forgotten. There were some gifted producers, true, but they were too few to make a real difference.

I discovered, soon after I joined, that Doordarshan was in the middle of a fairly major tussle about the Reliance World Cup Cricket Championship to be held in early 1987. The Board of Control for Cricket in India (BCCI) was considering an offer made by Kerry Packer, the owner of Channel Nine in Australia, to cover the matches, while Doordarshan was insisting that it could provide as good coverage. In fact, anticipating that they would be asked to cover the matches, Doordarshan had ordered new OB vans and mobile uplink stations—giant trailer-mounted dishes that could be moved from one venue to another and linked to a satellite from there. Nowadays, of course, mobile satellite uplinks the size of a suitcase are routinely taken by news teams to remote locations. Two decades ago, however, these monstrous trailers and their dishes were state-of-the-art equipment, a wonder to behold. New cameras had been ordered as well, including what the engineers called RF cameras, which could be taken to different parts of a stadium, from where they could send signals via radio frequencies back to the OB van parked outside.

The chairman of the BCCI, N.K.P. Salve, was not very sure that Doordarshan could cover the matches adequately. He felt that it would be more profitable to get Kerry Packer to cover them and was more than half inclined to accept his offer. The catch was that given the technology available then, Packer needed to have his signals uplinked to a satellite via Doordarshan's uplink stations, of which there were just two, one in Mussoorie and the other in Pune. Or he would have to borrow the mobile earth stations that Doordarshan was acquiring for itself.

Initially I was in two minds. Could Doordarshan cover the matches, which would be telecast internationally, given the wretched record it had? I studied how coverages were undertaken and discovered some interesting facts. For example, whenever a match was held in a particular city, the Doordarshan kendra in that city did the live coverage; there was no question of 'outside' staff being brought in. The result was that often persons with very little knowledge, let alone skill, manned the cameras and OB vans. At times even the producers were quite dim-witted. This could, of course, be changed. Another thing I discovered was that many of the staff involved, particularly the cameramen, had no knowledge of the game at all. At that time, this was not surprising, given the modest backgrounds from which they came, where playing cricket was beyond them in terms of getting bare necessities like bats, gloves and pads. But they were skilled producers and cameramen; if, then, they got to know the game, would they be able to cover matches with the same finesse as they did, say, the Republic Day Parade? I decided that we should take on this task, daunting though it was, but that we would cover the matches differently.

To begin with, I made it clear to all staff handling sports coverages in all the kendras that the Reliance Cup matches would not be covered by the local kendras but by three teams consisting of the best staff from all the kendras. They would move from venue to venue, with the OB vans and mobile earth stations, and the local kendras would give them all the help they needed. I threatened them all that any lack of support would result in some nasty consequences. Doordarshan's reputation needed to be built on this event, and I was determined not to let anything stop that from happening, even if it meant dismissing uncooperative or lackadaisical staff.

I then met the BCCI chief and informed him we would do the coverage ourselves. Initially he was sceptical, even uncomplimentary about earlier coverages done by Doordarshan. I explained how we planned to do it and, very reluctantly, Salve agreed, but suggested that we pay a fee to the BCCI for covering the matches. I was horrified. *Pay a fee?* I told him very firmly that far from us paying the BCCI a fee, they ought to pay us a fee for telecasting the matches to millions, which would, I stressed, increase the sums he could levy for advertisements within the stadiums. Salve was annoyed and spoke to the minister, Ajit Panja. Panja told me that Salve was a senior Congressman and that I should have spoken to him more respectfully. I told the minister I hadn't been disrespectful at all but I had to safeguard Doordarshan's interests. That meant I couldn't accept Salve's demand for a fee because the fee would have to be paid from public funds—would the minister approve that? That was a decision the minister deftly avoided.

So it was settled: Doordarshan would cover all the matches *and* be paid a fee by the BCCI for covering each match. That is a clear measure of the difference in attitudes between then and now. Today, far from being paid a fee, Doordarshan has to compete with private channels and pay millions to the BCCI to cover similar events. But Doordarshan was the only television network then, so the BCCI had little choice.

The news was not greeted with cheers by the press. There was wariness, among the mildest, and downright derision among others. They predicted that Doordarshan would make a mess of the coverage, and all kinds of horror stories were trotted out by critics who made it their business to excoriate Doordarshan for virtually everything it did. To be fair to them, some of the stories were true, particularly the one of the producer telling the cameramen during the live coverage of a Test match that the camera should be trained on the ball whatever happened so the viewer would know where it was going. Some of the cameramen took this literally, and even after the ball had hit a batsman on his pads and there was an appeal for lbw, the camera remained duly trained on the ball rolling away while maddened viewers screamed at their sets, wanting to see the players' reactions and what the umpire's decision was.

I was determined to change all that. To begin with, I sought help from Mark Tully, the BBC correspondent in India and a great lover of cricket. He immediately spoke to those who mattered in London; I followed up with a request to Michael Checkland for the best sports producer the BBC had to train our staff.

He was startled. 'Look,' he said, 'we've got the Pakistanis coming here in the summer and you want me to send you our best producer? I can't. I mean, we aren't a training school, you know.'

'I know. But the situation's desperate. This is the World Cup we're talking about. Don't you want it to be covered well? You can manage your home series with others I'm sure.'

'Well,' he said finally, 'I'll send him, but he's got to be back before the Pakistanis arrive.'

He was as good as his word. The producer arrived not very long after. I discovered later that Mark Tully had had to do a great deal of work behind the scenes to get him, even after Checkland had agreed.

I planned a training session for two or three weeks in Bangalore. It would begin with the coverage of a match to be played for the training camp, and would give the BBC man an idea of the problems with our coverage. Thereafter, once the training was completed, there would be a second match, and this time the results of the training would be assessed and the best performers picked out for the three teams to cover the World Cup. I got tremendous support from the Karnataka Cricket Association. Not only did they organize the two matches, they also got some former greats like B.S. Chandrasekhar and E.A.S. Prasanna to play in these matches. I couldn't have asked for more.

Just before the training sessions started I was told that some of the commentators had decided not to go because they felt they had nothing to learn; they apparently already knew it all. I told the deputy DG that if they didn't want to go that was their decision, but as far as Doordarshan was concerned they would never do the commentary in any cricket match again. I told him to explain to them what should have been obvious—this was really about building up a team, which included them, because they would be working very closely with the producer, commenting more on what the viewer saw on screen and on the replays and graphics the production people would provide. Eventually they went, but with bad grace, and stayed far enough from the sessions to make it clear to everyone that they were there on sufferance.

The airs of the commentators apart, the training obviously went well. I couldn't go to the camp myself, inundated with other work as I was, but those who had been sent for it were happy and certainly more confident about handling the coverage. The BBC producer was also satisfied with the results and with the final selection of technical and production staff for the three teams. He left on the eve of the visit of the Pakistan cricket team to the UK, but told me that he would be watching the World Cup anxiously to see how the coverage was handled.

The World Cup began and it became apparent fairly soon that the coverage was definitely better, much more professional and satisfying. Viewers were able to see individual bowlers, batsmen and fielders in action. The new machines in the OB vans meant it was possible for the producers to come up with instant replays in slow motion— a batsman hitting the ball for a four or a six, or making a mistake and losing his wicket. The cameras were able to zoom in on a catch being taken, then show it from different angles.

There were problems, of course. The pace was punishing, because the OB vans and mobile earth stations could only travel by road and rather slowly, owing to the delicate equipment they carried. The earth stations began to develop a particular problem, not a very major one but one that caused a great deal of worry. There was one part (a sort of glass tube) that kept breaking during every journey. The replacements were terribly expensive and the engineers looked gloomier as the series went on.

There were other incidents as well. At some venues officious men from the local cricket association objected to the placement of cameras, and that led to altercations with the television crew. On one occasion the crew decided to stop telecasting a match and were prepared to leave because of the obnoxious behaviour of the local officials. The BCCI representatives had to plead with them and the local officials to come to an amicable settlement and carry on with the telecast.

Such problems notwithstanding, the coverage was very good. For the first time television pictures came directly off satellites to the main transmitters and kendras and the picture quality was excellent—sharp, clear and with just the right richness of colour. We used new devices for high-speed rewinding so that shots could be played back almost instantly and in slow motion. Computers gave the commentators a wealth of information about previous games and the current one. The cameramen, now familiar with the game, were never caught unaware by the action, and the cuts to advertisements came only at the end of an over or when a new batsman was coming on, apart for the longer series of ads during the drinks interval.

When the World Cup ended, after that electrifying game in Calcutta between Australia and England, I was finally able to relax. And it was quite a pleasure to get faxes from several sources congratulating

Doordarshan on the quality of the coverage. Kerry Packer very generously sent a message saying he couldn't have done a better job himself. I also received very complimentary felicitations from Michael Checkland, the Australian Broadcasting Corporation, and from the BBC producer who had trained the teams. 'You cannot imagine how proud I am of my lads,' he said in his ecstatic message.

We had developed skills that were equal to the best in the world. The effort and the tension and the worry had been worth it.

Following this I was inundated with requests for live coverage of all kinds—a hockey match here, a football match there, some anniversary function somewhere else. While we couldn't oblige them all, we did try our best to cover as many other sports events as possible, especially football, hockey and athletics. Sadly, the numbers watching these sports were never as large as those who watched cricket matches, both Tests and one-day internationals. Sometimes, whenever I could snatch a few minutes from my harrowing schedule, I would watch the live coverage of a hockey or football match. Invariably I saw shots of empty stands; there were often more people on the field than in the stands. Tennis was a slightly different prospect. There was a great deal of interest in Wimbledon, and the French and US Open championships, and we tried to get the rights to these whenever we could. Usually the costs were prohibitive, but Wimbledon we did take, whatever the price. Even our own tennis tournaments were watched with a fair amount of interest, and Doordarshan always covered India's Davis Cup matches, for which there was a fairly substantial television audience.

The sad truth is that television coverage by itself can never kindle spectator interest in a sport. That needs to be nurtured by the organizers, by improving standards and the manner in which these events are presented. Today there is perhaps a little more interest in hockey, the difference being due to the quality of hockey played as India has become one of the best teams in the world. Sure enough, when India plays and the event is covered by television, there are sizeable audiences.

*

In the winter of 1988 I got a call from a south Indian colleague to tell me that he and some others wanted to know if Doordarshan could cover the aradhana of the annual chanting of the *kritis* of Thyagaraja at the Thiruvaiyaru temple not far from Tiruchi. I told him we could send a team to record the event—in fact, Doordarshan Madras was doing it anyway—and that it would be telecast at an appropriate time.

'No,' he said. 'We are thinking of a live telecast.'

A live telecast from a small village! Unthinkable at that time.

'You will bring so much joy to lakhs of people,' he pleaded. 'Most of us cannot attend; the chanting of the kritis by the greatest Carnatic singers as a tribute to Thyagaraja is a regular ritual. Couldn't you do it?'

On an impulse, I summoned Madan Mohan and told him of the request. He laughed at first, then, on a more serious note said, 'It will be very difficult to do, very difficult.'

I sensed something in the way he said it, the kind of technical challenge Madan Mohan enjoyed.

'Why not try?' I asked him.

'We'll see. I can't promise, but we'll see,' he said and left.

Some days later he came into my office. 'About the live telecast of the singing of Thyagaraja's kritis, I think we just might be able to do it.'

I told him to go ahead. He kept me informed of the preparations. It was impossible to deliver a mobile earth station to that area owing to the enormous size of the trailer-mounted dish and equipment, but he arranged for a microwave link set-up which would transmit the television signal from the temple to an OB van parked near Tiruchi. From there the signal was to be sent to Madras using a more powerful link made available by the telecom engineers, and from Madras it would be uplinked to a satellite and taken down in the MSR in Delhi. Delhi would then uplink it again so that all the transmitters across the country could download the signal on their TVROs and retransmit it terrestrially. Why couldn't the transmitters take the signal directly from the one sent by Madras to its transponder on the INSAT satellite? I believe it had to do with differing frequencies and bands.

Once everything was in place I rang my colleague to inform him about the live telecast, asking him to pass on the information to everyone he knew. He was speechless at first, then ecstatic. We also had this news of the live telecast advertised on Doordarshan. And early one cold January morning, the kritis of the poet-saint Thyagaraja sung by assembled artistes, including singers of renown, entered the homes of many viewers. All over India thousands and thousands of devotees of Carnatic music sat before their sets and watched a ceremony that they otherwise could not have seen.

The next morning my colleague came to thank me. His emotion was most embarrassing. I didn't know what to say.

'I couldn't believe I was hearing and seeing it,' he said. 'But I did hear it and see it. Sitting here. What can I say? There will be thousands all over the country who will want to thank Doordarshan.'

I mumbled something about it being a challenging task, if people had liked it what more could we ask for, and more drivel to that effect. After he left I rang up Madan Mohan, told him of this visit, and thanked him on my own behalf.

'Why don't you write to all those who worked on it?' he suggested. I told him I would. 'You see,' he continued in that dry, rather amused tone of his, 'this is what television is really about.'

'About what?' I asked him.

'Communication,' he said, and hung up.

It was true, I thought to myself. Television wasn't about broadcasting events, musical or otherwise; it was about *communicating,* about stimulus and response, about reaching out, overcoming that terrible solitude in which each one of us is wrapped, about the bond between people. I felt very humbled that day by that knowledge.

*

I should mention another kind of live telecast to offset this euphoria. In 1986 and 1987 there was a sense that India was rediscovering its forgotten culture, the traditions, crafts and arts in our villages and in near-forgotten communities. That this sense of discovery was limited mainly to a few of Rajiv Gandhi's friends who made up for their lack of knowledge or any real link with these traditions with their enthusiasm made it a little bizarre, even comic. Emblematic of all this was an event they put together called Apna Utsav (Our Festival); who the *apna* was is anybody's guess and there were, I must confess, some ribald comments made about this in Doordarshan. The name was chosen to indicate that, unlike the usual festivals organized by impresarios or government institutions, this event was organized by the folk artistes themselves. I suppose the organizers meant well. The trouble was that they wanted the opening to be covered live. It would be followed by coverage of the other events they had put together over the next few days—folk dances and singers and minstrels, craftspersons and suchlike. Covering the later events live was no problem at all; many were due to be held during the day out in the open, or in the evenings under bright lights. It was the opening ceremony that was the problem.

It was to be held in the evening, outside the Red Fort in Delhi. Processions of folk artistes carrying torches would converge from four different directions to present the events. They would hand these torches to the prime minister, who would be standing on a raised platform, and then dance, sing or, if they were jugglers or acrobats, perform in the light of these torches, which would be fixed in slots along the stage. It was all meant to be exotic and visually attractive. I quickly put my own personal thoughts about all this aside, but did point out something that was very much within my professional domain: live coverage would be pointless because viewers would see nothing more than little blobs of lights emanating from the torches. We didn't have Betacam cameras then, which are sensitive enough to register images even in shadow, and the organizers were adamant that no television lights be used. ('Positively *dreadful*, we simply can't have them ruin the *wonderful* ambience of the event.') Worse, the security staff around the prime minister wouldn't allow cameras too close to the platform on which he would be standing. Our cameras could zoom in, but only far enough to get something less than a midshot, and that too one which would be very blurred because of the feeble lighting. I did think for a moment that the organizers were getting carried away by images they had seen in various Hollywood films.

Unfortunately my explanations and those of the engineers and production staff were dismissed out of hand. The live telecast was to be done exactly as the organizers indicated, with the torches held high and the artistes in their colourful costumes dancing and singing. I looked at my people and they looked back gloomily at me.

'It won't work,' they told me later, urgently. 'It'll all be pitch black.'

It occurred to me then that this, in fact, was the key. With devilish glee I said firmly, 'We'll do it.' For I wanted these eager young people to see the mess which their eagerness would land them in.

The live telecast began and the screens all went black, with the voice of the joyous presenters describing what no one could see. Then, as the presenters became hysterical with excitement, a few blobs of light appeared on the screen, wandering, or so it seemed, aimlessly around. Then there were images of Rajiv Gandhi, barely visible himself, on the platform with his wife and the organizers. The producers cut from that to total darkness again, towards those bobbing spots of light, and back again to the prime minister. Finally, when the dances started, the screen was full of crazy little glow-worms, but there was not a trace of any artiste, any costume, any dance. It was completely ridiculous, and I was delighted.

The reaction to the telecast ranged, as I had expected, from bewilderment to derision. 'Doordarshan does it again' was the general assessment, and that was followed by a not very flattering account of Apna Utsav, seen by many as a huge waste of public funds on a pointless tamasha. I later gathered the prime minister was furious; I delicately had it conveyed to him through the minister that the live coverage was done expressly as it had been planned by the organizers, who were his close friends and associates. I also told Gopi Arora, who was still in the Prime Minister's Office then, what had happened and I have no doubt he briefed Rajiv appropriately. Needless to say I was never again asked to do a live telecast by these gentlemen.

*

Doordarshan did, however, move into a different kind of live broadcasting, owing to the imagination and persuasive powers of a young man called Prannoy Roy. Though he was an economist, Prannoy had established himself as a psephologist, having worked previously with David Butler, a highly respected psephologist, in Britain. Prannoy used to produce current affairs programmes for television, and because he was very relaxed and natural in front of the camera, as well as very good-looking, he was a television personality waiting to become a star. The first major step in that direction came when he dreamed up, with his partner Vinod Dua, a new way to report on an election—live. This marked a watershed in live telecasting on Doordarshan.

As mentioned earlier, of all the by-elections being held in 1987, by far the most interesting one was the contest for the Allahabad Lok Sabha seat between V.P. Singh, who had resigned from the Congress and had formed the Janata Dal, and Anil Shastri, the Congress nominee. The Congress was naturally pulling out all the stops to defeat V.P. Singh; Ghulam Nabi Azad had moved to Allahabad to supervise the campaign and all the Congress heavyweights were taking turns to address meetings there. V.P. Singh's platform was anti-corruption, and he linked this with the Bofors affair, which had just begun to develop into a major scandal.

Prannoy proposed that the actual counting of votes be covered live from Allahabad and the opinions of experts and the public be taken live from different locations all over the country. The main broadcast would be from a Doordarshan studio in Delhi, where a panel of distinguished journalists and political analysts, including representatives of different political parties, would comment on the results. From there Prannoy would go live to Allahabad, where specially picked persons from the newsroom would interview various political personalities and take the viewer into the counting hall. Then there would be live reactions from ordinary people in the streets to the results. Nothing on this scale had been done before. It would give thousands a ringside seat to an election for the first time—during the polling and after, during the more interesting time, when the votes are counted. I thought this an absolutely first-rate proposal and gave Prannoy permission to go ahead, promising him the equipment necessary to make all this happen.

Technically and operationally, it was a difficult task at that time. It meant stationing OB vans in the constituency at specified locations during the poll and then during the counting, at locations in the field and in studios across the country, and, of course, in Delhi, so that the two anchors could bring in live comments by the people. The coverage involved very elaborate arrangements, with links that used telephone lines at some places, microwave links at others and, of course, the very few satellite links we had available then. On election day there was a seemingly endless set of breakdowns: people couldn't be heard, the image was shaky, at times nothing at all came through. Again, you have to consider how very primitive the available equipment was then compared to what is used now as a matter of routine by virtually all the networks. In spite of all these problems, however, the broadcast was a resounding success, a pioneering effort that paved the way for other such broadcasts.

Why did I choose this particular by-election for a live telecast? There were several others being held at the same time. Could I not have covered them all? That at least would have made it difficult for furious Congressmen to criticize what they saw as an instance of Doordarshan deliberately highlighting a Congress defeat. In fact, the whole point of the programme was the coverage of an election in this intensive, direct manner. We simply did not have the resources to cover all the by-elections in the same way. We chose Allahabad because it was the most interesting contest: V.P. Singh, recently resigned from the Congress, standing alone against the might of the seemingly invincible ruling party. Besides, we didn't *know* the Congress would lose.

I do know now, however, that telecasting this particular programme did not add to my rapidly waning popularity in the ruling party. Sadly, I heard it said that even Rajiv Gandhi thought I had overstepped the mark. When I was asked about it, I explained that all the programme had done was reflect directly what the people had said and thought; there were no ulterior motives. Perhaps eventually even my detractors saw the point; frankly, I think they didn't, but had to hold their hand because of V.P. Singh's resounding victory.

Whatever else it did or did not do, the programme established Prannoy's and Vinod's ability to put together such telecasts, where studio discussions alternate with live interviews from the ground. They used the same technique later when they covered the presentation of the budget for the first time. This was again a very complex business as far as organization went: live telecast arrangements from Bombay, Madras and Calcutta, with studio discussions in Delhi, and live interviews in Delhi with the finance minister. Again there were glitches, but the overall impact was very good indeed. For the first time the budget presentation became a fascinating business, with comments from economists, captains of industry, political leaders and, of course, the finance secretary and the minister himself. And once again, this set a trend, a trend that has continued and developed into something much more refined than those early, fault-ridden telecasts.

6

Money Talk

By the time I joined Doordarshan the government had taken two terribly wrong decisions. The first was to eliminate licensing of radio and television sets; the second was to introduce advertising in Doordarshan. Both have been responsible for much of Doordarshan's present woes and travails.

The first, which some very foolish people in the I & B and finance ministries must have thought up, closed the door on Doordarshan's (and AIR's) ability to get a substantial and regular source of funds that would not affect government resources in any way. Given that today there are at least 8 crore television sets in the country and at least 15 crore radio sets, an annual fee of, say, Rs 1,000 for a television set and Rs 100 for a radio set would have brought in Rs 4,000 crore. Even after paying for the cost of collection and for an inevitable shortfall in collection, the amount left over would meet a truly professional public broadcasting network's operational expenses, costs of upgrading equipment and expansion plans. The BBC's estimated annual income is £1400 crore, with another £300 crore coming in from the sales of its programmes, DVDs, video cassettes and CDs. In a study done in 1999 by McKinsey & Company it was discovered that all successful public service broadcasters (they did not include Prasar Bharati among them) had large budgets and not only dominated but actually controlled the market. The most effective among them were funded by licence fees.

There would be an added advantage to this kind of revenue: no one from the corporation—Prasar Bharati or whatever—would have to approach gnomes in the ministry (who know as much about broadcasting as they know about piloting a spaceship) to bow and scrape for a few crores necessary for some activity or programme. In other words, the control of the ministry, which is financial more than anything else, would finally and effectively end.

Perhaps when the populist decision to revoke licence fees was taken, the political and administrative authorities involved may have felt the amounts were too small to matter—at that time, in the 1970s, the licence fees were Rs 10 per year for radios and around Rs 45 a year for black-and-white television sets, of which there weren't many. They simply did not see the virtual revolution that was coming; today the political authorities are plainly pusillanimous when it comes to a decision to reimpose licence fees. And yet, oddly enough, they have quite eagerly acquiesced to the imposition of the Conditional Access System (CAS), which is really a form of licensing—you pay extra to get the channels you want whereas earlier you merely paid the cable operator to get a cable connection. Is it only I or are there others who think this smells distinctly fishy? The government has, in a sense, handed over the right to levy what amounts to a licence fee to private channels and cable operators for reasons that are quite incomprehensible.

Having effectively deprived Doordarshan of a lucrative source of revenue, the government then took the second disastrously wrong decision—to introduce advertising in Doordarshan. This was in the form of regular advertisements put in at fixed times and also through sponsored programmes, where airtime was sold to private producers for an amount that was irrationally modest. In return, the private producers, who asked sponsors to pay hugely inflated amounts for their serials, got a certain amount of FCT that averaged out at between three and four minutes for a half-hour episode of a serial. This FCT was used to advertise the sponsor's products.

It was a system that made everyone happy. The sponsor, because his accountants calculated how much he saved. It would cost, at a rough average rate of Rs 30,000 for ten seconds, Rs 5.4 lakh for three minutes of regular advertising on television. For an episode, the sponsor paid a producer around Rs 2 lakh and an airtime fee of around Rs 50,000 to Doordarshan. He thus saved almost Rs 3 lakh by sponsoring episodes in a serial. Consequently he had every reason to be happy. The producer was just as happy. His actual cost for making each episode rarely exceeded Rs 80,000. He thus pocketed Rs 1,20,000 per episode (a substantial amount back then) and laughed and skipped all the way to the bank.

These are all very approximate figures but they aren't too far off. Mrinal Sen, who also did a serial for Doordarshan, once thanked me, in a slightly mocking, amused tone, for having telecast his serial. 'My cameraman has built himself a house,' he said, 'thanks to Doordarshan's largesse.' Saeed Mirza, who made the very popular serial *Nukkad*, told me much the same thing: 'I've bought a flat, and so has my cameraman.'

Doordarshan was also happy for its own reasons. Every minute of broadcast time cost it money and now this was not only being paid for, there was something left over, which wasn't bad at all. This is why there was a frenzy of proposals from frantic producers, like sharks who have scented blood in the water, a frenzy that had me and my officers caught up in a bewildering and endless set of meetings with producers every day—some indignant, some pleading, some suave and polite—leaving us weary and virtually unable to think when we dragged ourselves home.

My recollection is, though, that we made more money from 'spot ads', i.e., the regular advertisements put in before, during and after different programmes. These were over and above what went in as FCT, and in one of the revisions of the rates, I raised the prime-time rate for spot ads from some Rs 45,000 per ten seconds to Rs 71,000 for the same amount of time. This caused some indignation among various advertising agencies, but they accepted the logic behind it: raising airtime rates would dislocate the system under which sponsored serials operated, but raising spot ad rates would not. It would, in fact, improve it, by increasing the value of FCT. This would mean more sponsors willing to lay out more money per serial, and we would also collect more on the spot ads.

I disliked the whole business of commercializing television. I was spending far too much time on issues like rates and viewership figures and in discussions with producers who saw television as merely a commercial medium, including most of those who made much noise about being 'creative' film-makers. When it came to television they drove a mean bargain and were as sharp as any broker on Dalal Street.

I wanted to spend my time devising ways to showcase really good programmes. We did get some on, but they were the exceptions. Why couldn't we make better programmes in the CPC, I thought, especially since we had enough money with which to make them?

Enough money? You may well wonder. Indira Gandhi has been criticized for many things, but as far as television is concerned I think she had some very clear and correct ideas. She was opposed to advertising on Doordarshan, and it was only because of the persistent advocacy by the then finance minister and possibly some of those in the Prime Minister's Office that she agreed to it. However, she agreed only on her terms, and very well-thought-out terms they were. They were beneficial to the growth of Doordarshan and also frustrated the desire of the gnomes in the finance ministry to convert it into a goose that laid golden eggs which they could grab and take back with them into their burrows in North Block, giggling insanely.

Indira Gandhi directed that the money that came in from advertising had to be deposited in a special fund, called the Non-Lapsable Fund (NLF). This fund would be rather like a bank account and would not 'lapse' like budgetary allocations of ministries that remain unspent at the end of a financial year. The fund would be used to make 'good programmes' and suitable amounts could be drawn out by a committee consisting of the I & B secretary, the financial adviser, the DG of Doordarshan and a senior officer from the finance ministry's Department of Expenditure. Not all of the advertising revenue would go to this fund; some of it would go to meet the expenses involved in the process of getting the revenue, a notional figure that was worked out by the financial adviser. But that still left enough for the purpose Mrs Gandhi had in mind.

The NLF grew slowly at first, then very rapidly. By the time I came to Doordarshan, television advertising had begun to attract more and more advertisers; the NLF's balance was almost Rs 400 crore. For reasons I failed to understand, however, very little was drawn from it to make good programmes. But Madan Mohan, our canny engineer-in-chief, persuaded all of us that the phrase 'good programmes' meant good equipment as well. After all, he said in his quiet manner, you can't make good programmes unless you have good equipment. This was very convincing, which is why we were able to get state-of-the-art equipment for the new CPC. But what about the good programmes this wonderful equipment was meant to create? We never got money from the NLF for that, owing to the mindless obstruction of the finance ministry. We were meant to use the funds allotted in Doordarshan's normal budget to run the CPC. The usual argument was that if money was needed for programmes then it had to be provided for in the budget; if we used the NLF for this, we were, in bureaucratic terms, exceeding our budget, and so forth. Alas, yet another of the little tragedies that make up the picaresque story of Doordarshan.

One particularly bizarre story had to do with a shrewd, market-savvy agent who had a monopoly contract to market advertisements and airtime on Doordarshan. He decided—with sundry Doordarshan officials making a variety of noises expressing concern, disagreement, agreement, indignation and goodness knows what else—how much Doordarshan would earn in a year, and of course how much he would cream off from that. Perhaps that's not a very nice way of putting it—after all he was entitled, as most agents are, to a commission. But given the frenzied scramble for advertising space on Doordarshan, which was then the only television network in India, there was, it was whispered in advertising circles, a 'premium' on all spots, which was particularly high for prime-time slots. No prizes for guessing where that premium went.

The agent made a large fortune, as one would expect, and kept making an even larger fortune as the years passed. He had his head office in Bombay, and walked disdainfully among supplicants anxious for airtime. His contract, however, was coming to an end the year I became DG, and I was determined we would do the marketing ourselves, not through this 'sole concessionaire', as he was deferentially referred to by some in the ministry and in Doordarshan. As the last day of his contract approached I came under great pressure from the minister, the ministry, from within Doordarshan, from power centres in the Congress party and from some advertising agencies as well. Doordarshan does not have the expertise, you'll need staff, they'll need to be exposed to market strategies, and so on and so forth, they all said. I kept a stubborn silence. I was summoned to the ministry more than once and notes were sent to me on the subject, all of which I left on my table. Then the man himself came to see me. He was a very humble, simple man eager only to serve Doordarshan in his own way, he let me know with an oily smile. I played the village idiot and grinned back vacantly. But I think he got the message: his days of making crores from this network were over. The smile vanished before he left my room. And I did not renew his contract.

Had I made a terrible mistake which was going to cost Doordarshan a fortune? I wouldn't be truthful if I said I wasn't apprehensive, but I felt even more strongly that *Doordarshan* should get to keep whatever it earned. Would there be corruption in the sales set-up of Doordarshan? Perhaps. If I got evidence of it I wasn't going to spare anyone, I let that be known. I know there was corruption, but as often happens in government offices, I did not manage to garner even a single bit of evidence, however slight, to warrant a full-fledged enquiry, except in some cases involving lowly staff wanting 'chai-pani'. Whenever there was a whiff of something, it was referred to the CBI and investigations undertaken. One result of this was that, years after I had left government service, I kept getting summoned by various CBI courts from Jammu, Delhi and even Bangalore to give evidence that I had indeed sanctioned the prosecution of those accused—usually, as I have mentioned, minor officials. This notwithstanding, I still felt Doordarshan being responsible for its own marketing was better than putting Doordarshan's fortunes in the hands of an agent. With our own marketing set-up, primitive though it may be, we would have control over what we were selling and the rates at which we were selling it. With an agent, we never knew just what deal had been struck quietly—we had to accept whatever he had agreed he would deliver to the advertiser, even though some programmes or films could well have got us more.

I have already mentioned one reason why I disliked having to deal with the commercial aspect of Doordarshan. There was another reason for this: instead of spending what little spare time I had thinking up newer and better programmes, I was obliged to spend hours with importunate producers, each of whom brought a sheaf of proposals for serials, most of which were garbage. But they couldn't be rejected out of hand—most of them came with recommendations, pleas, peremptory demands and directions from the denizens in the corridors of power, ranging from members of Parliament to power brokers, recognized by their Gandhi topis (the older kind) or the white, collared kurta and churidar pyjamas (the more recent models).

I suppose the basic, underlying reason for my dislike of this commercialization of television was that it altered the very definition of television. It distorted perspectives and brought in a kind of schizophrenia among eminent people in various important positions in the government. They would speak of television's 'mission' in ringing terms one minute, and in the next demand that it earn its keep by becoming even more commercial. The fact that the mission implied television not be dependent on either advertising or government funds never seemed to occur to them.

Very early on in my tenure as DG, in Spetember 1986, I discovered, to my horror, that over 32,000 proposals for serials intended for the National Programme had not even been looked at. The harried officers simply hadn't had the time. Something had to be done. I formed a few teams with two or three officers in each and entrusted them with the task of going through these proposals and rating them on merit for rejection, a second look or for serious consideration. They worked for some weeks late into the night each day and finally we had a list of just a few worthwhile serials.

Naturally the matter didn't end there. There were furious, tearful and reproachful reactions from all those whose proposals had been rejected, but these were fielded by a smaller group of officers, and of course by the Dogsbody General—me. The process consumed a huge amount of time in useless work. Ideally we should have had controllers of programmes going out to talented producers asking them to make serials or films, rather than hordes of people who fancied they could make serials come clamouring to us with proposals that were often, literally, just pages torn out of novels. If anything skewed the nature of work in Doordarshan it was this one utterly unproductive messing around with serials and their frantic producers.

After about a year of this it dawned on me that Doordarshan had, in fact, been reduced to a mere renter of airtime: we gave a slot on hire for what was, given the amounts earned and spent on television advertising, a modest amount, getting nothing in return. The producer or the sponsor kept the copyright, depending on the agreement between the two, and repeats of popular serials or series meant paying a fortune to the copyright holder. Meanwhile the serials made in-house, by our own producers, some of whom were as talented as the best in the business, were either not shown or difficult to sell to sponsors. I suspect some canny agents were responsible for this, but it's only a suspicion; I never had any evidence.

The answer seemed to me for Doordarshan to commission serials. We could make the initial payments to producers once they had brought in a proposal to us which had a sponsor's backing, retain some of the FCT ourselves while giving the sponsor a part of it, and also earn revenue through spot ads, the number of which would depend on the popularity of the serial. One of the advantages would be that Doordarshan could keep the copyright to the serial and repeats would cost us nothing; another was that we would be able to use a mix of private and in-house productions. Most important of all, we would be able to control the quality of the programmes—the Ramanand Sagars of this world would not be able to get away with whatever they chose to make. I went ahead and called a press meeting where I announced our intention to switch over to this system.

The reaction to this caught me by surprise. There was a howl of protest from private producers of serials, perhaps because they were happily creaming off a good deal from the cost of each episode, which, once production was monitored by our executives, would not be so easy. But what really astonished me was that the I & B minister, H.K.L. Bhagat, who usually left me alone, called the press and told them emphatically that the system would not change and things would continue as they had always been. There were no consultations with me to find out why I had said what I did, just a plain contradiction. It was blatant interference with what was my business entirely, but I assume he made that statement because of pressure brought to bear on him by some powerful producers who had made it a point of getting close to the power brokers in the Congress party. They obviously wanted the statement made without loss of time and without discussing the matter with me, so that sponsors would not hold back the funds they were offering for various serials.

The system of hiring out airtime for serials in Doordarshan continues to this day. Interestingly, the private channels now operating in India all commission serials precisely in the manner I had sought to do, and very clearly with the same advantages.

*

There was, however, something very valuable that I did get from this whole business: the opportunity of meeting very bright, clear-headed people from the world of marketing and advertising. I learnt a lot from many of them. They belonged to a world that represented the future of private television and they were the ones who laid out the new guidelines.

Shunu Sen is without doubt the most memorable of them all. Shunu was then vice president of Hindustan Lever and the person who virtually built up television advertising in India, setting out the structures and the path it was to take. He also happened to be my second cousin (he was my mother's cousin, but many years younger than me); apart from the familial relationship we shared a close bond of affection and respect. I had known Shunu since he was a small boy going to Doon School but in the new equation we developed, he taught me a good deal about the complexities of television advertising without ever making me feel he was lecturing. It was as if we were sharing, discovering something together, except that I 'discovered' what Shunu very quietly and casually was showing me.

There was also Roda Mehta, then with Ogilvy & Mather (O&M). She was a very rational young woman professional who patiently took me through the labyrinth of ratings and the manner in which placement of advertising worked in a medium like television. I came to depend on Roda for sound advice that was not slanted in favour of advertising agencies or advertisers. She kept all interests in mind when she spoke to me. Roda was ambitious, as everyone in that profession was, and she had every reason to be: she was young, intelligent, and had accumulated a fund of knowledge and experience that made her invaluable to her agency. Perhaps it was this and her innate reserve—a manner that appeared aloof but was a cover, I suspect, for a very deep-seated shyness—that seemed to isolate her in her own line of business, an isolation that made her decide, finally, that she would not be a part of advertising except as a freelance consultant.

Then there was the genial, very friendly Mike Khanna of Hindustan Thompson Advertising (HTA), who gave me valuable, disinterested advice that stood me in good stead; Sam Balsara of Madison, shrewd but also perceptive, and cooperative when it came to doing something wildly unpopular, like raising the rates for advertisements on Doordarshan; and the irrepressible K.M.S. 'Titoo' Ahluwalia, head of MARG, the marketing research agency, with whom I often disagreed but nevertheless shared much laughter and good cheer.

I didn't realize what they in turn thought of me, although they were all very friendly and warm whenever we met. It was only after I had ceased being DG of Doordarshan that I found out: when they called me up to tell me that I had been awarded the ISA-Khatau Gold Medal for outstanding contribution to the world of advertisers and advertising on television. The citation said, among other things, that I had brought about a new understanding between advertisers and television. No better compliment could have been paid to me. It was heart-warming and touching. I don't know how true what the citation said was, but the fact that these people had a great deal of affection for me was enough.

Given that commercial television was distasteful to me, I nevertheless was concerned that since we did, in fact, have a commercial dimension, we simply weren't earning enough. True, the revenues had gone up from an annual Rs 99 crore to well over Rs 300 crore, but the rate of growth had begun to slow down. This, when we had no competition at all, was worrying. Part of the reason was the attitude of those in the commercial section of the organization. They weren't marketing men but Doordarshan officials who had been looking after production at some stage, then yanked out and put in charge of sales. They were given no training, not even any conditioning, just a set of advertisement rates thrust into their hands.

While marketing men from big newspapers and journals went to major clients and offered them packages of rates that induced them to place more ads, our men strolled into their office rooms like all other government officials, rolled up their shutters, in a manner of speaking, to announce they were open for business. The large number of people waiting to meet them to place ads only convinced them that all they needed to do was deal with them the way inspectors of civil supplies deal with ration card applicants. They got by with this only because there wasn't any competition; when it came, they were left stranded like beached whales, open-mouthed and gasping for air.

But it was clear right from the beginning that what Doordarshan needed was a set of professional marketing executives who could aggressively market time slots, particularly those that weren't very popular. But which executive worth his salt would look at a job in Doordarshan at the salary levels that we could offer? Finally, I thought of a way out. Just as we had recruited television journalists on a contract basis we could hire a professional marketing person on a fee that was equal to what the market was offering. That person could then decide what kind of organization needed to be set up, again by hiring people on contract, or 'staff artistes' in AIR/DD parlance.

Who might that person be? Where would I find someone who knew how Doordarshan's commercial side worked, would optimize revenues without affecting programme quality, yet remain impartial and level-headed when it came to working out rates, allocating time slots and, above all, marketing space for advertisements? I considered a number of alternatives and finally decided to ask Roda Mehta if she would take on the assignment. When I did ask her, she was understandably astonished but didn't say no straightaway, which I thought augured well for the reorganization I had in mind. I told her we couldn't match what she was getting at O&M, so perhaps, as some kind of public service, O&M wouldn't mind making up the difference between what we could give and what she was currently earning. She didn't have any idea if this was possible, but promised to get back to me. When she did, it was to tell me that S.R. ('Mani') Iyer, the MD of O&M, would be visiting Delhi and perhaps I could talk to him about it. I got in touch with him as soon as he arrived and over a quiet dinner Mani Iyer, with great tact and, with hindsight, wisdom, advised me against the whole idea. He said for one thing O&M couldn't spare Roda, and even if she were to be released, the business of contributing to her emoluments would immediately raise questions of bias that could harm both Doordarshan and O&M. It would be best, he suggested gently, if I looked for someone from within the organization; anyone from outside would not find the work culture easy to come to terms with, which might become a major problem. I reluctantly had to agree, since what he said was realistic, and regretfully put the idea on hold.

Meanwhile the CPC was coming up reasonably fast. I located some attractive space at the back for the sales unit, which had been functioning from squalid cramped accommodation in Parliament Street. We planned and built a more spacious office, with a comfortable, elegant room in which everyone coming in to place ads or buy airtime could sit, and equipped the sales office with PCs that made the process of placing an ad and preparing bills much more orderly.

I still felt we needed a truly professional marketing unit, not just offices where one could book ads. If we were going to increase revenues it had to be by going out to advertisers and persuading them to buy more time and place more ads, while raising the rates from time to time, depending on the popularity of programmes. But in the hurly-burly of events I had to wait for a more opportune time, and that came later, when I became secretary, Ministry of Information and Broadcasting.

7

Cameos in the Periphery: The Kendras

It becomes almost inevitable for a story about Doordarshan to dwell on what happened in Delhi, in the headquarters of the DG, and with the National Programme. But Doordarshan was really the sum total of a number of television centres—the kendras as they are known—and a good deal happened there of immediate relevance to the viewers of those programmes, which was a pretty substantial number. This should come as no surprise: give a person outside the cow belt the choice of watching a programme either in his mother tongue or in Hindi and you can be sure that he'll invariably prefer his own language. This has nothing to do with politics or understanding a language better; in fact, many are as comfortable in Hindi as in their mother tongue. It's a question of response, of contextuality, of a familiar social ethos to which the viewer relates completely.

Before satellite hook-ups and the National Programme, the kendras were the focal point of television in their respective states, sometimes in an area greater than just the state. We have had a glimpse of just how all this worked in Calcutta when the television centre there began to function under the direction of Mira Mozoomdar. As in Calcutta, so in other cities where television centres had come up—Bombay, Madras, Jalandhar—television attracted a wealth of creative talent from the performing arts. Theatre, dance and music programmes abounded in television schedules, much of it by distinguished artistes, musicians and playwrights.

Perhaps they realized that this new medium reached right into viewers' homes without losing any of its immediacy, whether it was a news programme or a serial or a film. They were also curious, I think, to try their own skills and talents in this new medium, and recognized that it was like no other medium in which they had worked before. It wasn't a medium suitable for a regular play (because of various limitations, not the least of which was time); it also wasn't a medium for a regular feature film. But it was brilliantly suited to present dance, and this the kendras did well, at least those located where dance was a living creative form, like the Madras Kendra. It also gave birth to a genre called the telefilm, which the Czech film-maker Jiri Menzel once disparagingly labelled the poor man's film. Poor man's film or not, the kendras helped present some fine telefilms, which were telecast nationally later on. Satyajit Ray made *Sadgati*, and Girish Karnad made *Cheluvi*—just two of several good telefilms that Doordarshan presented.

The National Programme destroyed much of the creative energy in the regional kendras. At the appointed time every evening—8 p.m.—the kendras stopped transmitting their own programmes and started relaying the National Programme. They stopped being stations which originated programmes and became mere repeater stations. They resumed their original identity again at around 11.30 p.m. when the National Programme ended—they were allowed to have a local presenter say in the local language, 'You've been watching the National Programme of Doordarshan, and that brings us to the end of our transmission for today. Good night.' And then all kendras went off the air. Thus, while private producers of serials thronged the corridors of Doordarshan's headquarters, only the makers of some rather unprepossessing serials came to the kendras. The numbers were by no means small, because there were substantial audiences for programmes in the mother tongue. By then, however, the damage had been done; the earlier enthusiasm and commitment in the regional kendras had evaporated, to be replaced by apathy and ennui. The fact that successive directors of these kendras were not able to lead by example was no help at all. Most kendras were riven with internal dissension and politics. Every visit I paid to these kendras meant having to listen to endless complaints about practically everything.

The director of the Lucknow Kendra is a curious case in point. He virtually withdrew from the kendra and the pressures and internal intrigues that plagued it and spent all his time making serials. This was fine—he was totally dedicated to making these programmes and spent a great deal of time working out scripts and shooting. While I was all in favour of letting the staff indulge their creative impulses, I found it rather irritating that every time I went to Lucknow on some official commitment or other, the fellow was invariably away 'on location', shooting some serial or film. If he was going to spend all his time doing only that, he had, I felt, no business being the director as well. The director of a kendra necessarily has to handle a great deal of administrative work, and at Lucknow this was all being done by some listless deputies, which made the overall working of the kendra shoddy and lackadaisical. I suppose I should have removed him from the director's post and let him make serials in the CPC, but he refused to budge from Lucknow. Indeed, when he had to retire he went to court to get a stay on his retirement! Fortunately, he didn't get it.

Meanwhile, more and more kendras kept coming up. The Bangalore and Hyderabad Kendras were pretty enough, and tidily small. Each had a single studio around which the station was built. But both were miles outside the city, which was, and still is, a major problem when you have to get news footage across to the studio for the local news bulletin or send to Delhi for the national news, and also when you have to get local artistes to come to the studio for programmes. It was also a daily ordeal for the staff, who had to travel a very long way to get to office on time. Some residential quarters were planned across the road from the kendra, but they were not nearly enough.

In 1987, the new kendra in Jaipur was being built so far from the city that we simply had to provide some residential accommodation for the entire staff. I pleaded with the then chief minister for some forty-five flats in a large state-built housing estate that was coming up next door. He was very obliging; he called in the housing commissioner and issued orders that as many flats as could be made available be provided to Doordarshan. I stuck my neck out and said we would of course pay for all these flats at mutually acceptable rates, but the officers of the civil construction wing of AIR remonstrated that they didn't have the money for the purchase of these flats. I went back to Delhi and pleaded that this money be taken from Doordarshan's construction budget (I did not, you will appreciate, have control over my own budget in actual fact, regardless of the fiction that was trotted out in reports and official documents). Fortunately, the financial adviser in the ministry agreed, though not for the entire amount. But something was better than nothing.

I faced a problem of an entirely different sort in Kohima. The kendra was, as in other cities, rather far out, and when I went there I discovered that it had no water supply at all. Nor could water be supplied because the source lay within the territory of a local tribe, and the chief refused to make any water available to a place that was not of any immediate benefit to the tribe. This was a major stumbling block; the tribal chiefs' writ ran in their areas, and there was nothing the state government could do except request their help, which was sometimes given, sometimes not. It depended on whether the terms satisfied the local chief. At that time, the chief and the government in power were on less than cordial terms, and the consequence was no water for the kendra. I was told there was nothing the state government could do about it. Then the bright young man from AIR who had been assigned to me as translator suggested I talk to the chief myself, and tell him that I had nothing to do with the state government. I did that and the chief was pleasant enough but came swiftly to the point: what was in it for the tribe? I said I would employ a certain number of local youngsters from the tribe in the new kendra. This worked, and I noticed a smile of approval from the translator. I bent my head, acknowledging with grace my translator's contribution to this solution. His contribution was, I found out later, a little more than just a bright idea. He was a member of the tribe, and I have no doubt had worked out the deal with the chief before he suggested it to me.

The problems with the Kohima Kendra were, however, not over. At a meeting of local writers and artistes, I asked them what the language of the broadcasts would be. Again, it was my young translator who had alerted me to the fact that this was a major problem in AIR Kohima and that I shouldn't leave Kohima without resolving it. I hesitantly suggested Nagamese, the lingua franca used practically all over the North-east, a mixture of Naga languages and Assamese. The suggestion was dismissed with derision and contempt. 'Bazaar language' was how most of the people at the meeting described it. So what then? I asked. All the languages spoken in Nagaland, they said. Not dialects, *languages.* The trouble was that Nagaland had twelve of them. All right, I told them, programmes will be in all twelve; we would allot a fixed time every day for a particular language, so speakers of a particular language, say, Angami, would know that programmes in Angami would be aired on Tuesdays at 3 p.m. It would mean increasing the staff strength beyond the prescribed norms. I dreaded having to do battle once again with the ministry on that, but I knew there was no other alternative. Before I left I promised the bright young translator from AIR he would be the first to join Doordarshan Kohima. He grinned widely, no doubt dreaming of the television programmes he would make. I hope he has been able to; he had enough imagination and enthusiasm.

I have mentioned the demoralizing effect the National Programme had on the kendras because it deprived them of the best programming time, from 8 p.m. to 11.30 p.m. every day. This notwithstanding, proposals for serials in the local languages kept coming to the kendras, low-budget proposals mostly, but even in these there was money to be made by the producers, given the prevalent formula of renting out airtime for sponsored serials. In fact, the markups in price by the producers to the sponsors were large enough to warrant some producers bribing some of the staff at the kendras to get their serials cleared for telecast. Some of the staff were caught and suspended for this; the CBI took up a number of cases against them.

For some reason, this kind of action seemed to petrify many officers against whom there hadn't been complaints of this nature. In fact, I received complaints of a different kind against the director of Doordarshan Madras. The complaint was that *no* serial was being cleared. I sent a deputy DG to find out why and he came back amused and exasperated. He said the man had indeed not considered any proposal—the deputy DG had found a room in which all the proposals, numbering several hundred, had been locked away. When he had demanded an explanation from the director, the latter is said to have whispered 'CBI' and looked at the deputy DG in terror. He was clearly convinced that if he cleared a single serial the CBI would come down heavily on him. To put the poor man out of his misery I moved him to Delhi.

There was one special feature though of practically all kendras. I had noticed that, of all the kendras I visited, the one where there were hardly any complaints or internal tensions was Bombay. Work there went on briskly and everyone appeared cheerful, caught up in their daily schedules. It took me a little while to find out what lay behind this benign atmosphere. Practically all the production staff—cameramen, lights people, sound recordists and producers—were moonlighting. Bombay had rapidly developed into the biggest centre for sponsored serials, so trained staff was in great demand there. Where would one get them? Each episode of a serial took some four or five days to shoot and edit, rerecord the sound and so on; and it was over in just twenty-three or twenty-four minutes of airtime. Television is an insatiable monster: it needs to be fed constantly and in vast quantities. This made producers desperate for trained staff, and they went quite naturally to those in Doordarshan.

One can't really blame them. The kendra wasn't making full use of them, with just about three and a half hours of programming, a part of which consisted of sponsored serials in the language of that particular state. The rest of the time was spent telecasting the National Programme. And private producers offered good money. That is why the staff in Bombay was such a contented lot. I found out, over time, that there was a varying degree of contentment among the staff of other kendras as well. One could, in fact, have worked out an equation which could be applied to all kendras: the level of contentment in a kendra in a particular city increased in direct proportion to the level of local, privately sponsored production of serials, ad films and other programmes such as documentaries and current affairs programmes. The key to it lay in the degree of moonlighting.

Did I do anything about the moonlighting? Not really. It seemed pointless to stop something that would happen anyway. Besides, the production people were obviously being taken on because they were good; one could only hope that they would do equally good work in the kendras. The sad part was that they did not, a direct result of the apathetic atmosphere in the kendras. This, in turn, was a result of the National Programme, which was the root cause of a great many ills that afflicted Doordarshan then. Looking back, it seems that I would have done Doordarshan a service by removing the National Programme from the main channel. It could have formed a part of what came to be known as DD Metro, and regional kendras could have downloaded via the satellite only those programmes they felt would be of interest to local viewers, like the national news. This would have kept alive the enthusiasm of the staff in the kendras, and made them centres for production of good programmes that could be taken by other kendras if they were considered good enough.

*

This seems as good a place as any to relate the genesis of DD Metro, a channel that had immense potential to present commercially attractive programmes of a fairly high quality. When the first usable satellite (INSAT 1B) was in orbit and its transponders began to be used by Doordarshan, it became possible to link the kendras in the metropolitan cities through this. But there was always the danger that this link could get interrupted due to some technical reason; after all, we were just starting up satellite transmission and nobody knew what lay ahead. So our engineers, led by the wise old Madan Mohan, had set up a microwave link as a backup, after coming to an agreement with the telecommunications authorities. They would provide a twenty-four-hour microwave signal with enough bandwidth to take an audio-visual television signal between Delhi, Bombay, Calcutta and Madras.

Within a year or so, however, the Indian Space Research Organization (ISRO) had launched another satellite and we had access to even more transponders, so a backup to the first satellite link was available in the form of the second satellite link. This made the microwave link unnecessary; but not to Madan Mohan.

'Why not use that for a second channel?' he asked me. 'You always wanted one.'

Why not indeed. I had been talking of a cheerful, lighter channel, not nonsense or garbage, but programmes with more vitality and energy, if you will. Taking the cue from Madan Mohan, we started the second channel. It was initially made available to the four metropolitan cities through the microwave link (hence the name DD Metro), but soon we were able to link other cities as well. The new channel rapidly became very popular and the minister was besieged with requests not just for transmitters but also for the metro channel.

One of the cities to get this link was Hyderabad, in the days when N.T. Rama Rao was chief minister. The formal inauguration of the channel was planned with great care. An elaborate ceremony was held with Ajit Panja and N.T. Rama Rao doing the honours, followed by a dinner hosted by the chief minister at his official residence.

What happened was an experience out of Kafka. I arrived at the chief minister's house around 7.30 p.m. and was shown up to the first floor, into a hall foggy with incense smoke. Near the entrance sat a man at a desk facing the wall, motionless. I have no idea who he was or what he was doing. I was taken past this man to the centre of the hall, where, through clouds of incense, I could see a throne set between a row of chairs on one side and a set of benches on the other. Next to the throne was a small table with a telephone on it.

When I came in some state government officers were already there, all of them sitting on the benches to the left of the throne. I was asked to sit on the second chair from the throne, on the right. Doordarshan officers—the engineer-in-chief, a chief engineer, and the director of the kendra, among others—were given chairs next to me. Finally, Ajit Panja walked in, wreathed in smiles, and was taken to the chair immediately to the right of the throne, adjacent to mine. The smile vanished. He looked a little bewildered; I think he expected something less weird, and frankly so did we all. Only the state government officers seemed unsurprised.

Several minutes passed while Ajit Panja became distinctly uncomfortable. Then a door to one side was opened dramatically and N.T. Rama Rao appeared, with some flunkeys in attendance. He came to the throne with a swish of silk, and I noticed he was wearing an orange sari. Not a dhoti, *a sari.* (I had heard stories that he had been told he would become prime minister if he wore a sari because Indira Gandhi used to wear saris; this may well be apocryphal, but that evening he was definitely wearing a sari, whatever the reason.) We all stood up and he imperiously motioned to us to sit down. A strange silence ensued. He said nothing. Panja said nothing. No one else ventured to say anything. Clouds of incense smoke eddied and swayed among the motionless silent people sitting on their respective benches and chairs.

Then a man came and whispered something to N.T. Rama Rao, who suddenly announced, 'We will have dinner.' He got up and strode to the next room, making no attempt to take Ajit Panja with him. The latter followed his host sulkily. We trooped in and were ordered by NTR to sit at various places at a long, large table laid out for dinner. We were joined by two of the chief minister's sons-in-law, but I cannot remember if Chandrababu Naidu was one of them.

Food was served to everyone on the directions of the chief minister. 'Give him that,' he would tell one waiter, gesturing to a guest. 'Give that person one more helping,' pointing at another.

There was no scope for argument. You took what you got and ate it. Fortunately I got off lightly. But one of the sons-in-law, poor man, was not so lucky. When plied with large amounts of food for the third time he shook his head and declined.

'You are not going to eat?' his father-in-law demanded thunderously.

'I . . . I am full, Appa,' the young man said timorously.

'What are you saying?' bellowed Rama Rao. 'My people go hungry in the villages and you say you are full? EAT!!' He gestured peremptorily to the waiter, who, terrified, piled large amounts of rice and vegetable curry on the wretched son-in-law's plate. We waited in embarrassed silence as the young man painfully swallowed the food. I thought he was going to throw up any minute but he managed to hang on.

As soon as he had finished and the sweet had been served, Rama Rao rose.

'Good night,' he said to Ajit Panja and shook his hand. Then he strode out of the room. A little after we heard the sound of cars starting up and the chief minister left the house, sirens wailing.

Ajit Panja looked at me incredulously. 'What sort of creature is this?' he asked me in Bengali.

The chief secretary said apologetically, 'He will go to his ashram now, sir, which is forty miles away. He actually stays there, not in this house. He is a man of very regular habits.'

'Yes, yes,' a visibly annoyed Panja said and left. One by one we trickled out back through the incense-filled hall. As I went out, I noticed the man sitting at the desk facing the wall. He had not moved. Perhaps, I thought mischievously, he's a son-in-law being punished by not being given his dinner. Or a mere assistant not exalted enough to be asked to dine at the chief minister's table. Whoever you are, I thought, you're a lucky man.

Thus was the second channel in Hyderabad inaugurated.

DD Metro could well have become the national channel, an *alternative* to whatever was being given to audiences in every state from their own kendras. Some programmes, as I said, could have been taken off it by the kendras, and the kendras would have been on air right through prime time to the close of transmission. I think it may have worked well, but, like many good ideas, it came to me too late, long after I had left Doordarshan.

8

Of Cabbages and Kings

Perhaps it was Rajiv Gandhi's extraordinary interest in television that made him decide to personally select someone to head Doordarshan. Whatever the reason, it certainly made me feel as if a floodlight had been turned on when I joined, and this was reinforced by the messages I got through the channels of power—by way of the Prime Minister's Office or the I & B minister—about something that had displeased him or, more rarely, something he liked.

Soon after I had taken over he summoned the minister, the secretary and me to a meeting. Not in his office in South Block, and not in his office at Race Course Road, but 30,000 feet above the earth in his special Air Force Boeing 737 on the way to Bagdogra, from where he was continuing to Darjeeling and elsewhere to address some meetings. We were not the only ones who had meetings scheduled with him on the plane. There were other ministers and officials as well, all of us carrying every conceivable piece of paper we thought would be remotely useful during our exchanges.

We were shown into the prime minister's cabin in due course. Instead of asking us how Doordarshan was doing, or something similar, he began with, 'Oh, here you are. I've been doing some thinking on what the organization of Doordarshan should be. Here, take a look at this.' And he pulled out some sheets of paper on which he had drawn a few organizational charts. One had as many as eleven additional DGs under the DG. I suggested, hesitantly, that these were a few too many.

Rajiv Gandhi responded instantly, almost eagerly. 'No, not at all. You see, the problem as I see it is that the DG is inundated with a great deal of unnecessary work. Well, perhaps it isn't unnecessary, but it takes up a lot of his time. Now, these eleven chaps will do all of it and leave the DG free to think, to look at the whole network, and decide how best it could be improved.'

Girish Mehra, the secretary, suggested that we take a little time and study the structure outlined and then come back to the prime minister with our suggestions. After some more discussion, Rajiv Gandhi agreed, but before we were shown out he said, in his usual way, 'Don't go to sleep on this.'

When we came out, Girish Mehra looked at me in astonishment. '*Eleven additional DGs?*' he asked. I told him the number did seem, to put it mildly, on the high side, but that I would work on it and try to preserve what Rajiv wanted—freedom for the DG to study and think about major issues and policies—without creating a vast bureaucratic empire.

At Bagdogra we disembarked from the special plane. Rajiv Gandhi left in a flurry of activity, security people scurrying about. Soon the whine of turbo-jet engines and the rhythmic, thumping swish of the giant rotors of his helicopter drowned out all other sounds. The big MiG 17 rose into the air, followed by a second, and moved towards the line of mountains which stood, hazily blue, over the airfield, climbing higher and higher. How familiar those mountains were! It hadn't been so long ago that I had been divisional commissioner of that area. This was territory I had known for years, since I was a probationer doing my revenue settlement training, later as additional deputy commissioner, Darjeeling, and then as divisional commissioner and secretary, Department of Hill Affairs in the state government. I had spent many hours in those mountains, walking through many forests and along many mountain paths, through the years.

The foothills were partly visible from the airfield; I could see the familiar huts and dwellings with their distinctive corrugated iron and aluminium sheet roofs, banana trees, a stream flowing swiftly over pebbles and stones. I felt an ache for a time when life had seemed more leisurely, when one had lived among all this without surprise, without a sense of alienation. Those aluminium-roofed huts and buildings, the forests, the clear streams and the rocky beds of seemingly placid, gentle and narrow rivers had once defined my world and what happened in it.

I felt I had moved into an impersonal world, one from which I could never return. And, sadly, I never did.

I flew back to Delhi on a regular commercial flight and worked on the organizational plan Rajiv Gandhi had sketched out. Eventually, after several attempts to define the specific nature of the work to be done, I was able to trim the proposed structure to three additional DGs, one deputy DG, a few more controllers of programmes and some corresponding increases in the engineering wing. I sent this off to the ministry, directly to the secretary, since he had been part of the discussions, and that was the last I saw of the plan. It may have gone to the prime minister with the minister's clearance, or perhaps it just sat on Ajit Panja's desk.

The next time I saw Rajiv it was later the same year, 1986, and it had to do with a fly. The occasion was a live hook-up with leaders around the world, including Margaret Thatcher, the Secretary General of the UN and others, all of whom would speak on the importance of preserving wildlife and our planet's natural environment. While the other leaders were being linked through satellite connections from their offices, Rajiv Gandhi had to come to the studio because we didn't have the facilities to take a live feed from his office and uplink it from there. Taking it back to the studio via a microwave link would have meant a one-way connection; this programme required that the leaders talk to and hear each other. That, given our technological progress at the time, was possible only from the studio in Delhi Kendra.

The studio was scrubbed and cleaned days before he was to arrive. It was a rather untidy place; part of the back was used to store bits of sets used for different programmes, props and other objects, since there simply wasn't room elsewhere to keep them. But they were decorously covered and the studio made to look as neat as possible. The prime minister arrived, went into the studio and sat down. He smiled briefly at me as he passed, and seemed to be in good spirits. The lapel mikes were duly fitted and we waited for the moment when the programme would go live the world over. An engineer who was in touch with his counterpart in London signalled that we were live. Then, the fly appeared.

It flew lazily out of the stuff stored at the back and as Rajiv Gandhi began speaking, flew right across his face. He continued to speak, pleasantly, without reacting to it, but when it made a few more passes in front of his nose, he waved it away and continued speaking. We watched apprehensively. I asked the director of Doordarshan Delhi in a whisper what sort of cleaning he had done and he replied that they had spent hours cleaning every bit of the studio.

As soon as the programme was over, Rajiv Gandhi ripped off the lapel mike, his face dark with anger. He strode out of the studio, and turning to the wretched director, who had the misfortune of being the nearest, told him what he thought of his standards of cleanliness in very explicit language. Then he got into his car and the convoy swept away. There were recriminations, angry expostulations, frightened explanations from the director and his staff. The minister demanded that someone be punished, but I managed to persuade him and the secretary that that would be taking things too far. It seemed a bit excessive to transfer someone, or demote him, because of a fly. The presence of the fly was inexcusable, but I felt a strong verbal dressing down was enough. Better inspections, a greater use of insecticides—that was what was needed. I conveyed this to the director and asked him to inspect his studios himself every day.

Clearly, that was not enough. That fly was cleverer than we thought. A few days later I was asked to see the minister.

'This is really disgraceful,' he said angrily. 'I was with the prime minister and as we were talking he looked at the television and some lady was singing and there was a fly in front of her face! She was waving it off. The PM is very angry.'

I was dismayed and decided something drastic had to be done. The minister was, however, a little more canny than me. It helped that he was a lawyer, I suppose.

'I need evidence,' he said conspiratorially. 'What you must do is ask for a recording of that song. Say nothing about the fly. Just say you liked it and want to see it. Then we will see the fly and they cannot deny it.'

I duly asked for a recording of the song. I rang the station director and told him I had rather liked the song and wanted a copy of the recording. He was very pleased and said he would send it over immediately. The tape arrived the same evening. I watched it in my office. No fly. I watched it again. No fly, not even a brief glimpse of anything remotely like a fly. Just the singer singing and occasionally waving her hands as classical singers sometimes do when singing a long *gamaka* or taking a high note.

I marched into the minister's office with the tape.

'Sir,' I said loftily, with as much injured pride as I could muster, 'if we do something wrong we certainly need to be told about it. But it is not fair to accuse us of what did not happen.'

Then I showed him the tape. He was dumbfounded.

'You see, sir,' I said with excessive politeness, 'there is no fly.'

'But I saw it,' the minister said, looking bewildered. 'The PM saw it. All of us saw it.'

'What you saw, sir,' I explained with some condescension, 'was the singer making some movements with her hands. Singers do it, you know. Sometimes it could look as if they were waving off a fly.'

'Yes,' the minister said doubtfully, 'I suppose that's true. But . . . I saw the fly!'

I gave him the tape. 'Would you like to see it again, sir?'

'No, no,' he said.

'I suggest you show it to the PM, sir. He may like to see it for himself.'

'Yes, I will show it to him,' the minister agreed. I left, making a dramatic exit in my best theatrical style, and noticed that the minister was still looking bewildered. A few days later he called me to his room and handed back the tape.

'The PM has seen it. He said he must have made a mistake.'

I returned to my office and sent for the director of Doordarshan Delhi. When he came, I gave him the tape.

'Nice recording, Grewal,' I told him genially. 'I enjoyed watching it.'

'Thank you, sir,' he said, beaming. 'She is a very talented singer, sir. But we had some trouble with the tape, sir, I am telling you frankly.'

'Trouble?'

'Yes, sir,' he said and laughed. 'It was the fly, sir. The recording was made before the PM's visit, and that fly was in the studio. It was sitting on the singer's face and she had to wave it off. When you asked for it we did not want you to see the fly, so we edited the tape and removed the fly.'

I stared at him. Finally I said, 'That was very considerate of you, Grewal.'

'No sir, no sir,' he said happily. 'You liked the ghazal, and so we had to give you a *very* nice copy. No fly.'

No fly. Oh yes, I thought as I watched him go out of my room, no fly. The fly had been officially edited out and edited out it would stay. But I went to the kendra the next day, with the engineer-in-chief, and got all the junk removed from the studio, which was then sprayed dense with insecticide. I told the director, who thought I had taken leave of my senses, to have it sprayed every day from then on.

'No, Grewal,' I told him, 'I'm not the one who's mad. A director who keeps his studio so dirty that there are flies in it as if it was a dhaba needs to have his head examined.' Not long thereafter I moved him out of Doordarshan Delhi. The fly had nothing to do with it, of course.

*

These were some of the occasions when I met Rajiv Gandhi. There were also a number of messages relayed to me through various sources: sometimes the minister would tell me that Rajiv was not happy with such and such programme, or sometimes I was informed by the secretary of some observation about a particular programme he had made. Occasionally the phrase 'the prime minister desires' was dispensed with and the instructions of the functionary in the Prime Minister's Office were delivered to me directly.

I received one such instruction from T.N. Seshan, who was secretary in the Ministry of Environment, but also the secretary in charge of the prime minister's security. Rajiv Gandhi had concluded a rather useless visit to Sri Lanka; this was just after the Indian Peace Keeping Force (IPKF) had been recalled and there was a good deal of resentment that Indian troops had been deployed there. During the ceremonial send off, he had to perform the usual inspection of the guard of honour at the airport. As he was doing so, a naval rating, who was part of the guard of honour contingent, reversed his rifle and tried to hit Rajiv Gandhi on the head with it. Had he succeeded it may well have proved fatal. More than anything else it was Rajiv Gandhi's own agility and quick reflexes that saved him. He darted to one side and at the same time the officer in charge of the guard of honour leapt at the man and pushed him aside, an act that caused the blow to lose some of its force. Nevertheless the rifle struck Rajiv Gandhi a glancing blow on his shoulder. A split second later one of his Special Protection Group (SPG) men grabbed the rating and threw him to the ground.

A Doordarshan cameraman who was shooting the departure for the news bulletins caught all this on camera. He hadn't allowed the incident itself to fluster him and had kept on shooting. As a result he had a record on videotape of just what had happened. Soon after the prime minister had been hustled on board the IAF aircraft and was airborne, Seshan came to the cameraman and demanded to see the footage. The cameraman tried to explain that he didn't have a VCR, so he could only show it through the viewfinder of the camera. Seshan was apparently annoyed but agreed to this. Then the poor cameraman in his nervousness couldn't locate the particular cassette that he had used. He had taken it out of the camera and put it with all the other tapes used to film the entire trip and couldn't find it in the heap of cassettes in his bag. If he hadn't been harried by Seshan he probably would have been able to locate it quickly enough, but with an angry Seshan breathing down his neck he fumbled for a few minutes. By the time he found it, Seshan had reached boiling point. He raged at the poor man, called him all kinds of names and assured him of the most severe punishment once they reached Delhi.

True to his threat, he rang me up as soon as he got to Delhi.

'Ghose,' he said in the half-snarl he always used when he had lost his temper, 'I am speaking to you as a complainant. I have a grievance and demand redressal.' Even when he was in a foul temper, his love of the dramatic did not leave him.

I asked what his grievance was. He told me that the cameraman was utterly inefficient and not the sort of man who should have accompanied the prime minister on his tour. He was brainless, Seshan told me, as well as clumsy and incompetent. He went on to give me his version of what this clumsy, incompetent man had done, informed me that the prime minister was very annoyed by it all, and then demanded that the cameraman be placed under suspension. I assured him I would look into the affair personally.

I then spoke to the cameraman and after I had heard him out, felt his version was more credible; he had nothing to gain by antagonizing the security adviser to the prime minister, much less the prime minister himself. And, after all, what had he done? He had merely said he didn't have a VCR, which was true, and then hadn't been able to find the cassette with the footage of the attack quickly enough. This again was understandable; there were some fifty or sixty cassettes since he had covered every bit of the visit. I rang Seshan and told him that I didn't think it was necessary to take any action against the cameraman because he had done nothing wrong.

Seshan was silent for a bit and then said, again with the familiar growl, 'You're very lucky you aren't working under me.'

'I am,' I told him. 'I can't tell you how fortunate I consider myself.'

He hung up.

*

When I joined as DG I had some idea of the work I was expected to do, but no idea at all of how to do it. I knew that Rajiv Gandhi wanted fresh ideas, newer programmes that embodied some values, and that he wanted Doordarshan to function more independently. As long as he was a powerful prime minister, his leadership of the party not in question, this was all right. My initially small and gradually more comprehensive attempts to pull away from the government's almost stifling control bore fruit, owing in no small measure to the strong support I got from Girish Mehra. With the passage of time, however, Rajiv Gandhi's position became difficult, mainly because of the Bofors issue. This brought into the open a whole lot of resentment, a great deal of envy, anger and a desire to pull him down a peg or two. These feelings were fanned by frequent reshuffles of the council of ministers, wherein some lost their posts, and others, like Ajit Panja, were moved to posts that were really sinecures. The party was used to patronage being doled out to its functionaries and when this did not happen, coteries of the disgruntled began to form and spiteful comments were made in the drawing rooms of those affected.

Among the dissatisfied was a group of Congress MPs from West Bengal, including some others like Santosh Mohan Dev from Bengali-speaking Tripura. Ajit Panja was prominent in this group, and made much, apparently, of the manner in which he had been demoted, as he saw it, from being in charge of a high-profile ministry like information and broadcasting to being a mere minister of state in the Ministry of Finance. He blamed my handling of Doordarshan for his misfortune; he was convinced that the prime minister had moved him out because I had shown 'anti-Congress' stories in the news and aired 'anti-Congress' current affairs programmes.

In fact, I had not shown any anti- or pro-Congress programmes but, yes, there were programmes by talented film-makers on problems faced by the common man, such as drinking water and unemployment, and also the manner in which ordinary people lived in the midst of the terror that had gripped Punjab. But regardless of what I thought about these programmes, they had become the focal point of resentment. I was labelled Jyoti Basu's man, and this was conveyed to those close to Rajiv Gandhi.

One other factor probably worked against me as well, namely, the fact that I paid little attention to some of Rajiv Gandhi's friends who felt they had the authority to instruct me about what needed to be shown. The one exception was Suman Dubey, who was a pillar of strength. He was a very close friend of Rajiv's and had agreed to become an information adviser in the I & B ministry only to help him. He never told me what to do. If I asked for his opinion, he gave it; often we put our heads together to work out just how some programmes could be done. We understood and valued each other's opinions and ideas.

I mention this because, unlike Suman, others would make comments to Rajiv Gandhi (I heard of these from various unexpected but reliable sources) about how dreadful Doordarshan was, that nothing was going to change, that bureaucrats would never be able to make a difference, and other such remarks. They may have been casual comments, but when such comments are made over and over, they do make a difference. Once, Romi Chopra, one of Rajiv's friends, came to my room and said that the prime minister was furious at the manner in which slogans on various social issues—conserve drinking water, adulteration is a crime against humanity—were being telecast. He said that Rajiv thought they were dreadful and wanted them changed at once. I had no means of knowing if Rajiv really felt that way except for Romi Chopra's word, and I said as much. In reply, he told me that he had informed me of how the PM felt, and if I knew what was good for me, I would do something about it, otherwise there might be unpleasant consequences.

*

During my tenure as DG there were three I & B ministers—four, if you count the minister of state along with the last minister. The first of these was V.N. Gadgil, a scholarly, gentle person. I found him very easy to get on with, a person who listened and tried to help in whatever way he could. His problem was that he was a little too eager to please the powers in his party, and this eagerness was, I think, seen as weakness. He or his private secretary sometimes interfered with the day-to-day work in Doordarshan, particularly the news, but he was never overbearing. If he did ask for some event to be covered, it was always because he had been asked to do so by someone he couldn't afford to alienate.

His exit was rather sudden. Word had gone about that Rajiv Gandhi was going to reshuffle his council of ministers, and one morning when I went for a meeting called by the minister, Girish Mehra told me that the reshuffle was due to take place right then. As we entered the minister's room, he was preparing to leave for Rashtrapati Bhavan.

'The PM wants to remove a few ministers,' he confided, and mentioned two who probably would be dropped. 'I have been telling them to be careful,' he continued. 'But they simply wouldn't pay heed to my advice. Anyway, we will have our meeting when I come back.'

We went back to Girish's room and waited. About half an hour later the principal information officer rang up and told Girish that two ministers had indeed been dropped from the council of ministers. V.N. Gadgil was one of them.

'Bhaskar,' Girish said, 'we ought to go and see him. He's been good to us all, and this must have been a great shock to him.'

We went to the minister's house and were shown into his study. He sat there looking stunned. Girish Mehra said something to the effect of how very sorry we were and that it was a shock to us all.

'It's all Raman's fault,' Gadgil said suddenly. 'He never carried the stories I asked him to. That's what annoyed the PM.'

I was taken aback. C.V. Raman had never been that difficult; if he had been blocking stories he must have had good reasons for it. In any case, I never thought Rajiv Gandhi would remove a minister for something like that. He had always encouraged openness, within some limits of course, and had wanted the government to 'take its finger out', as he had told me.

We left Gadgil looking forlorn and miserable. He never became a minister again. I think he became spokesman for the party for a while, before his untimely death.

The new minister was Ajit Panja. I had known him as the health minister in West Bengal in Siddhartha Shankar Ray's Cabinet. He was, besides, a lawyer and a good friend of my brother-in-law, Samaraditya Pal, who was also a lawyer. He had been a jovial, cheerful man then. When I met him in the I & B minister's room he seemed quite glad to see me, but I sensed that his cheerfulness was a little perfunctory. I thought it would be pleasant working with someone whom I had known earlier and went back to my office quite pleased.

A few days later, a strange event occurred which permanently altered the initial cordiality. One of his personal staff rang up and told me in a distant, condescending tone that the minister wanted to interview all the presenters and newsreaders, to assess for himself how suitable they were. I was a little incredulous.

'The *minister* said that?' I asked.

'Yes,' the flunkey replied. 'If you want, you can ask him. He wants to start with someone he noticed introducing a music programme last night. Some western music programme.'

I checked with the programme staff. The programme was a Doordarshan Madras presentation, a piano recital by Handel Manuel, introduced by the very pretty and very competent Jennifer Arul.

The next day I was in the minister's room for a meeting on something or the other. As it ended, I asked him about the planned interviews.

'Do you really want to interview all the presenters and newsreaders, sir?'

'Yes, yes,' he said carelessly.

'And you want to start with the presenter of the music programme you saw two nights ago?'

'Yes, she seems quite good, but I wish to find out,' he said impatiently.

'I'll get her to come to Delhi,' I said. Then, I added innocently, 'Of course, she may need a few days. It may not be easy for her to leave Madras at only a day's notice. Did you know, sir, that she's the daughter of the inspector general of police?'

Panja paled. 'Inspector general of police?' he said. 'I think you need not disturb her. I . . . I will speak to her when I visit Madras.'

'And the other presenters and newsreaders, sir?' I asked.

'Yes, yes, I would like to interview them.'

'Of course, sir,' I said in my most oily manner. 'When should we come?'

Panja looked surprised. 'You will come also?' he blurted out.

'Naturally, sir,' I said earnestly. 'My minister wishes to meet some of my staff. I have to be there in case you have some instructions for me. The deputy DG news will also be there.'

Panja was visibly dismayed and annoyed. 'All right, all right. You ask my PS to fix up a time.'

'Certainly, sir,' I said meekly. Then I added, 'Sir, I would be grateful for your instructions on one point.'

'What?' said the minister curtly.

'Your assistant private secretary was asking for the addresses and telephone numbers of the presenters and newsreaders. There is a convention that these are given to no one, not even to me. Should I have them given to your APS?'

There were some other officers still in the room from the previous meeting, listening silently to all this.

Panja flailed about in confusion. 'What?' he said. It was clear to me he wasn't speaking the truth. 'Who asked for these addresses and phone numbers? No, no. What do I want with them? I never asked for them.'

'Thank you, sir,' I said. 'In that case I'll tell our officers to disregard all such requests.'

The minister looked at me for a long while. I realized I had made an enemy, but my enthusiasm and, yes, a certain amount of vanity I had then made it easy for me to disregard the fact. I discovered only later how wrong I was to have done so.

I have already related the trouble I had with Panja when we began recruiting people for the news division, and his reaction to what he perceived as sacrilegious remarks about the Congress in one of the current affairs programmes by Ramesh Sharma. He seemed to think that there were other occasions when I had got Doordarshan to carry stories in the news that did not flatter the ruling party. I cannot recall now which ones they were, but the fact he thought me culpable was evident when, in early 1988, he was appointed a minister of state in the finance ministry, which he saw as a demotion because in the finance ministry he had to be content with whatever the minister allotted to him. From all that I heard then, he ascribed his demotion to me. He thought the prime minister was annoyed with him because of the kind of programmes Doordarshan had been showing, little knowing that it was the prime minister himself who had given me the mandate to open out the programmes to views other than the constipated official ones.

This said, Panja was not a minister who interfered or bullied; he had some areas of interest, usually in connection with Doordarshan Calcutta, where, to buy peace, I let him have his way unless what he wanted was blatantly political and partisan. He seemed content enough to appoint a few people to some low-level jobs in the kendra; in Delhi he kept away from most programming decisions. I cannot recall him ever trying to manipulate the news.

There was, however, one strange incident when he suggested that a story be aired in a particular manner. It had to do with Benazir Bhutto's visit to India when she was prime minister of Pakistan. She and Rajiv Gandhi apparently got on fairly well, well enough for a joint declaration of some kind to be made that seemed to augur well for relations between the two countries. This was, remember, a few years before terrorism hit Kashmir. The declaration came not long after an unpleasant exchange of public statements between India and China, an exchange that had caused indignation at home.

Just after Benazir and Rajiv signed the joint declaration, Panja rang up and asked me to see him. He was very excited and as soon as I entered his room, took me aside and said in a conspiratorial tone, 'Bhaskar babu, do you remember there was a football match some time ago played in Calcutta between a Chinese team and an Indian team where we scored one goal against them?'

I couldn't remember.

'Yes, yes,' he said, all excitement. 'You give the story about the Indo-Pak friendship and then show India scoring the goal against China. From the old recording.'

I was flabbergasted. Panja's attempt at international diplomacy seemed no better than India's international footballing skills. I hemmed and hawed and finally said I would try to locate the footage. I went back to my office and rang up one of the secretaries in the external affairs ministry and told him what the minister wanted.

'Are you totally insane?' the officer asked me. 'This is incredible. Don't even think about doing anything so foolish.'

I told Panja that external affairs didn't think the idea very opportune, and he accepted it with good grace. 'But it would have been nice,' he said.

Panja was followed by a Cabinet minister, H.K.L. Bhagat, and a minister of state, Krishnakumar. Bhagat was also Minister for Parliamentary Affairs and that kept him rather more busy than his duties as I & B minister. He left me strictly alone, except on one occasion when, as usual, there had been shrill cries of 'anti-Congress' reportage by Doordarshan. He called me and said that a number of MPs were upset by some of the stories being carried by Doordarshan in the news and by the current affairs programmes.

'Just be a bit careful,' he said, and that was it.

I realize now why Panja had left me alone and why Bhagat did as well. It had to do with Rajiv Gandhi's political position within his own party. As long as he was the undisputed leader, able to do just what he wanted, no minister dared oppose him. They knew that he had chosen me to head Doordarshan, hence the hands-off approach. Panja was moved while Rajiv Gandhi was still a formidable power, but soon after Bhagat became minister, things began to change. By then Rajiv had lost all the elections in which he had campaigned. He lost West Bengal in 1987, which all of us who had served in that state knew he would. He lost Tamil Nadu, where for the first time in several years, and in a move that was epic in its foolishness, the Congress decided it would campaign on its own without the support of its erstwhile ally, the AIADMK. And he lost all the by-elections, including the prestigious Allahabad by-election.

All these events weakened Rajiv's position. To add to his troubles, the president, Giani Zail Singh, had begun to make some not very covert moves to isolate him. As his position grew more and more precarious, Rajiv tried desperately to keep the loyalty of the Congress MPs in the Lok Sabha. The MPs realized that he was no longer the unquestioned supremo of the party and became more strident in their demands. One of these demands was that I be removed from Doordarshan. H.K.L. Bhagat was an old Indira Gandhi loyalist and therefore loyal to Rajiv, which was why he left me alone for some time. Then there occurred a little incident which made him change his attitude.

He called me to his house one evening, which I thought rather odd. He had never called me to his house before; all our work, such as it was, had been in his office. I went to the large bungalow, one appropriate to his rank as a senior Cabinet minister, and was shown into a tastelessly furnished room. There were Rexine-covered sofas in garish colours and portraits of Bhagat receiving all kinds of felicitations on the walls; a framed photograph of Bhagat with Indira Gandhi graced a table.

Bhagat came in with a young man. 'Ghose,' he said, his eyes hidden, as usual, behind dark glasses, 'I want you to meet my son, Deepak. He is very interested in films.'

'That's nice,' I said for lack of anything else to say.

'Doordarshan is showing *very* bad films,' the young man said assertively. '*Very* bad.'

'Are they very bad?' I asked. 'Well, you know, we can't really pay very much by way of royalty . . .'

'I will get you good films,' the young man said. 'I know many people in Bombay. Very good films.'

Then the penny dropped. 'Really?' I said feigning enthusiasm. 'That's wonderful. Now, I happen to have a list of really good films. Can you get me any from among them?'

I gave him a list from among the papers I was carrying, a sort of wish list one of the officers had prepared some time earlier when I had had a meeting with some film-makers from Bombay. Deepak looked at it and his jaw dropped. The first film on the list was *Sholay*.

'Yes, yes,' he said. 'These are good films, but I also have . . .'

'These are the films that the viewers want,' I interrupted him. 'We did a short survey and these are the films they want to see.' Lies, of course. I hadn't conducted any survey.

'Why don't you try, beta?' Bhagat asked his son. 'Mr Ghose has done a survey, you see. We must give the people what they want.'

'Ah . . . yes, Papa . . .' the young man fumbled for words. 'I will try, Papa . . .'

'Don't worry, sir,' I said to the minister breezily. 'Leave it to me. Deepak and I will work something out.'

'All right,' the minister said. 'You can talk freely to Mr Ghose, Deepak,' and he left.

As I had expected, Deepak wasn't able to get even one of the films on the wish list. They were very popular films, and most film-makers believed that once they were shown on television their box-office value would drop. Right or wrong, they refused point blank to let these films be shown on television. I knew that, but I needed to go through the charade to stymie Deepak's little game.

I succeeded, but that probably didn't stop Deepak from telling daddy just what I had done. And that, as far as Bhagat was concerned, was the end of the road for me. No angry meetings, stern instructions, nothing. It wasn't his style. He simply decided I had to go, and by that time Rajiv Gandhi was politically in no position to refuse a request from Bhagat. But he set about it methodically, so that Rajiv would have no argument left to justify my staying on at Doordarshan.

I was also left pretty much to myself by Girish Mehra. He had been additional secretary in the Ministry of Defence when I was a joint secretary there; I had met him then a few times and found him friendly enough. When I came to Doordarshan he soon became not only cordial and friendly, but also a source of support. I made it a point of keeping him fully informed of all that I did; he not only approved of the initiatives I took but backed them strongly, which helped me a great deal.

The one thing he was very concerned with, and which he insisted on deciding himself, was the choice of commentators for the international cricket matches that India played and which Doordarshan covered exclusively in those days. This wasn't just for Doordarshan; he was equally concerned about the commentators for AIR. His interest led him to discuss different aspects of commenting directly with the commentators and with the sports producers of both AIR and Doordarshan. I kept out of all this for two reasons. One was that, if he had wanted to, he could have been an S.S. Gill, actually running Doordarshan himself—after all he was, administratively, my boss. But he scrupulously kept himself away from any day-to-day interference with the way I managed Doordarshan. If, then, there was one area where his love of the game made him take a more than usual interest in how it was covered and who the commentators were, I felt it was quite all right. The second reason was more mundane and in a way linked to the first: I knew little about the game, certainly much less than Girish Mehra did, and so was quite content to let decisions about its coverage be taken by him.

Girish Mehra left the ministry about a year and a half after I joined. He was moved to the Ministry of Heavy Industry, from where he retired, and then became high commissioner to Canada for some years. His place in the ministry was taken by Gopi Arora, who was—and continued to be—a key figure in the Prime Minister's Office. I had known Gopi earlier so I found it very easy working with him, but there was a world of difference between him and Girish Mehra. Gopi wanted to know a great deal about how matters were handled in Doordarshan and discussed virtually every aspect of it. But these discussions were in no way a laying down of instructions on how to do things; they always remained mere discussions. Out of these emerged some new and better ways of handling matters, but they were never thrust upon us.

I have wondered, occasionally, just what role Gopi played in my removal from Doordarshan. He became I & B secretary when Rajiv Gandhi was politically vulnerable. One would have thought that at a time like that he would have kept his closest advisers near him; why then did he send Gopi to I & B? I knew that Gopi continued to do some work for the Prime Minister's Office but I hadn't the faintest idea what it was. Gopi had some personal staff from the Prime Minister's Office and handled some files from there with their help, never using the personal staff he had been given from the I & B ministry.

It was after he came to the ministry that the chorus of resentment at the way I was handling Doordarshan, headed by the redoubtable Ajit Panja and ably supported by other MPs from West Bengal, became more and more vociferous. Not that Gopi was responsible for any of that—he was the one person who kept reassuring me that it was the sort of thing one had to live with, and advised me to go about my work without giving it too much thought. I am just putting together certain events here that occurred around a particular time, like stars that move into a certain zodiac sign or 'house'.

However, while I trusted Gopi greatly and sought his advice on much of what I did, I always felt there was an area which he kept within himself, a sort of secret place where all kinds of facts and developments were stored, something that made him appear just a little reserved, preoccupied, sometimes abstracted. It made me wonder just what he was so preoccupied with.

He told me a strange story long after we had both left the government. Apparently at one time Rajiv Gandhi had actually wanted to dismiss me from the IAS when the chorus against me was at its most shrill, and had said as much to Gopi, who was aghast. He informed Rajiv that he couldn't dismiss an IAS officer unless there were very good grounds and only after a high-level inquiry had been conducted into the misdemeanours, and there were none, he pointed out, as far as I was concerned. According to Gopi, the prime minister persisted, and Gopi told him if he did issue dismissal orders I would go to court.

'Let him go to court,' Rajiv is supposed to have said. 'We'll face him there.'

Gopi put his foot down and told the PM that even if such orders were issued, he would not carry them out. Rajiv expressed some surprise at that, but Gopi vehemently repeated that he would not carry out orders that were blatantly wrong.

All of a sudden, Gopi recounted, Rajiv's position on the matter changed right then. He was known for doing that—he would pursue one line of thinking and then suddenly change to something diametrically opposite.

'All right,' he told Gopi. 'You don't have to get so excited about it. We'll just transfer him from there.'

This is what Gopi has told me and I have only his word for it. If Rajiv had indeed said it, it must have been to Gopi alone. At the same time, however, I simply cannot believe that Rajiv Gandhi was deceitful. Shortly before I was moved out, I met him one last time in his room in Parliament. I had accompanied the visiting DG of Syrian television, an event shot by the Syrian television crew accompanying their DG. The formalities were over, and I was leaving, when Rajiv Gandhi called me back.

'Bhaskar,' he said, 'just stay on a minute.'

Rajiv Gandhi personally went to the door that led to the main corridor of the Parliament building and locked it.

'What's all this I hear about your being anti-Congress?' he asked.

'*Anti-Congress*, sir?' I said, completely surprised. 'I'm not anti-Congress or anti or pro any party.'

'That's what I thought,' Rajiv said. 'But all these Bengal MPs in the Congress are saying your news is slanted against the Congress. They say you're Jyoti Basu's man.' He laughed in that very contagious way he had.

'I'm only doing what you told me to do when I joined, sir,' I said. 'I've been trying to keep the news objective and credible.'

He nodded. 'I know. I watch the bulletins.'

Then he came up to me and put an arm around my shoulder. 'Look, Bhaskar. You're doing a fine job. Just keep it up. But be a little careful. There are some people who don't wish you well. Go on doing what you're doing, and remember,' he smiled disarmingly, 'I'm always there.'

There was a knock on the inner door, and Sheila Dikshit, then minister in the Prime Minister's Office, B.G. Deshmukh, the Cabinet secretary, and Serla Grewal, principal secretary to the PM, came in.

Seeing me there they froze and their faces darkened. I knew it was time for me to leave. I made a discreet exit. I also knew that I was going to feature in their discussions with him, but I nevertheless felt that I had Rajiv Gandhi's unqualified support and he understood that all the complaints were trumped up. It seems to me quite unbelievable that the same Rajiv who was so encouraging then could have told Gopi that he wanted to dismiss me from the IAS.

It was after this brief encounter with the prime minister in late 1988 that I went down to Pune to meet the newly appointed television correspondents who were going to start their training. Which is why when some of them expressed misgivings about not being allowed to report freely, I confidently told them, 'Don't worry. I'm there, and I'll make sure you do.'

I returned to Delhi and tied up the next part of their training, which was due to start after their three-month training as television people. This was an orientation with news agencies, including Reuters, PTI, AP, the London *Times* and other major papers. The *Times of India*, the *Hindustan Times* and the *Indian Express* were also happy to give the new correspondents such exposure as they needed. FES had pledged to send two English-speaking television journalists who would work with the new recruits for a whole month after their press orientation. The new news unit was, I thought, finally beginning to take shape.

And then, one Sunday afternoon in October 1988, I got a call at home from Gopi Arora. Gopi worked on Sundays; come to think of it I never have found out when he didn't work. He asked me to come and see him in his office. I asked if I could see him on Monday, as I had some guests over for lunch who had already arrived. No, he said, I was to see him immediately. I excused myself and went to Shastri Bhavan.

'Bhaskar,' Gopi said, 'I have some bad news. You have to handover as DG of Doordarshan.'

I looked at him blankly. It didn't register for a time. All I could think to say was, 'But today is Sunday.'

'All right, hand over on Monday.' Then he stopped and added, 'Bhaskar, I am really very sorry. I tried hard to stop it, but I'm afraid I couldn't.'

'Where are they sending me?'

'That's it, you see,' he said almost angrily. 'I told them, at least give him a good posting. He's more than deserved it. But they wouldn't listen to that either. They're sending you to the Department of Culture as additional secretary. There's not enough work for a secretary but they've created a post for you there.'

I got up, picked up the transfer order and left. There was really nothing to say.

'Oh, Bhaskar,' Gopi called after me, 'see Serla Grewal. She's very anxious to see you.'

I drove almost mechanically to her house, parked the car and went inside.

'You see, beta,' Serla Grewal told me anxiously, 'the PM is very keen to have a really good officer in culture. He feels it's being neglected badly, and he wants you to revive it.'

I heard her out. I suppose she meant well. Then I drove back home, and somehow got through the lunch, being genial to the guests, laughing at witticisms and all the rest. Finally, they left. I got into my car and drove aimlessly through the streets for hours. In the evening I went to Kaka Nagar, to Usha Rai's flat. She was my brother's sister-in-law, someone whom I had known since she was sixteen. She could make out something was wrong and asked me what had happened. Perhaps it was the way she asked, the concern in her face, or just the built-up tension of working in the exasperating but exciting medium of television, I don't know. But I suddenly found tears coursing down my face and I broke down completely.

Usha quietly rang my brother and within minutes he and my sister-in-law, Viji, arrived. Viji sat next to me and told me in a very matter-of-fact way that these things happened and I should not let a post matter so much. Nothing, she said, matters that much.

'But I worked hard, Viji,' I told her. 'I worked so very hard. Every day, every Sunday . . .'

'I know that,' she said calmly. 'But it still doesn't matter. Come on, just accept it and get on with the new job. *You* know you've done a good job. That's all that matters.'

The next day I went to the office and called all the officers in. I told them I had been transferred. There was complete silence. I asked Shiv

Sharma to take charge till a new DG was appointed—in all likelihood it would be Shiv himself. And I asked that the papers that one has to sign when leaving a post be brought so that I could get it over with. Then Shiv told me that he had, in fact, been told of my transfer by R.C. Sinha.

Sinha was a joint secretary in the ministry. An IAS officer from the Maharashtra cadre, he had made it his business to be as offensive and superior as he could. He would send me semi-official letters (this is government-speak for letters, plain and simple) that always began sniffily 'My dear Ghose', even though he knew I was senior to him and deserved to be addressed in a less condescending manner. I avoided him as much as I could. I would go straight to the secretary with whatever business I had at the ministry, and I once told him that if he had something to say he should address it to one of the deputy DGs, not me. I dealt, I told him loftily, only with the secretary and minister. Yes, it was arrogant of me, I know now. But in those days, heady with trying to bring about change in a network as gigantic as Doordarshan, which was the object of steadfast attention from the press, I tended to be reckless. Much of the distrust and coldness towards me that Panja developed was, I have no doubt, a result of the sly egging on that Sinha was very good at.

His great day had now come: he had the privilege of formally sending me my transfer orders. He not only sent them, but rung up Shiv Sharma and told him, 'See that he hands over charge today itself.' I was going to do that anyway, but when Shiv told me of Sinha's eagerness to ensure I depart that very day, I decided I wouldn't. I told Shiv to inform Sinha that I would not handover charge that day. This was childish perhaps, but someone who has just been asked to leave a post where he has tried his best to do a good job isn't always cool and rational. Shiv looked rather concerned but I made it very clear that I wasn't going to go till I had decided to go. What could they do, come and physically push me out?

The next day I left my office for the last time. The foyer was full of staff and officers, standing there silently. A few of the women were crying, but mostly everyone was silent. I got into the DG's car for the last time and drove out of the grounds of the new building, into which

I had moved with such enthusiasm only a few years before.

In the days that followed I often wondered what I had actually achieved and learnt in the years that I had been associated with Doordarshan. My achievements were, by any reckoning, modest. I had tried a number of things—the Doordarshan Society, reorganizing the news division, showing good films at special times, starting a number of current affairs programmes, live coverage of election results, telecasting the World Cup cricket matches—but they did not seem to add up to anything that I could point to and say, 'Look, *this* is what I have achieved.'

What had I, an IAS officer who had served mostly in the field as a district magistrate and a commissioner, brought to Doordarshan? I would venture to say that at least I hadn't made things worse. I had shown it was possible to argue with the ministry, even resist unfair or blatantly partisan orders; that it was possible to think of new ways of doing things even if it was something as trifling as a signature tune. I had, I think, succeeded in engaging people—advertising people, producers, media analysts, creative people—in the exciting discourse of television, laden as it was with tremendous potential. These achievements may not have amounted to much, but they did make for a change in attitude. And in this lay my personal satisfaction.

*

The general elections were held in 1989, about a year after I had been removed as DG, and the Congress lost. The new Janata Dal government was never a very stable one, with a variety of people in it who weren't really compatible. V.P. Singh became the new prime minister; he had come in on an anti-Congress wave, as the brave fighter for openness and truth who had resigned over the murky Bofors deal. Singh made P. Upendra from the Telugu Desam party Minister for Information and Broadcasting. Upendra made it clear that he wanted me back in his ministry, not because of any particular love he had for me, but because he thought he would be cocking a snook at the Congress by bringing me back. Fairly soon I was moved back to the Ministry of Information and Broadcasting as additional secretary, where Suresh Mathur was secretary.

After my removal as DG of Doordarshan the ministry had kept dithering about whom they wanted as my replacement. Finally, when poor Shiv Sharma went to court, the ministry went through the proper motions and appointed him DG on the advice of the UPSC. But when I was brought back he was still, technically, only holding charge of the post. Upendra directed that I oversee the functioning of Doordarshan and issue Doordarshan 'suitable directions'. This did not suit Shiv at all and he came to the ministry and protested to the secretary. I fancy these orders didn't suit Suresh either, but I made it clear to both that I had no intention of running Doordarshan from the ministry. There would be no 'directions' from me that were not proper government directives duly approved by the secretary and the minister. That quietened Shiv.

It was a bad time for the country; terrorism had ceased in Punjab but was growing at an alarming rate in Kashmir. Two Doordarshan Srinagar newsreaders had been killed, and soon after I joined the ministry the director of the station, Lassa Kaul, was killed. He had, for most of his working years, been an AIR man, and had only recently joined Doordarshan. A few weeks later there was a grenade attack on an AIR relay station on the outskirts of the city. The staff in both the Doordarshan and AIR stations were terrified and demoralized. In fact, for some time, news bulletins of Doordarshan Srinagar were actually prepared in, and telecast from, Delhi, and relayed from Srinagar, as if they were being broadcast from there. This was not a very clever way of showing that broadcasting was going to continue as if nothing had happened. Indeed, everyone in Srinagar who watched the bulletins knew that they came from Delhi, because the newsreaders were either from Delhi or Srinagar staff brought down to Delhi. But there was little else one could do. No one in Srinagar was prepared to present the news.

As if these events weren't gloomy enough, I discovered that the news division I had so carefully set up had been completely dismantled. The new correspondents had been sent to the news agencies and papers for their training, but no one really bothered to keep a watch on what they were doing. The final part of their training with the television journalists sent by FES collapsed: very few of the correspondents were sent for this part of the training, no arrangements were made for a place where they could be trained, no equipment was provided. One of the two trainers returned to Germany in disgust; the other persevered for a few weeks with the handful of utterly demoralized young correspondents sent to him, and then, when they stopped attending his sessions because they were assigned some work in the station, he too went home.

None of the cameras designed specifically for news coverage that I had ordered were made available to the news units; they were taken over by different station directors for routine use in the studios. All the Gypsies I had purchased for the news teams were given to the engineering wing or to the civil construction wing of AIR. The correspondents themselves were posted to different stations and most of them were given little or no work. One or two got some inconsequential, light stories to do, that was all. The news editor in Bombay, obviously a very foolish woman, complained that neither of the two correspondents sent there—one a Tamilian and the other a Hindi-speaking young woman from Rajasthan—knew Marathi. Their repeated pleas that they were meant for the *central news unit in Delhi* and therefore had to report in English and Hindi, that they were not expected to report for the local news bulletins, did not appear to penetrate her very thick skull. She sent them off to do stories of little consequence, most of which she didn't even bother to see, let alone send on to Delhi.

Not that the Delhi news unit was complaining. They, too, were totally indifferent to what these correspondents were doing, or not doing. And I soon found out why: in my enthusiasm to set up the news division I had overlooked the officers of the IIS who had been manning the news division and were still doing so. They saw the induction of the new correspondents as an end to their stay in the news division, and they were right. Had I stayed on as DG, had the correspondents finished their training and joined, I would have sent back the IIS officers for posting elsewhere. They were not a bad lot (some were very good, in fact), but they were essentially government officers, whereas I wanted a completely fresh set of people who would bring with them a new work culture. My mistake was to have been so uncompromising about this.

I should have kept on some of the better IIS officers and integrated them with the others. But I had not, and that was what destroyed my plan. No sooner had I left Doordarshan than the IIS lobby, headed by the principal information officer, I. Ramamohan Rao, moved in and persuaded the minister and secretary that the scheme was terribly flawed. Aided enthusiastically by the redoubtable R.C. Sinha, they wrote off the new scheme. This resulted in the new correspondents being used merely as extra hands to write up news reports and perform sundry inconsequential tasks.

I felt angry and bitter; I could hardly keep it in check. But there was nothing I could do about it. Suresh Mathur had made it clear, in his seemingly hearty, pleasant way, that his decision about the news unit was final. Most files relating to Doordarshan were sent to him by Sinha directly. The ministry had once again taken to running Doordarshan from Shastri Bhavan, and there was little that Shiv Sharma could do about it. He had to follow the orders given to him, and these were many, some on the most trivial matters. Sinha also told Suresh plainly that he would not take orders from me. According to him, apparently, he was on the verge of being promoted to the rank of additional secretary. As it happened, he never was, and had to go back to his state cadre unpromoted.

This was one of the most unpleasant periods in my relations with Doordarshan. There was the barely concealed defiance from Sinha; Shiv and all the others who had been colleagues were embarrassed at my being there because they knew Suresh was watching what I did very carefully and who kept in touch with me. Perhaps, who knows, Shiv was apprehensive that I would try to get back as DG, something I wouldn't have done had I been paid twice my salary—the thought was positively repellent. For me it was over and done with, but maybe Shiv and the others didn't realize that, which was a great pity, because I sensed not just a wariness but a positive coldness from those who had earlier been supportive. I often heard of meetings concerning changes in programming, or about policies regarding different aspects of the network, being held in the secretary's room, but I was rarely invited to attend. What came my way were routine files about minor promotions or pension cases, and routine reports to be sent to the finance ministry or somewhere else. To think Upendra had wanted me to 'take charge' of Doordarshan! I did not tell the minister anything about the real state of affairs. It seemed petty, just the sort of bureaucratic gripe that politicians delight in hearing about. But it was clear that while the minister had wanted me back, for whatever reason, none of the officers in the ministry, or indeed even in Doordarshan, did.

I survived being sidelined for two months and then, out of the blue, I was called by Upendra and told that George Fernandes, then railway minister, had been put in charge of a special cell to look after Kashmir matters, and that he wanted me to head it. He asked me if I really wanted to go; after all, I had much more experience with Doordarshan. Did I want to go! The speed with which I gathered my papers, such as they were, and left Shastri Bhavan for the unfamiliar environs of Rail Bhavan would have won Superman's admiration. This rapid exit ended my mercifully brief, miserable stint in the Ministry of Information and Broadcasting and an uncomfortable two months of involvement with Doordarshan, which I had nearly forgotten till I had to write about it here.

9

Remote Control: Secretary, I & B

I joined the tiny Kashmir Affairs Cell as its administrative head, working directly under George Fernandes, who had been given additional charge as Minister for Kashmir Affairs, along with his main charge as railway minister, by V.P. Singh. After an exciting, tension-ridden few months, George Fernandes discovered that V.P. Singh was neither going to help rein in the governor, Jagmohan, who had an agenda quite different from Fernandes's, nor was he going to sort out the differences that inevitably cropped up between him and the then home minister, Mufti Mohammed Sayeed. Typical of the man, he resigned his Kashmir affairs charge promptly. This meant that all those serving under him had to be posted elsewhere. I waited till all the officers and the staff had been given berths, and was wondering if I should go on leave till I was given a post, when the Cabinet secretary, Vinod Pande, called me up and told me I had been promoted as secretary, but there was only one post available, namely, secretary of culture. Would I take it, he asked. I had earlier been additional secretary there and had become quite fond of the ministry. I agreed to take it. I went on to spend a very rewarding and absorbing three years there, learning many things about which I had no knowledge at all. They were perhaps the most enriching years in my career as a civil servant. Then, quite suddenly, things took a dramatic turn and my idyll came to an end.

On 6 December 1992 the Babri Masjid was destroyed, an act which horrified many of us, more so because during the entire day it took to bring down the building, a virtual running commentary on the events was given to the then prime minister, P.V. Narasimha Rao, who had a force of some 40,000 paramilitary men on hand, but chose to do nothing. Only after the building had been razed to the ground did he have the BJP-led government dismissed and President's Rule imposed in Uttar Pradesh. Late that night I received a call from the Cabinet secretary who asked me to take over as I & B secretary the very next morning. Ashok Chandra, who until then had been the secretary, was being sent that night as one of the advisers to the governor of Uttar Pradesh.

I was a little surprised, mostly because the minister for information and broadcasting was none other than Ajit Panja, reinstated by Narasimha Rao. That morning, I thought it only proper to inform the minister, so I rang up his residence and asked for an appointment. The man who answered the phone said the minister was busy.

'Well, I'll wait till he can see me,' I said.

'He is not here,' the man replied coldly. 'He has gone to meet the prime minister.'

I immediately knew why—he had heard of the midnight appointment. Sure enough, when I went to my own office in the Department of Culture, the Cabinet secretary rang up and asked if I had joined as I & B secretary. I said I hadn't, because I hadn't received any formal orders to do so.

'There's some little hitch,' he told me. 'Just wait for a while.'

I went about my work and didn't try to get in touch with Panja's office again. That afternoon Vinod Pande asked to see me.

'What's Ajit Panja got against you?' he asked when I went into his room.

'Well, it's a long story,' I replied and proceeded to tell him about what had happened in 1988.

He smiled. 'So that's it,' he said. 'He saw the prime minister this morning and was ranting and raving about never having you as secretary. He said you were a BJP man.'

I was astonished. 'He accused me of being a CPI agent the last time.'

'Well,' said Vinod, grinning, 'you've obviously changed sides. But anyway, the net result of his shouting and protesting is that the prime minister has decided to send someone else as secretary, Mahesh Prasad.'

'Just as well,' I told him as I left. 'I wasn't looking forward to working with Panja at all.'

I thought that was the end of the matter, but I was wrong.

A few months later, early in 1993, Panja was moved out and replaced by K.P. Singh Deo. Shortly thereafter the new minister spoke to me. He told me he was very anxious that I should become the secretary of his ministry and that he had spoken to the prime minister about it. The then secretary was Raj Bhargava and the minister made no bones about being keen to see him go. Bhargava was due to retire in September.

'But I can't wait till then,' Singh Deo said. 'You must join as Officer on Special Duty (OSD) for a few months and then take over from him. You can understudy him for that period.'

I didn't like the idea, but agreed, only because of one reason: I liked K.P. Singh Deo. Several years earlier, when I had been joint secretary in the Ministry of Defence, he had been brought in first as deputy minister and then as minister of state under the defence minister, R. Venkataraman. Right from the start he had been a model of politeness and warmth. I remembered that whenever I had gone to his room, he had stood up, much to my embarrassment. Ministers never stood up when even the seniormost officers walked into their room, leave alone a joint secretary. He explained why he did it.

'It's not for you, Mr Ghose,' he said. 'It's for the post. If I don't give the post the respect it deserves, the rank-conscious defence services never will.'

This was not all. If I did take a matter to him that was complicated or needed intervention at a higher level, his first reaction was, 'Let me see how I can help.'

He was kind, courteous and friendly, never displaying any displeasure or anger. He was hospitable as well. Once, after a meeting held in Bhubaneswar about the acquisition of some land for a military installation, he invited us—the army officers and me—to his palace in Dhenkanal for dinner. Had the princely states and titles not been abolished by Indira Gandhi, he would have been maharaja of Dhenkanal. When we got there, he and his mother personally served us an excellent meal in a large, ornate dining room, which had obviously seen better days. Neither ate with us; it was a custom in his family to eat only after serving the guests. Small wonder that all of us were full of admiration for this gentle, unassuming, graciously hospitable minister.

When I was divisional commissioner of north Bengal, he had come to Darjeeling for a meeting of the governing council of the Himalayan Mountaineering Institute. I had made his visit a major event for the town. Apart from other functions, I organized a dinner in his honour and called all the leading personalities, including the district officers and superintendents of police in my division, because I wanted them to meet a minister who, to me, had broken the mould, was not like any other minister—he was an honourable, kind and supportive person, who never stood on ceremony of any kind.

So when he asked me to join the I & B ministry as OSD to succeed the outgoing secretary I agreed only because of my admiration and liking for him. Ordinarily I would not have done so; why would I need to understudy a secretary whose work I knew fairly well from earlier years? I was warned though by a number of colleagues to be careful. Singh Deo had changed, they told me; he had become a very difficult man to work with. I dismissed all this as bureaucratic gossip. I had worked with him, and I knew the sort of man he was.

However, this time round, things were indeed very different. Shiv Sharma had retired; the additional secretary in the ministry—they never abolished the post Upendra had created for me, but then, very few posts at a senior level ever are—had just been given charge of Doordarshan as well. He was Ratikant Basu, a very dynamic, intelligent IAS officer from the Gujarat cadre. R.C. Sinha had gone, and the new joint secretary (broadcasting) was Navin Chawla, once a very powerful secretary to the Lieutenant Governor of Delhi during the Emergency because of his close friendship with Sanjay Gandhi. The secretary, Raj Bhargava, was a rather embittered man who felt he had not been treated well and who resented having me come in as OSD, but could do nothing to stop it.

'I suppose you'd better start seeing all the files,' he told me caustically. 'After all, you'll be handling them very soon in any case.'

A confused, rather comic set of events had led to his growing distance from the minister. In 1993 private television networks had only recently arrived in India. Their satellites sent down programmes beamed up from foreign countries (Hong Kong, Singapore, and for a while Russia). Their advent had brought officials in the ministry and in Doordarshan close to a collective nervous breakdown. The initial reaction was: 'Private television networks? What private networks? We are not aware of any such thing.' While this was said loftily in public, in the security of their rooms they were running scared. Then, when the Star TV network began to make waves with its channels Star Plus and Prime Sports, and providing BBC, MTV and, a year later, Zee TV, panic set in and there was a frantic attempt to get transponders to carry five new channels (corresponding to the five Star channels) which would air programmes made by Indian companies. These they hoped would lure viewers away from these foreign networks. With the help of the Department of Space they managed to get the transponders. But the content?

Raj Bhargava had worked out what seemed like a novel idea: the ministry would auction airtime on the five new channels. The eagerness to get a slice of this airtime was so great that private entrepreneurs camped for nights on end in front of the ministry's office to be the first to put in their bid. There was dreadful confusion over whether the new channels would be assigned on a first-come first-served basis, or to the highest bidder, or by some other process. The result was a number of court cases, and all action to get these channels leased or auctioned was stayed. But the transponders had been hired; something had to be done. The ministry turned to Doordarshan and directed it to start five new channels at once.

Doordarshan officials, headed by a man called Krishnan (a deputy DG who had been officiating as DG), couldn't do much. After all, how does one produce programmes for *five* different channels overnight? So the poor people in Doordarshan did the only thing they could—they started showing old programmes over and over again. Nobody watched them and the channels began to be called, derisively, the 'invisible' channels. The minister, furious at the mess into which he had been dragged, moved Krishnan out at once and brought in Ratikant Basu.

All this had not endeared Raj Bhargava to the minister either, particularly when the prime minister himself complained that he had seen one particular old film three times on what was called the sports channel, and could they please show something else. This is why the minister was so anxious that I join. He expected me to become the de facto secretary, wave a magic wand and set everything right. But I knew that strange administrative arrangements never work. I sensed how resentful Raj Bhargava was and I was determined not to add to this. I made it clear that I would see whatever files I was sent, but just see them was all that I would do, nothing other than that. Even then there were a few occasions when Raj Bhargava ticked off some officer for taking 'instructions' from me without informing him. 'I am still the secretary,' he is said to have shouted, 'and will be till I retire.'

This was just a minor aspect of my few months as OSD. The real eye-opener was K.P. Singh Deo. He was very friendly with me, repeatedly telling me and whoever else happened to be in the room how good it was that I was there, how he and I had worked so well together in the Ministry of Defence, and so on. But in meetings with officers from AIR and Doordarshan he became a totally different person. It didn't take me long to realize that all the warnings I had been given before I joined were true and that I should have taken them seriously.

Singh Deo had indeed changed. Physically, he had put on weight, and his eyes looked inflamed. But the major change was in his personality. Dr Jekyll had gone, to be replaced by Mr Hyde—a short-tempered, arrogant man with a sharp tongue. His meetings would, for one thing, go on for hours, often from about 10 a.m. to 2 p.m., sometimes longer. *All* the senior officers from both the programme and the engineering wings of both media units, AIR and Doordarshan, had to be there. There was never a fixed agenda; the minister asked random questions, wanting to know what was going on, e.g., how many transmitters had been put up, and if an answer was not to his liking, he would spend a good fifteen minutes berating the hapless officer in charge, threatening him, shouting at him, warning him that he would be transferred to some remote region for being grossly negligent.

I was shocked by this change. Gone was the polite, helpful minister I had known; in his place was a person of uncertain temperament, who could be very jovial and friendly on one occasion, and viciously nasty at another. I was told of an incident that had occurred before I joined the ministry and which I had no reason to disbelieve, given what I was seeing of Singh Deo's personality now.

During one of those interminable meetings where different officers were administered tongue-lashings, in between anecdotes he would frequently relate by way of humorous interludes, Navin Chawla asked for permission to leave the room for a few minutes.

'And why do you wish to leave the meeting, Mr Chawla?' Singh Deo asked him in an excessively polite manner.

'The secretary's called me, sir,' Navin explained nervously. 'To discuss a file I had sent him. He asked me to be in his room at 11.30 a.m.'

'Oh, I see,' Singh Deo said in the same polite way. 'So you think it's more important to attend a meeting called by the secretary than to attend a meeting being taken by the minister.'

'No sir,' Navin said, becoming more nervous. 'It's just that the matter was urgent and . . .'

He stopped, because the door opened and Raj Bhargava came into the room.

'Go on, Mr Chawla,' Singh Deo said. 'You were saying you wanted to go to the secretary's room.'

'Yes, but . . . now he's here, sir,' poor Navin stammered. 'So I could perhaps—'

'Oh no, Mr Chawla,' Singh Deo said. 'You wanted to go to the secretary's room and so you shall.'

'But he's here, sir,' Navin countered.

'I know he's here,' Singh Deo said, suddenly changing his tone. 'I sent for him. But *you* wanted to go to his room. So you will go.'

In the presence of a roomful of officers from Doordarshan and AIR, Navin was made to go up to the secretary's room, *touch the door,* and return to the minister's room. I gather a chaprasi was sent with him to make sure he did just that. This, from a minister, I told myself when I heard this squalid story, who, some years earlier, would stand up whenever a joint secretary entered his room.

I had, however, burned my boats and was now in the Ministry of Information and Broadcasting. I had to accept the situation as best I could. And I will say this of Singh Deo: he never blocked or stopped any of the projects that I, or for that matter the DGs of AIR and Doordarshan, took up. His obsession was with transmitters—he wanted more and more put up, not so much to ensure access to television to remote areas as for political compulsions. This, and his never-ending passion for commissioning programmes on various regiments of the army.

Now, there is no question that the role played by the army in securing the borders of the country and in times of natural calamities deserves the highest praise and needs to be brought to public attention through, among other things, television programmes. But a series on *all* the regiments, one by one, seemed a bit much. Nonetheless, he gave summary orders that they should be produced, and even indicated the order in which these programmes should be taken up. Money was not an issue. If the funds allocated for commissioned programmes were all used up, he simply ordered that more be appropriated from other heads, a task that gave the financial adviser nightmares.

Apart from these army programmes, he left me on the whole to myself. Now and then he would call me in to those never-ending meetings he had about transmitters and related matters, but he never objected if I excused myself from them after a while. Nor did he give me instructions I could not follow because they were improper, except for two bizarre incidents that I shall relate presently.

Ratikant Basu was one of the first persons I met after I came to the ministry. He had introduced himself soon after I had joined. A very intelligent and shrewd officer, he was quick to see the essential nature of a problem and to work out a solution. He was also cheerful and regaled me with stories of the minister's eccentricities, which, as he said, one needed to be amused by, or otherwise one would become a nervous wreck. One thing we immediately agreed to do was close down the 'invisible' channels; the transponders were put to other uses by the engineers.

He filled me in on the state of affairs in Doordarshan. It was pitiable. Revenues were dropping and very few producers wanted to bring their serials to Doordarshan, even though Basu offered them attractively low rates. The craze at that time was to get your programme aired on the private channels. Something had to be done to turn things around. I explained that I would not interfere in any way in the running of the network, and I would ensure that no one in the ministry would, either.

I told him, however, that if he ever wanted any advice or support he was welcome to come over. I thought this laying down of the basic rules of engagement, as it were, was necessary. He knew I had been DG of Doordarshan, and I sensed that he was apprehensive that I would try to run it again from my office. I wanted him to know from the outset that that would never happen. Precisely because I had been DG, I was never going to interfere in his work.

I think this reassured him. Soon he began to come over fairly frequently to discuss various problems that he was facing, and new things he wanted to do. I noticed that he was not really interested in reviving my scheme to set up the news service division; he had Bimla Bhalla, a senior IIS officer, as additional DG (news) and he clearly wanted things to stay the way they were. It saddened me, but I was determined not to make him do what he did not want to; perhaps he didn't want to revive it because it had been my idea, I don't know. Whatever it was, he kept the news division just the way it had always been—dependent on the news fed from the general newsroom of AIR and from PTI and UNI, supplemented with some visuals from different sources. I knew that Bimla Bhalla, who was a good officer, had little experience of news work. She had been head of the Directorate of Advertising and Visual Publicity (DAVP) for years. Harish Awasthi, the officer who did know something about the news (he was one of the first to have been sent to the BBC and to the Thomson Foundation in the UK for training in television journalism), had fallen foul of K.P. Singh Deo, who had had him summarily moved out of the newsroom and posted as head of the research and reference division, an obscure office under the ministry. Given this, and Basu's good equation with Bimla Bhalla, I let things be.

So my dream of a professional news service, manned by trained television journalists who did their own news-gathering and then wrote and presented the news, finally died. One by one, the young men and women we had recruited and arranged to train began to leave. Many of them came to see me before leaving; I could see the disappointment in their eyes, and sense that I had in some way let them down and muddied the waters as far as their careers were concerned. It was true, and as they left I always felt a lump in my throat. Something I had built and nurtured was slowly dying; and yet, I told myself, at least they had had some training as television journalists, however flawed it may have been. That, I hoped, would stand them in good stead. Indeed, a number of them joined NDTV, the television company started by Prannoy Roy, rated as one of the finest new television companies.

Soon after I took over as secretary, the first of the two incidents involving the minister occurred. To be fair to him, his involvement was indirect, but definitely there. He sent for me one day and said, quite frankly, that he had received a great deal of help from a certain deputy general manager of South Eastern Railways during his campaign and now the officer had requested him to arrange to air a dance recital by his daughters' on the National Programme of Dance. He could have told the DG to do it, but Basu happened to be away on tour, hence the summons to me. I told him that only performances carefully selected by a committee of experts were shown on the National Programme of Dance; we simply couldn't put in two teenagers in such a programme. It had already been tampered with enough in years past, and I pleaded that in his time he should help build it up as the finest dance programme on the network, not compromise its quality. His face hardened; he had given his word to the officer and the two girls' programme simply had to be shown, he reiterated. I tried a compromise: I would ask Doordarshan to show it, but not on the National Programme of Dance; it would be shown at the same time as that programme, but on another day.

'No, Mr Ghose,' he said coldly. 'I have told him it will be on the National Programme of Dance and it has to be on that.'

I then explained what an uproar there would be; it could reach Parliament, the papers would pick it up, and it would do him no good. Finally he agreed, with very bad grace, that I could show it at an appropriate time, but it had to be shown that week. I spoke to the director of the Delhi station, who said he would have it telecast two days later at 10.30 p.m.; the National Programme of Dance was due to be telecast on the previous day. I told him to go ahead.

On the day the National Programme of Dance was to be telecast, I got a call at around 10.15 p.m from the duty officer at the Delhi Kendra and he sounded hysterical. He was ringing me because Basu was still on tour and I was his former boss. The reason for his near hysteria was that while trying out the tape for the National Programme on a video recorder, it had got jammed, and it could not be taken out without dismantling the recorder. No engineering staff was available to do so at that time of night. Besides, he said, there were just ten minutes left for the National Programme to start and taking out the tape would take at least half an hour.

'Use the standby,' I told him. I knew there was always a standby programme with the duty officer.

'That's the problem, sir,' he replied. 'The officer on duty in the previous shift has taken the key to the almirah where standby tapes are kept, by mistake. I have telephoned him. He is sending it back. But he lives in Pitampura.'

'Well, break the damn thing open,' I snapped. Time was running out.

There was silence. 'I cannot do that, sir,' the man said weakly. 'You see, it is a steel almirah. Breaking it will take a lot of time.'

At that moment I really was at my wits' end. I was thinking of asking him to replay the previous programme—the tape would still be in the control room—when an odious voice on the phone interrupted my thoughts.

'Good evening, sir,' the voice said. 'This is Rajesh. Rajesh Tiwari.'

Rajesh, who used to be a rather boyish, ingenuous young fellow when I first met him, was now an assistant private secretary to K.P. Singh Deo and the boyish eagerness had been replaced with a rather oily cunning. His presence in the ministry had disconcerted me at first but I learnt to keep my distance and be careful about what I said to him, because I knew that every word would be relayed to the minister.

'Yes Rajesh?' I said.

'Sir, I had come here to deliver the tape of the two girls' dance programme,' he said smoothly, 'and I heard of the crisis. Sir, the only alternative is to show this programme. Isn't it, sir?'

Damn and blast. I was trapped. I knew it. Rajesh Tiwari knew it. I knew that he knew. He knew that I knew that he knew.

'Give the phone to the duty officer,' I told him as curtly as I could. When the duty officer came back on the line, I told him to broadcast the tape Rajesh Tiwari had brought. 'But,' I told him softly, 'tell the presenter to apologize for not being able to show the National Programme of Dance. Tell her to say that another dance programme recorded earlier is being shown instead. And don't tell Rajesh Tiwari what I've told you.'

'All right, sir,' the man said, sounding very relieved.

Ten minutes later I got a call from Basu. He sounded excited.

'Have you seen the rubbish being shown on the National Programme of Dance?' he asked me.

'No,' I said, and then narrated all that had happened.

'Sir,' he said in an astonished voice, 'just turn on the television set and look at what's being shown. Two chubby little girls capering about! I feel like smashing the TV set!'

'But didn't the announcer say that—'

'Yes, yes,' Basu said. 'But who listens to that carefully? This is the slot for the National Programme of Dance. Everyone thinks it's the National Programme. I've been getting angry calls ever since it started.'

There was nothing that could be done. 'Just turn off the television set and take your phone off the hook,' I told him and hung up.

The next morning, a smiling Rajesh Tiwari met me outside the minister's room. 'Good morning, sir,' he said. 'And how did you like the National Programme of Dance last night?'

It suddenly dawned on me that all of it had been a charade: the jamming of the tape, the apparent taking away of the key to the almirah, everything, just to get this programme on. I looked at Rajesh Tiwari speculatively and promised myself that one day, in some form or the other, I would get even with him. Meanwhile, I had to dissemble a cheerfulness I wasn't feeling at all. The minister was undoubtedly highly satisfied, but I had the mortification of reading some of the most acid comments I have ever read about this programme in the regular reviews of Doordarshan that used to appear in the newspapers. I need hardly mention that the most virulent and forthright of all of them were those made by Amita Malik, the doyenne of all critics.

*

Even though I tried, I couldn't keep myself away entirely from

Doordarshan. I didn't interfere with any of its work, true, but I did get involved in trying out new things, such as setting up a new channel. I had always felt there was a category of people whom no channel was really addressing—the more discerning viewers, the opinion makers and leaders, the captains of industry, the decision makers, people who wanted more than dumbed-down serials and talk shows, however glitzy they may be. They may not have been very many such people on the ground, but these were people who would look for the very best on television, whether it was a film, a discussion or a documentary feature. The idea was to create a channel that would not necessarily make money but one that would stimulate and provoke new trends of thought and perhaps new ways of looking at issues and even at the creative arts. It would carry news and debates, and also news about market trends and the very latest business information from around the world.

It was a daunting charter but I felt we had to try and put such a channel together. I called in Ratikant and bounced the idea off him. I made it absolutely clear that I was merely making a suggestion; if he didn't like the idea, it would be scrapped. His was the final word as DG. Fortunately, he liked the idea and was just as enthusiastic about it as I was. He gave Jai Chandiram the task of putting the channel together and I have to confess I prompted him a little in this. Jai was the only Doordarshan officer who had been with television right from the start; she had not spent a day handling radio. Trained in the US, she happened to be one of the most intelligent and discerning persons in Doordarshan, even though she could be abrasive and had a quick temper. But I knew she would never accept anything she thought was second rate. I had known her for a very long time; in fact, we had acted together in *The Seagull* in 1965, when I was secretary to the Lieutenant Governor of Delhi and she was a young officer with the experimental television wing of AIR.

Jai got down to work with an organized dedication that was admirable. We put together a small committee of people whom we considered perceptive, intelligent, discriminating and uncompromising on quality. They were to select programmes that would fit in with the style and identity we wanted the new channel to have. We called the new channel Doordarshan III, or DD III, as it came to be known.

The committee set about its work with great enthusiasm. They were not just uncompromising as far as quality was concerned—they were very severely uncompromising. Producers with programmes that were not considered good enough were told so in very explicit terms. It did not make for good relations all round, but it did mean that what passed through this inquisitorial process was truly of high quality in terms of content and production values.

While the committee was going about its work, a visit from an old friend, Zafar Hai, resulted in a most interesting and rewarding idea. Zafar was a film-maker; he had made one feature film, *The Perfect Murder*, which though very professionally made had done poorly at the box office. He had also made some excellent documentary films. What was more, Zafar had close connections with C & A, a formidable Hollywood agency that looked after the interests of stars like Julia Roberts, Kevin Costner and Tom Cruise, among others. C & A was headed then by one of the most influential men in the film world, Michael Ovitz. Zafar suggested I talk to them about sourcing some good international programmes.

I took his advice and called them. Initially they were not only cautious but almost reluctant. They really weren't in the business of sourcing programmes for television networks, but acted as agents for film stars, they said. However, since it was Zafar Hai who had made the initial request—they obviously thought highly of him—they would look around and come back with some possibilities. And they did: they sent me a list of BBC programmes, a few Canadian programmes and a number of US programmes like *Twin Peaks*. I was delighted with this and sent the list on to the committee, who chose some of them for the new channel.

Ratikant and I worked on the hardware as well. I was determined that the new channel had to be as clear and sharp as the best satellite channels and ordered four NEC high-power transmitters from Japan for the four metros. I had a rather low opinion of the high-power transmitters made by BEL and GCEL here in India—their pictures were grainy and fuzzy and I was told this was the best we could expect 'given the price and the quality'. It was the last thing I wanted for DD III. Along with the Japanese transmitters, we got AVID computer facilities to link the programmes together seamlessly, with announcements, promos and ads leading into the programme without a hitch. These and a host of other new equipment came in while we were preparing for the launch of the new channel.

DD III was to have live current affairs programmes instead of the insipid sanitized kind that Doordarshan usually carried. There were to be debates on issues where participants would be free to say what they liked, subject, of course, to what the moderator felt was necessary or appropriate. These programmes were to be the high point in the content of DD III. It was a mistake, and, had I given it a little more thought, I would have realized it. I had assumed, naively, that these programmes wouldn't be questioned, just as the programmes which I had done when I was DG had not been. I had forgotten that Rajiv Gandhi was no longer prime minister. The calculating, coldly political P.V. Narasimha Rao, whom I didn't know at all, was in charge. He had yapping around him a creature called P.V.R.K. Prasad (an IAS man, I am ashamed to say) as his information adviser. Prasad had been the returning officer of the constituency from which Narasimha Rao had been elected to the Andhra Pradesh legislature years earlier, and had become one of Rao's favourites ever since. He was one of those officers who didn't just carry out orders—he was servile, and did whatever was asked of him. He was rewarded by being made information adviser when Rao became prime minister. (The gentle, dignified and scholarly H.Y. Sharada Prasad had occupied this post in Rajiv Gandhi's time.) It was rumoured that P.V.R.K. Prasad was one of the very few who could walk right into Rao's bedroom to get him to look at papers or brief him on something. Prasad was obviously deeply suspicious of what I was putting into DD III, and my unwarranted assumption that I could go ahead with such programmes because there was some kind of support from on high was to be my undoing.

Meanwhile, the second and much more unpleasant incident involving K.P. Singh Deo occurred. I relate it here only because it brought a degree of coldness into the relationship I had with the minister. Narasimha Rao was due to go abroad and a few days before he did, the minister sent for me and told me in hushed tones that a 'conspiracy' was afoot. He had it on good authority that Bimla Bhalla was sending one of her trusted officers to cover the trip, and the real reason this person was being sent was to assist Bimla's husband, who had a leather export business, in selling his wares. I was astonished, to put it mildly, and pointed out to the minister that a news correspondent covering the prime minister's visit hardly has a minute to herself during the day, rushing from venue to venue with the cameraman and then working late into the night to prepare the feed for the newsroom.

Singh Deo brushed my observation aside impatiently and said that he knew there was a conspiracy. Bimla Bhalla had been spotted walking in Lodhi Gardens the night before with the principal information officer, S. Narendra, who was also apparently part of the plan. Something, the minister said darkly, was up. I managed to keep a serious face; when I came out of his room I told Basu all this. He was highly amused. But then we soon realized the minister was in deadly earnest; he did think something nefarious was going on and that something had to be done to stop it. That something he had in mind was the summary removal of Bimla Bhalla from the Doordarshan news division.

I knew that behind the minister's suspicions was his erratic private secretary, Abhijit Bhattacharya, a wispy young man who, for reasons best known to him, kept a long flowing beard. Among his other attributes, Abhijit had a very pronounced obsession with the dramatic, the sinister and all things related to undercover activity. I think he may have had a stint in RAW, but I'm not sure. Abhijit's passion for the world of undercover activities had made him put a few unrelated incidents together which he had then related to his boss in the manner in which he always spoke—short, staccato half-sentences. He would on occasion tell me things like 'Sir! File passed on to private producer! Deal being done in DD! CBI!' Oddly enough—or perhaps not so oddly, given the fact that both were eccentric in their own ways—Singh Deo believed Abhijit implicitly. He was convinced, therefore, that this particular conspiracy theory was true.

We thought the best course would be to put all this down on paper, point out that Bimla was doing a good job as head of news in Doordarshan, and that it was highly unlikely that she was part of any conspiracy to further the leather sales of her husband's firm by suborning a news service correspondent to do some selling while also covering the prime minister's busy schedule. Basu wrote a reasoned note to this effect and I endorsed it and sent it to the minister. The reaction was even more startling than the conspiracy theory.

The minister sent the file back with a long note saying that since both the DG and I were so impressed by Bimla Bhalla's work he had, naturally, to accept our assessment, and consequently he ordered that she should be immediately appointed DG of Doordarshan. Basu was to function as additional secretary in the ministry, the post he had been appointed to originally. To this the minister added another rather spiteful order concerning me. When I had joined the ministry as OSD he had passed orders that I should be chairman of the National Film Development Corporation (NFDC). Technically, a secretary to the government ought not to head a public sector undertaking, though many were doing so with no questions asked. When I took over as secretary, this particular prohibition slipped my mind as other things took up all my attention. In any case, the NFDC was being looked after by the managing director, Ravi Gupta, and I had, literally, nothing to do with it. But the minister pointedly drew my attention to my continuance as chairman, and said that I should immediately resign as chairman of NFDC. I lost no time in doing so and sent my resignation letter to him at once, with copies to the NFDC office in Bombay.

This, however, was just a rap on the knuckles for me. The main directive he gave was to post Bimla Bhalla as DG of Doordarshan. I explained to him that this was not possible; for her to hold charge of the post we needed the approval of the Appointments Committee of the Cabinet (ACC), which is headed by the prime minister himself. In fact, I pointed out, Ratikant Basu had been appointed to officiate as DG of Doordarshan by the ACC. I sent him the note from the ACC to this effect. Back came the file saying the proposal sent to the ACC for Basu's concurrent appointment to the post of DG had not been sent with his approval, and since proposals to the ACC had to have the minister's approval, *the ACC appointment was, ab initio, void!* I once again pointed out that the ACC's approval could not be set aside except by the ACC itself, and added that I had consulted Zafar Saifullah, the Cabinet secretary, who had confirmed this.

The minister was undeterred. He sent back the file saying that regardless of what the Cabinet secretary may have said, his orders had to be implemented instantly. I then went to Zafar and told him of the antics of the minister and that it had now got to a stage where I could do nothing more. Saifullah advised me not to pay any attention to these insane orders and carry on as before. I gather he then went and talked to the prime minister and later rang up the minister and gave him to understand explicitly that Rao did not approve of his actions and that he was to follow the orders already passed by the ACC. That, thankfully, ended the farce, but it resulted in my having to pay a price. I sensed that I had not only lost the minister's warmth and trust, but that it had been replaced with a simmering resentment. I had made an enemy, one who still smiled and was pleasant when we met, but beneath that veneer of friendliness was waiting for an opportunity to get his own back.

He got that opportunity soon enough. Work on DD III had gone on smoothly and the channel was formally inaugurated in October 1994. Soon after, I received an urgent summons to 7 Race Course Road, the prime minister's office. I arrived to find Singh Deo already there, and P.V.R.K. Prasad darting between the room where we were and another room in the house where Rao was. He had a triumphant grin on his face, and I soon realized why. After a while, Narasimha Rao came in and asked if it was true that DD III was showing live current affairs programmes. Since the minister said nothing, I answered, yes, there were live current affairs programmes, but care had been taken that they would always present a balanced picture.

Prasad excitedly told Rao that the programmes were being aired live; what if someone said something anti-Congress? The prime minister then turned to me and said that the channel should be taken off the air. I was aghast. I began telling him that we had entered into contractual obligations, that we had spent almost Rs 20 crore on the channel.

The PM waved all these objections aside. 'Twenty crores,' he said dismissively. 'We cannot have live broadcasts. It is too dangerous.'

He got up, indicating that the meeting was over, and left the room. I was numb with disbelief, but did notice a rather satisfied smile on K.P. Singh Deo's face. Through all this he had not said a word, even though I had scrupulously kept him informed of all that we were doing, and had obtained his approval on the expenditure.

I informed all those who had laboured to make the channel something unique of the decision, and told Basu to allocate the money kept for DD III elsewhere. I later learnt from people in the media that the initial damage had been done, perhaps unwittingly, by a journalist, Kalyani Shankar, who was known to be close to Narasimha Rao. She was among those invited to a preview of the channel's programmes and apparently she had subsequently asked Rao if he knew that live discussions were being telecast on DD III. Then Prasad had gotten into the act and convinced the prime minister that the channel would subvert the nation, or at least his government.

Prasad had obviously not prepared Narasimha Rao for the sharply hostile reaction of the press to this decision. It was condemned as yet another example of the way the government would never allow any autonomy to Doordarshan, as a stifling of the freedom of expression, and everyone put the blame squarely on him. Rao was depicted as intolerant of dissent, not bothered about quality television, interested in nothing but his immediate political gains.

Two months passed. The banning of DD III became something of a *cause celebre* in the media. In January 1995 I got a terse note from the redoubtable Prasad saying that 'the PM desired' DD III be restarted immediately, without, of course, the live discussions. This ought to have pleased me but it actually put me in a quandary. The financial year ends in March, and for that current financial year money that had been earmarked for DD III had been reallocated to other activities after the channel had been stopped by the prime minister himself. How, I wondered, was I going to find any money to restart a channel that had been talked about so much? Getting through the few months of that financial year was bad enough; what was truly worrying was that we had made no provision for DD III in the budget for the following financial year (1995–96). In other words, we would have to start the channel with the little bits one could take out from other committed activities. It was clearly not going to be the channel I had envisioned it to be, where quality would be the only criterion and funds never a problem.

Nonetheless, Jai and her team began putting together what they could and, as unobtrusively as possible, the channel went on air. It never attracted many viewers. The programmes were good, but some major elements, like live stock market figures from Bombay, were not possible because of the cost. None of the programmes we had agreed to take from C & A actually came; we had no money, they lost interest.

*

This was certainly not the only occasion when I got involved in Doordarshan's activities. When I became secretary, DD Metro was on the verge of collapse. Producers were actually taking programmes away from it, saying they didn't think there was an audience for it. This was, in fact, the first problem Basu had mentioned to me when I joined. But then a determined effort to increase the area covered by DD Metro by fixing extra transmitters to existing terrestrial transmitter towers, juggling with rates and numerous calls—including many by me—to producers and film-makers helped to halt the decline. Most of it was thanks to the determined, unflagging efforts of Ratikant Basu and his colleagues. They not only halted the decline but turned the channel around, using a variety of methods, including new logos, slicker presentation of programmes with computerized switching from one programme to advertisements to another programme, and so on. These measures were such a success that a study made at the time by Jardine Mathieson on the rating of channels based on 1994 viewership figures began by saying that the findings excluded DD Metro because it was so far ahead of all the other channels that it simply could not be brought into a meaningful field of comparison, and this, they said, was owing to the very skilful handling of the channel by its managers.

We also hit upon a means of changing the viewership of Doordarshan's regional channels, almost by accident. One day Basu came to my room with a proposition. The regional stations of Doordarshan, he said, were closing down at 8 p.m. when the National Programme started. Now, if instead of that they continued to broadcast as satellite channels, regional viewers could continue to watch them via their cable operators or by installing a dish antenna—something many were doing at the time. The problem lay in the bands that were being used. The regional stations uplinked their signals to S-band transponders on the INSAT satellites; these were taken down by the terrestrial transmitters, amplified and rebroadcast terrestrially across the state. When the National Programme came on, the terrestrial transmitters shut off the link to the regional centre and switched to the C-band transponder carrying the National Programme being uplinked from Delhi.

What Basu put to me was this: why not persuade cable operators in different states to invest in S-band dishes so that they could carry the local Doordarshan station as a satellite channel and provide it to their viewers along with the commercial channels? The local stations could then continue broadcasting during the National Programme and even after 11 p.m., as they used to in the 1970s. Many viewers, particularly in the south, would be only too happy to continue to watch the Doordarshan channel broadcasting in their mother tongue. All they needed to do was switch from their own antenna, which received Doordarshan terrestrially, to a cable connection. He felt many would not mind spending the extra money to do this. But what about the revenue, I asked him, from the National Programme? He was not worried; he felt that it would continue to grow as long as the national segment contained entertaining, attractive programmes, and in any case, if the viewership of Doordarshan's regional channels picked up, it would only add to the kitty.

There was just one obvious problem. All the commercial satellite channels were on the C-band and cable operators in every state had the hardware to download these signals; would they invest in S-band dishes for just one channel? We then discovered that in some states the National Programme was being transmitted on S-band transponders. Light suddenly dawned; I remember both of us realizing almost simultaneously where the solution lay. I rang the engineer-in-chief of Doordarshan, N.J. Nair, and asked him if he could switch *all* the National Programme transmissions to S-band transponders in every state. He said it was possible, since all the regional kendras were broadcasting their own programmes via S-band transponders anyway. Then I asked him: if he did that would he then have some free C-band transponders, the ones currently carrying the National Programme? Yes, he said, he would. How many more would he need, I asked him urgently, for all the states to broadcast their regional programmes via the C-band? He gave me a figure and I told him to ask ISRO if they could let Doordarshan have that number of C-band transponders.

He rang me back in a little while and said they could give him some, but he needed to get one from the telecom people to make up the numbers. Again I told him to use his goodwill with them and trade off an extended C-band transponder for a regular C-band transponder. The former was not really used for television as no cable operator had the equipment to downlink at that frequency, whereas all operators could and did downlink from regular C-band transponders. He informed me a little later that they had agreed but had added that the price would be an extra transponder on the next INSAT satellite. I told him to go ahead and promise them that, and then Basu and I sat back and considered with excitement and anticipation just what we had achieved.

It would now be possible, we knew, to get cable operators to take the regional Doordarshan signals on the C-band dishes they already had, so that every state could get the local Doordarshan programmes as a cable channel just like the other commercial channels. Even as we were congratulating ourselves on having solved the problem, another far bigger dimension to this dawned on us. *The footprint of each C-band transponder covered the entire country. What then prevented cable operators from taking, say, Doordarshan Trivandrum signals down in Delhi or Shillong? Or Doordarshan Jalandhar in Chennai?* In other words, the thousands of people who lived far from their home state would be able to watch programmes in their mother tongue. The very large Tamil population in Delhi, for example, could watch Doordarshan Madras as a cable and satellite channel; Bengalis settled in Bombay could watch Doordarshan Calcutta, and so forth. All of a sudden, the viewership of these channels would become all-India. For thousands and thousands who lived far from their own states it would be the next best thing to being back home. And this meant that the regional kendras would come to life again; they would be terrestrial till 8 p.m. and then become cable and satellite channels, and remain on air till 11 p.m. (Sridhar, the enterprising director of Doordarshan Calcutta, actually continued transmission throughout the night, broadcasting classical music and dance. He tested audience reaction by putting in a simple quiz at 3 a.m.

and offering modest prizes. The first week he got some 150 replies, and from the second week on over 2000!)

I called in the officers of the ministry and we prepared a proposal; the minister saw the political advantage of this arrangement and agreed to it promptly. Formal orders were given to Doordarshan and soon television sets all across the country were able to access programmes in their own preferred language. I thought back to the first live broadcast we had done of the Thyagaraja kritis and could not help a slight feeling of nostalgia. What a long way we had come! Now, watching the Thyagaraja kritis would involve merely switching to DD Madras. Watching the Mahalaya programme would involve merely switching to DD Calcutta.

*

With all good things, however, come events that are less pleasant. One of the worst, inevitably involving the minister, took place in 1994. Singh Deo had made it his mission to please as many of his MP friends and ministers from his party as he could by acceding to their every request, no matter how absurd or, as in this case, dangerous. Usually these requests involved the installation of transmitters in their constituencies, on which he overspent grossly; at times they involved awarding commissioned programmes, i.e., programmes for which Doordarshan would meet the production costs, to producers recommended by them. These favours were done by sending little scribbled or typed notes directly to Basu. I was never told, nor did I want to be, because if I had been in the loop, I probably would have objected and there would have been more unpleasantness. Unfortunately there was one affair that brought me into direct conflict with the minister. It concerned the starting of a news bulletin in Urdu from Doordarshan Bangalore. Veerappa Moily, then chief minister of Karnataka, had urged his good friend Singh Deo to start this news bulletin. It was clearly a move aimed at endearing himself to Muslim voters. Typically, Singh Deo issued peremptory orders to Basu to start the bulletin. Basu was troubled and sought my advice.

I went to the minister and raised the subject of the bulletin. He told me brusquely that he had already passed orders on the matter. I pointed out that perhaps we should consider consulting the home ministry before we took this step. He then told me in a condescending tone that Moily himself asked for it and, as a man of the people, the chief minister was better placed to judge the wishes of the people than bureaucrats in the home ministry. In any case, he said, again resuming the peremptory tone he had started with, he had passed orders. He directed me to find out why Basu had not carried them out yet.

I went back to my room reluctantly and told Basu that as the minister was adamant he had better go ahead. But, if I remember correctly, we did keep the home ministry informed. Meanwhile, the minister left for Hiroshima, where he was to be an umpire for the rowing events in the Asian Games. The bulletins started, and within a few days trouble began to brew, as I had feared it would. There were angry demonstrations outside Doordarshan Bangalore; the police had to intervene to maintain order. I rang up the minister in Hiroshima and told him. He merely asked me to keep watch. The trouble grew worse; there was arson, rioting and then, inevitably, a person was killed in police firing. That sparked off violence and arson throughout the state. I kept the minister informed of all this and recommended that we take the bulletin off till things calmed down. He asked me to do what I thought best and hung up.

The trouble escalated; widespread rioting and arson spread to other cities of the state as well. Basu and I discussed the situation and decided, on our own, to stop the bulletin. This may well be seen as a retrograde decision, a caving in to communal elements, but, as I saw it, the provocation was from our side, and we had gone into it without preparations of any kind. Had the chief minister been more aware and sensed the antagonism, he would have politically conditioned his people to accept the bulletin before letting it go on air. Now it was a question of taking steps to stop the killing, which could be achieved quickly only by taking the bulletin off the air. Indeed, the trouble subsided and calm returned to the state, but thirty-nine people had died.

After he returned from Hiroshima, Singh Deo travelled to Bangalore. There he went through the usual motions, offering condolences to the families of those who had died, declaring how grieved he was by the violence and loss of life. He then told the press that *it was a matter of regret that he had not been kept informed of what was happening by the I & B secretary*! When I read this in a newspaper, my anger spilled over. I went straight down to the minister and showed it to him. He shrugged it off. He said that I had, in fact, not told him of the magnitude of the trouble. I was completely horrified. I told him that I had spoken to him every day, and that since this reflected on the manner in which I worked, a contradiction should be issued as an official press note. He refused. I told him that I would have no choice but to place all this before the Cabinet secretary.

'Place it before whom you like,' he snapped.

And that is exactly what I did. I sent a detailed report to the Cabinet secretary, telling him the reason I was sending it was because I did not want him or the prime minister to feel that I had been remiss in my duties as secretary. I don't know what happened to that note but I didn't hear of it again from either the minister or anyone else. Nor did he ask me why I had overruled an order of his and stopped the news bulletin. But, as you can imagine, relations between us thereafter were very cold indeed.

*

There was yet another Doordarshan dream which I had discussed with Basu: I wanted to take Doordarshan overseas, to make it an international channel. Representatives of Panamsat, a company that had earlier launched PAS 1, a satellite which carried signals from the US to Europe and vice versa, had come and met me. They were launching a new satellite, PAS 4, which was to be placed in a geo-stationary orbit 35,000 kilometres above and just west of India and which would have on board some very powerful transponders. A C-band transponder on this satellite would have an enormous footprint extending from the western parts of Indonesia to the south-eastern tip of Britain. It could pick up a signal from India which could be downlinked all over North Africa, the Middle East, eastern and central Europe, Central Asia and western Europe right up to the coast of Britain. What they offered us was a bargain—if we agreed to take the C-band transponder on this satellite, they would downlink the signal in Germany and uplink it again after amplifying it, boosting the signal strength to a level which would make it possible for it to be downlinked in Britain. *Free of cost.* Moreover, they offered to take the Doordarshan signal from the UK to PAS 1, their satellite over the Atlantic Ocean, whose footprint covered a substantial part of the eastern seaboard of the United States. From there we could, once again, tie up with cable operators and have the signal delivered across the US. This special treatment was because if we hired the transponder we would be one of the first customers for PAS 4.

There was more. Should we take the C-band transponder they were offering, they would give us an option on a Ku-band transponder on the same satellite that would cover all of India and South-east Asia. This would be on a lien for just $840,000. The price in the market was about $1,000,000 then. A Ku-band transponder carries an extremely powerful signal transmitted at a very high frequency. While this makes the footprint smaller, within that footprint the signal can be received by a dish with a diameter of less than two feet. In other words, the cable operator could be totally eliminated because a user with a little dish would be abe to receive the signal *anywhere* in the country. He could, for example, receive all the Doordarshan channels in a remote corner of Ladakh or Arunachal Pradesh (provided, of course, he had a power source for his television set) without needing transmitters of any kind.

I discussed this with Basu and his officers exhaustively and decided it was too good an offer to pass up. We concluded the deal with Panamsat and decided to make use of the C-band transponder first. We had made the deal conditional to the signal being received in the UK because I wanted our signal to go to the UK more than anywhere else. Our engineers went to the UK and were warmly received by British Telecom, who sent a team to a location in Kent, where they reported that they had indeed received the signal, though it was very weak. This was not a problem, of course—the signal would be amplified before it was fed into the cable system in the country. Basu, meanwhile, spoke to the BBC, CNN, Viacom (which operated MTV), and some television channels based in the UK. All of them offered generous help; in particular, they offered to help Doordarshan work out deals with cable operators concerning the time slots during which they would carry the Doordarshan channel.

We called the new channel Doordarshan International. It was to carry news and recorded current affairs programmes, as well as select entertainment programmes. I was clear about one thing—we were not aiming merely at the South Asian immigrant population in Britain, but all British viewers. The entertainment we planned to offer on this channel would be more in the nature of dance, films with subtitles and other such programmes. Basu worked out a package that would be transmitted at different times to fit into different time zones. From my experience as secretary of culture, I knew that viewers in the Middle East and North Africa were deliriously fond of Hindi films, and I was determined to use them to make the channel popular.

Things now came to a point in early 1995 when it became essential that Basu travel to the UK to finalize the agreements with cable operators. All the networks that had offered to help informed him that they had done the preliminary negotiations; now he had to go and tie everything up. That was when the first problem arose, a seemingly minor one: the finance wing pointed out that Doordarshan's budget had no funds for Basu to go to the UK. I asked them to divert funds from the AIR budget; this was too important an opportunity to miss out on. But that was again considered improper, and finally, with a great amount of persuasion and the intervention of a very sympathetic expenditure secretary in the Ministry of Finance, funds were allocated for his trip.

It happened, as with all other things I planned for Doordarshan, a little too late.

10

Fade Out

One morning in April 1995, I opened the newspaper and read, to my astonishment, that Basu had been transferred as secretary, Department of Electronics. According to the news report, K.S. Sarma, who had been Provident Fund commissioner, Delhi, had been posted as joint secretary in the Ministry of Information and Broadcasting and would be holding concurrent charge as DG of Doordarshan. What astonished and angered me was that I, as secretary of the ministry, had never been informed of any of this. No one, not even the Cabinet secretary, had said a word to me about it, let alone ask for my consent or advice. I spoke to Basu, who told me he had heard it the night before while watching the Doordarshan news bulletin. He was DG of Doordarshan and had learnt of his posting from a Doordarshan news bulletin. In other words, the newspeople in Doordarshan knew about it before he did! I went to the office and wrote out a letter seeking premature retirement from the IAS. I had some four months leave due to me and requested that, at the end of that period, I be allowed to retire (I would have been retiring the following year in the normal course anyway). I then went down to the minister's room to hand over the letter, with a request that he endorse it to the Cabinet secretary, who could then process it for the necessary approvals.

The minister was no longer K.P. Singh Deo. The volatile, eccentric Singh Deo had been replaced by P.A. Sangma, the suave, ever-smiling, erstwhile labour minister. Some months prior to Basu's transfer, Sangma had taken on the task of answering Parliament questions concerning the I & B ministry while Singh Deo was in Hiroshima for the Asian

Games. I had occasion to meet him then and found him very genial and understanding; in fact it had been a pleasure dealing with him. So when he came in as I & B minister I was relieved and happy that a sensible and rational person, who was also cheerful and pleasant, would now be heading the ministry. What I did not realize was that of all the ministers I had worked with he would be the most difficult of them all. Beneath that cheerful exterior was a man who could be shrewd, calculating even. Sangma didn't rant and rave like Singh Deo; he merely acted.

Sangma wanted Basu out, not because of anything the latter had done, but to enable him to put a man of his choice in Basu's place. He had selected K.S. Sarma because he had worked with him as labour minister and he obviously considered him loyal, which Sarma certainly was. Sarma's mission was to please his minister in whatever way the minister wanted. Indeed, this is the kind of officer ministers look for, not for someone who might ask inconvenient questions, or give unsolicited advice, or even have the gall to refuse to carry out orders the officer considered wrong.

Sangma had worked quietly, behind my back. All the orders had been signed and ACC approvals obtained without my suspecting anything. He was a most efficient minister, I'll grant him that. When I took my request for leave and premature retirement to him, he was the picture of distress. He dissembled so well that he had me fooled for a few days. He claimed he himself had had no idea that all this was going on, that he himself had been told only the night before, and that Sarma was being brought in at the behest of P.V.R.K. Prasad.

'It is because of the elections, Ghose,' he said. 'What could I do? I am a Congress man. I had to agree since the PM wanted it.'

He wouldn't hear of my going on leave or taking premature retirement. Don't leave the ministry, Sangma pleaded, I'm new here and I need you to advise me. It was all so convincing that I believed him and stayed on. It was only a few days later, however, that I realized I had been made a fool of—Sarma was someone the minister knew, so how could he have been brought in from among the large number of officers of his seniority available for the posting unless it had been with the minister's concurrence? And not merely concurrence—*Sarma was his choice.* It had all been worked out carefully by him and P.V.R.K. Prasad, in absolute secrecy.

Initially I tried to make the best of a messy situation. My first task was to get the new DG to go to the UK to finalize the agreements with the cable operators so that DD International could become a reality. It was, in fact, already a reality, and was being received in the Gulf region, but I needed it to reach Europe. I called Sarma in and briefed him in detail, explaining to him that it was imperative he conclude the agreements with the cable operators in the UK; the agreements had to be in place so that the channel could be made available to viewers in the UK. I told him that, as a bargaining point, he could waive all fees from any advertising put on the channel by the operators.

He seemed to understand, nodding vigorously from time to time, and left for the UK. Days passed. I heard he had returned, but he neither called nor came to see me. Then one day I was sent for by Sangma and went to his room to find Sarma sitting there looking sanctimonious.

'Sarma tells me that no one can see your DD International in England, Ghose,' the minister said. 'And it is very expensive.'

I was flabbergasted. I told the minister that Sarma had not had the courtesy to see me after his return and report on his visit, so I wasn't aware of just what he had told the minister. I explained that he had been sent precisely because no one could see the channel; like every signal coming from a satellite it was weak and needed to be amplified before it was put on the local cable networks. *That was why he had been sent to the UK*—to conclude agreements with the cable operators for which the initial groundwork had already been done. I wondered if he had bothered to get in touch with the BBC and others at all, or with the cable operators.

Sarma began to look a little uncomfortable. The minister told him in his usual pleasant manner that he should have seen me on his return, to which Sarma mumbled something about having been very busy or some such rubbish. Then the minister asked him what he had done during his visit. Sarma, eyes opened wide in feigned earnestness, said that no one had come to see him and that no one from the BBC or any other network had contacted him. It was clear he had done nothing at all, and that his visit had been a colossal waste of money.

Back in my room I thought over the entire matter. Sarma, I had come to learn from the usual bureaucratic grapevine, was a very smart cookie, shrewd as they come. Why had he gone to London and done nothing at all? Just to be doubly sure I rang up the minister (information) in our high commission in London and asked him about Sarma's visit. The minister spoke of him in contemptuous terms, saying he was a pompous fellow who had apparently sent word to the BBC and other networks that 'the DG of Doordarshan had arrived' and would be free to meet them on an appropriate day and time. Naturally no one bothered to return his calls; he seemed to expect that they would all come running to him cap in hand, and they hadn't. Finally, he had returned to India. 'A totally useless visit,' the minister concluded.

It became clear to me that Sarma had done this deliberately, because the entire Doordarshan International project was a follow-up of what Basu and I had worked on. It was not his idea, and thus had to be scuttled.

This was about the time when I began to lose interest in all matters related to Doordarshan. I had never thought it could happen. It was an organization that had caused me much anger, distress, exasperation, but also great joy, euphoria and excitement. Every day had seemed to bring wonderful possibilities in this new, growing field, and I had never thought I would come to a stage where I would find it of no interest, even distasteful.

I soon saw the smoothness with which the Sangma–Sarma axis worked. Sangma had a personal assistant who accompanied Sarma to Doordarshan and sat with him all day. Between them they decided which programmes would run and which would not. Soon after he joined, Sarma ordered that a rather good programme, a talk show anchored by Mallika Sarabhai, be taken off the air. Just like that, no reasons given. Mallika came to see me, completely bewildered.

'What's with this guy?' she asked. 'I wasn't told what was wrong, if anything was wrong. Nothing. I was just told the DG wanted the programme stopped.'

I rang Sarma up and asked him why he had done it. 'I didn't like it,' was what he told me in his usual devious way. It dawned on me later that he had done it for the same reason that he had sabotaged Doordarshan International: Mallika's programme had been an initiative of Basu's and not his.

From then on I decided to keep as far away from Doordarshan as I could. I merely signed and sent back any files requiring my signature. But habits die hard. While I distanced myself from all operational plans and activities of Doordarshan, I kept an eye on two construction projects that apparently interested neither Sangma nor Sarma, namely, the unfinished Delhi Kendra, which was part of the complex coming up on the site of the old Mandi House, and some new studios for Doordarshan Bombay. The building for the Delhi Kendra was part of the dramatically brilliant complex of buildings Raj Rewal had designed. The first portion, which I had moved into during my first months as DG, was the DG's office; the other was the Delhi station. Work on this had started when I was DG but since then, for some reason or the other (chiefly because whoever was DG had taken no interest in it), the building activity had come to a standstill. When attempts were made to start it again, the construction costs had shot up from the original Rs 34 crore to Rs 165 crore. Not surprisingly, the finance ministry had flatly refused to accept this impossibly high rise in costs.

Soon after I joined the ministry I had taken up this matter with my batch mate and friend K. Venkatesan, who was secretary (expenditure) in the Ministry of Finance. Venkatesan was very helpful indeed; he pointed out how it was impossible for him to clear this astronomically high figure for a building to which nothing had been added since the original estimates. The answer, he said, was to reduce some elements in the building to lower the costs and he would, on his part, do his best to justify some increase. I sat with the Doordarshan engineers and I called in my old colleague and friend Shashi Kapoor, who was now DG AIR, to help. Between us we cut down the number of studios and other rooms and, with Raj Rewal's help, modified some other features. We removed the amphitheatre at the back and an entire wing consisting of two large studios and all the continuity booths.

I went back to Venkatesan with this drastically pruned-down project, which was now going to cost Rs 118 crore.

'I simply can't bring it down further,' I pleaded with Venkatesan.

'Don't ask me to cut it down even more.'

Venkatesan looked through the revised project carefully and then said, after some time, 'All right. But on one condition. Work starts on the project immediately. I will not countenance any stoppage or any request for a single rupee more.'

I promised him we would not ask for more money and that work would start at once. I told the engineers I would visit the site once a month and that they had better stick to their targets or else things would get difficult for them. Work did start and I made it a point to go to the site every month and spend an entire morning there checking on the progress. I continued this even after Sarma joined, busy as he was pleasing Sangma and Prasad, and producing, I believe, little programmes promoting P.V. Narasimha Rao. The 1996 elections were less than a year away. He occasionally did come along on my monthly visits, stay for some time and then leave. It mattered little to me. When he was there I ignored him; he was, in any case, totally ignorant of the project itself, and I dealt only with the engineers.

While this was going on I had to do a little rescue act on the additional studios and buildings for Doordarshan Bombay as well for which funds had been allotted and on which work had started. The project had been approved a long time before, during my tenure as DG, and, as usual, had run into a bog of bureaucratic procedures that had slowed the work down to little more that the odd worker laying a brick or two. When Raj Bhargava became secretary, he visited Hong Kong on a study tour and happened to see the Star TV studios. This was in 1992; Star had only just started up. Bhargava found that Star operated out of two tiny studios that were little bigger than telephone booths, the sort of studios our engineers called continuity booths. It was enough for their needs; all they wanted was a little space where Kamal Sidhu and Danny McGill would sit together smiling at the audience and introducing programmes. The rest of the work consisted of uplinking recorded programmes, which was done from a control room doubtless of the same size. Doordarshan didn't operate like that at all; programmes were produced in studios and there were live shows with studio audiences. We needed large studios for these and for a variety of other activities, like the live coverage of election results by Prannoy Roy and

Vinod Dua. But Bhargava wasn't having any of it. He declared that all we needed were small booths, no studios, and he convinced Singh Deo of this as well. The result was that the Bombay project had come to a halt. It remained incomplete, after several crores having been spent on it. This didn't seem to bother either Bhargava or Singh Deo one bit.

It took me a while to convince Singh Deo that Bhargava had been talking through his hat, that we needed those big studios since we worked in a way which Star TV didn't, and even though he was initially set on the small studios, I finally did get him to agree to let the Bombay project be completed as planned. Back I went to Venkatesan and pleaded with him to let me restart the Bombay project. He agreed, and I went down to Bombay and arranged to have a dedicated construction team start immediately. I visited the project every time I went to Bombay in the three years I was secretary, and it was a very rewarding moment when I saw the building finally up and ready for the installation of equipment. Two large studios and a smaller one had been added. These, together with the two studios Doordarshan Bombay already had, went a long way to ease the heavy demand for studio space and time.

Thus my involvement with Doordarshan came to be restricted, in my last few months as secretary, to the monitoring of these two construction projects. But I found a strange new satisfaction from doing this. Here was work not beset with intrigue and pressures; it was visible, physical work whose progress could be measured. True, it had none of the heady excitement of planning new ventures, trying them out on audiences and seeing the ideas take off. But it was satisfying work in its own way. Additionally, it gave me time to look at some of the other units of the ministry in which the Sangma–Sarma combine had no interest, such as AIR. I also spent a good deal of time, almost inevitably, thinking of the exciting days that had passed. Basu was now secretary for electronics; my erstwhile colleague and friend Shashi Kapoor was DG of AIR; Shiv Sharma had retired; Madan Mohan, the first engineer-in-chief of Doordarshan I had worked with and who was as much a teacher as a colleague, had died. It seemed to me that a dark shadow had descended on the organization to which I had once dedicated so many dreams. It was now part of a propaganda machine run by little people of limited comprehension and driven only by the need to fawn on and serve their political masters.

Sarma soon gave up the ritual of calling on me in the ministry; he went straight to the minister and got his approval to whatever he wanted; then, as joint secretary, had government orders issued if he thought them necessary. I was glad he did that; if he had involved me in what he was doing, I would have felt I was touching offal.

Meanwhile DD III dwindled into an insignificant channel. Jai Chandiram was given some other work to do, and DD III shared time with other programmes on the same channel. Except for the one at Madras, the remaining NEC transmitters were moved to other locations, presumably to satisfy some political personage. DD International remained a stunted channel reaching mainly the Gulf region and no place else. All the plans that we had had for it to be received all across the globe were forgotten or put away in the graveyard reserved for new ideas. For this inconsequential transmission to the Gulf, Panamsat was being paid $1 million for the C-band transponder! The figure would have been more than justified had the DD signal gone all over Europe, North Africa, the Middle East and the US, but given the insignificance it had been reduced to, the expenditure was totally wasteful. In addition, the plans we had prepared to start a direct-to-home (DTH) service for Doordarshan channels, for which we had taken out the option of leasing the Ku-band transponder on PAS 4, were allowed to lapse because Sarma hadn't a clue about any of this and was too filled with a sense of his own importance to ask—it was, after all, an initiative that Basu and I had taken.

Months passed. I occasionally heard of some semi-political event being held at Doordarshan—inaugurations, festivals, things of that sort—but never bothered to go. The summer of 1995 saw me in the UK. I had been invited by the Foreign Office of the British government to a seminar held at Wilton Park, a gracious old mansion set in over 100 acres of rolling green land, where a select group of persons, considered to be of some consequence in their field, had been invited to spend time talking to and at each other. I was flattered, of course; I never thought I was of any consequence in that sense, but it was a good enough reason to visit this beautiful historic manor and talk about the advent of transnational broadcasting. There was a mix of journalists, academics and broadcasters from around the world, and it was interesting to discover that transnational broadcasting evoked a variety of responses from different people. Representatives of international broadcasters like the BBC said, expectedly, that it was inevitable, while others pointed out that, unlike radio, television actually influenced cultures and attitudes and was therefore a medium that could be an agent of change, which was not always for the good. I argued that if a culture was vigorous and dynamic, as I thought ours was, if only because it was so diverse, it had nothing to fear from transnational broadcasting, although it had brought in a concept of broadcasting hitherto unknown in India, namely, broadcasting as a purely commercial activity, done for profit.

I took a day off to visit the nearby research facilities of the BBC, where I was shown their latest creation, Digital Audio Broadcasting (DAB). It was to FM what a CD is in comparison to an audio cassette. The sound was superb, with bell-like clarity, and didn't fade as the FM signal sometimes does, especially in a car. It could be sent to a satellite and be received by special radio sets over as wide a range as a satellite footprint. For a moment the old excitement overcame me—what a change this could bring to AIR's broadcasting! We could have a radio signal audible all across the country uplinked from just one station. And with more uplinks we could have a situation similar to what we had with television: radio programmes from every major station in the country could be heard anywhere! True, the cost of a DAB radio set at that time was £1000, but I was assured by the BBC engineers that costs would come down as DAB became more popular. Soon, however, my enthusiasm waned; I remembered the new realities at home, and thereafter my interest remained purely academic.

I also met some of the old BBC hands I had met earlier, among them Bob Phillis, then deputy director general of the BBC and managing director of BBC World. He met me at the door in a theatrical attitude of one who has been grievously wronged.

'How could you do this to us?' he cried, arms outflung. 'To *us*?' He was referring to Doordarshan having agreed to carry CNN news programmes for a brief period every day. 'The BBC and Doordarshan have been *so* close! And you go and tie up with . . . with *that* organization!'

We had a good laugh, but I did explain to him that CNN had

offered us a very good deal at that time. (Of course it all went haywire once CNN found a transponder of its own.) Then Bob asked for help in locating land for a 1000-watt transmitter to carry the BBC World Service into India and the surrounding countries with greater clarity and strength. I told him we wanted AIR's external service to reach the UK; he promptly said that they had a transmitter they weren't using in the north-east of England and would be happy to offer it free of cost in return for a location in India for their transmitter (for which they would pay). I promised I would get the engineer-in-chief of AIR to speak to his counterpart in the BBC about this.

I returned to India and to the distasteful state of affairs that I had to be associated with as secretary of the ministry. I told the engineer-in-chief of AIR about my conversation with Bob Phillis and he nearly had a fit. *Give the BBC place for a transmitter within the country?* I explained to him that we weren't 'giving' it, they would buy it, and that if we didn't give them a location, they would situate the transmitter close enough to India anyway, perhaps in Central Asia. This way we got, in return, a transmitter for AIR's external service within the UK free of cost. He finally saw the advantages of the agreement and promised to talk to his counterpart in the BBC. I never found out what happened to the deal. Someone in our ministry or in some other ministry must have blocked it. Or maybe the engineer-in-chief of AIR, a conservative man, just put the papers away, knowing that I was on my way out, and not very close to the minister.

Sangma, like Singh Deo before him with Raj Bhargava, was not able to wait for me to go. He got my successor, a batch mate of mine called Gopalan, who had worked with Sangma as labour secretary and with whom he got on very well, to come in as OSD, just as I had come in when Raj Bhargava was secretary. There was only one difference: I had scrupulously avoided doing anything to undermine Bhargava's authority till his last day as secretary, whereas here I told Gopalan to go ahead and sign and approve whatever he liked. He was a little uncomfortable, having to function in the way he did; we had been probationers together, and his wife, Sarala, was also an IAS officer and a batch mate of my sister's, though my sister was in the Indian Foreign Service. But he was essentially a good man, even if his first and complete loyalty was to Sangma. When Sangma became speaker of the Lok Sabha in later years he took Gopalan there as secretary general, the first IAS officer to hold that post.

Fortunately the months passed quickly enough, with the film festival in Bombay and other events engaging my attention. Soon it was time to go, to leave government service after nearly thirty-six years. I paid a last visit to the site where the new Delhi Kendra was coming up. A large group of engineers had gathered. The 'inspection' was just a formality; I think they knew I had really gone there to say farewell, not just to that project but for all the years I had spent with Doordarshan, and it did my heart good to see all of them there. Raj Rewal, who had become a friend whom I respected and admired, had made it a point of coming. I said goodbye to everyone, sat with all of them in the improvised site office and talked of times past.

A different kind of farewell function had been organized at Shastri Bhavan, all ritual and insincerity, where Sangma dwelt at length in his inimitably convincing manner on what a fine officer I was, how he thought I was very knowledgeable and all the rest of that. Flowers were given, others said the things people usually say at such events, someone clapped and it was over. Later, in my room, I signed my last paper, collected my personal things and left the ministry for the last time.

In the car going home I found that I had no feeling of regret at all. I was leaving something that had become foreign to me—a world where hypocrisy, deceit and dissembling were the order of the day, and where all that mattered was advancement, personal and political. There was no room left any more for new ideas, new plans or projects. It was not the world I had been used to, certainly not as DG of Doordarshan and not in the major part of my three years as I & B secretary. That world was gone and forgotten. It was as if a door had finally closed, not just for me, but for an era. As I entered my house, I had a strange, amusing feeling that another door had opened through which I walked with a lighter, happier heart.

11

Reflections

The story of Doordarshan is essentially a tragedy. It is the story of a publicly funded organization deliberately twisted, distorted and made into a mediocre presenter of programmes lauding the government of the day, and doing so badly for the most part. Above all it is the story of its owners, the Ministry of Information and Broadcasting, in particular, and the Government of India, in general, not comprehending or wanting to comprehend the nature and identity of the organization.

These could appear as serious charges, but they aren't charges as much as conclusions that have emerged from a look at the organization as it is now and as it could have been. Let us first consider what it could have been, beginning with the mission of both radio and television as professed by the government: they are public service broadcasters, that is, they have to educate, inform and entertain listeners and viewers. To use the language of the times, they were supposed to be 'agents of change', to sensitize audiences to the values inherent in our traditions, culture and civilization. This mission of Indian radio and television was not very different from that given to public service broadcasters across the world. The mission statement of the BBC, for example, states in part that its programmes should 'inform, educate, entertain and enrich the lives of audiences in ways which the market alone will not; bring people together for moments of celebration, common experience, and in times of crisis; and help broaden people's horizons'.

The aim was admirable and it is not too much to expect a government that was so committed to the development of its people, providing them with basic services like drinking water, roads, education and hospitals, to also have taken on this responsibility with the seriousness it required. It seemed for a while to have been so for AIR. For Doordarshan, or AIR-TV as it was called initially, the first few years of broadcasts in the 1970s by stations not linked to one another (Bombay, Jalandhar, Madras, Calcutta and Delhi) seemed to be going the same way. But the advent of satellite television, which linked all the transmitters in the country and created the National Programme, changed all that. The power of television soon proved to be too heady; the ideals and the mission did not survive.

In the 1970s the government took that monumentally foolish decision to abolish licence fees for radio and television sets. The reason given was that the cost of collection, which was done through post offices, was greater than the amount collected. The real reason was that someone, possibly the finance minister of the day, wanted some cheap popularity. With the abolition of licence fees, Doordarshan and AIR became a financial liability for the government, specifically, to the Ministry of Information and Broadcasting.

This did not mean that every year or every quarter the government handed an amount of cash over to both units. It meant that throughout the year officials of both AIR and Doordarshan had to visit various underlings in the ministry to plead that a file be 'put up' to the next level so that eventually a decision on some financial matter could be taken. It meant that in all money matters, from complex issues like the kind of equipment to put into earth stations to the kind of cameras to be purchased for outdoor use and for studios, the decisions were taken in the ministry, not in Doordarshan. This is not peculiar to Doordarshan, of course. As is well known, all major decisions on the acquisition of hardware by the armed forces is taken by the Ministry of Defence, not by the army, navy or air force. The reason why the ministries take these decisions is a very simple one: they want control, and financial control is the best form of control.

As an inevitable consequence, the ministry began instructing Doordarshan not only on matters relating to the acquisition of hardware but also on the kind of programmes it should broadcast. Some secretaries actually ran Doordarshan, with the help of pliant, subservient DGs. S.S. Gill, for example, was known to boast that he was the chief producer of Doordarshan. This eroded not just the freedom of Doordarshan executives to determine what kind of programmes they would broadcast, but also destroyed their confidence in being able to do so. The mission given to Doordarshan and the ideal vision outlined in the detailed P.C. Joshi Committee report and in that admirable monograph, *A Vision for Indian Television*, brought out by NAMEDIA were all forgotten in the face of the only goal that the executives set themselves—carrying out the orders of the secretary. Gill will in all probability say that he had to do it given the calibre of the executives he had in Doordarshan, but that is a specious argument. He himself knew as much or as little about television, about programmes and how they are made as Doordarshan officers. Which was natural enough—he was an IAS officer, not a broadcaster.

I, too, was only an IAS officer, but I had been involved, since my college days, with theatre. This stopped while I was at Doordarshan, but I continued to be involved during the other positions I held in Delhi, although I never let theatre come in the way of my official work. The wonderful people I worked with at Yatrik (the theatre group to which I still belong) were generous enough to wait for me till 8 p.m. for rehearsals, which then went on late into the night. Only for the performances did I take casual leave for a day or two if the shows weren't on weekends. I had major, mostly leading, roles in a number of plays: Chekov's *The Seagull* and *Uncle Vanya*, an adaptation of Morris West's *The Devil's Advocate*, Arthur Miller's *The Crucible*, Christopher Fry's *Venus Observed*, twice Jean Anouilh's version of Sophocles' *Antigone* (playing Creon on both occasions, first in 1979 and then fifteen years later in 1994), Ariel Dorfman's *Death and the Maiden*, Gurcharan Das's *9, Jakhoo Hill*, and Willy Russel's *Educating Rita*. I also acted in two Hindi plays, playing the lead in one of them. Acting was not all; I directed an equal number: the first *Antigone*, Fry's *Venus Observed*, Kamal Kapur's *The Curlew's Cry*, Shakespeare's *A Midsummer Night's Dream*, and Ugo Betti's *The Queen and the Rebels*.

I have enumerated these theatrical productions only to make the point that my theatre work was considerable. At Yatrik we don't perform merely for the fun of 'doing a play'. We take our artistic work seriously, give it our time and effort, concentration and study. Above all, we approach it with discipline and training. We hold workshops, for example—intensive sessions with those who have established themselves in the world of theatre, including Roger Martin, who directed the celebrated play *Equus* in London and Broadway, and Roshan Seth, among others. All this stood me in good stead at Doordarshan: I made it clear that deadlines had to be respected, that preparation was as important as performance, and that I would not tolerate shoddy preparation. I also think that the years on stage had given me a 'feel' for what was good in a programme and what was not. Television and theatre are not the same thing, of course, but they are close enough for me to be able to spot what is bad, or good, in a performance or a production. And this was an area in which I refused to compromise. If I found that someone was indifferent to his work, or just not good enough, I would find him some harmless work in a different department. Several persons in Doordarshan who had also worked in theatre understood, I think, what was behind the various decisions I took.

Returning to Doordarshan's story: as the years passed, it degenerated into nothing more than a propaganda machine for the government, carrying boring programmes on different development schemes, on what was happening abroad and in the country as given to them by the Ministry of External Affairs and the Ministry of Home Affairs, and broadcasting 'cultural' programmes that someone influential wanted shown, irrespective of how disgracefully shoddy and cheap they were. To call Doordarshan a public service broadcaster was to invite a great deal of amusement among professional broadcasters around the world.

The fault did not lie with the executives in Doordarshan; many of them were, in terms of talent and experience, no less than the best professionals in public service broadcasting networks around the world. The fault lies squarely with the government, not the Ministry of Information and Broadcasting alone, but on a host of others, including the Ministry of Finance, the Planning Commission, even the Prime Minister's Office, except when Rajiv Gandhi was prime minister. Things would have been totally different for both AIR and Doordarshan if the government had had the larger vision of a publicly funded radio and television network, and not treated it as a creature of the ruling party and its hangers-on. That is, if the bureaucrats in the ministries and offices I have named had thought not like petty clerks but with a degree of far-sightedness that one would expect from officers occupying important positions. And the ironic fact is that these officers of grave and concerned mien were actually exceptionally wise when it came to matters of state of other kinds. It was only when they had to deal with radio and television that all of them—from Montek Singh Ahluwalia and Arjun Sengupta, otherwise shrewd, intelligent economists, to the street-smart, ambitious and clever N.K. Singh—became pear-shaped.

Both as DG and later as secretary, I had to attend the annual ritual organized by the Planning Commission where the plan budget for the next year is finalized. The first time I had to do this as secretary, I & B we spent days preparing for it, collating figures, projecting trends, obtaining accurate information on coverage, reach, and a host of other details. When we were called into the meeting and were making our presentation, I was immediately interrupted by the member secretary of the commission with an utterly fatuous remark: 'Why did you stop showing that serial about the woman police officer? I used to enjoy that. Now you've got something boring instead. Can't you show a good serial?'

Words failed me. I tried to say something when the equally exalted secretary (expenditure) in the Ministry of Finance, said, 'But did you see that film, that old Dilip Kumar film? Terrific, I say. But it was a bad print. Ghose, why do you get such bad prints, yaar?'

This nonsense went on for a while, then suddenly the member secretary dropped his seemingly idiotic manner and said, 'Anyway, the fact is all I can spare for AIR and Doordarshan is so much.' He named a figure that was well below the amount we had projected as our barest minimum.

'Ghose,' he said to me kindly, 'you can split it up between AIR and Doordarshan any way you like.'

'This is absurd,' I began indignantly. 'It doesn't even cover the basic requirements we . . .'

'Everyone wants more than they're given,' he said, now curt and unsmiling. 'If you need more, raise the money. As it is you really ought to be paying your own way.'

This was a pattern that was followed every year, so after the first year I avoided any serious preparation. I knew the farce that would be enacted and did not want to waste my time. But it saddened me that these otherwise intelligent and sagacious officers never thought it necessary to question the need for government to exercise control on these media units, and to look at ways in which they could be funded by means other than state sponsorship.

There were very few points on which I agreed with the government's views on the electronic media, especially after my bitter experience with DD III and Doordarshan International. The government saw them as a means of spreading 'knowledge about the government's achievements', as they so elegantly put it, and of airing third-rate programmes made by cronies and fawning toadies in return for favours of other kinds. But there was one issue on which my beliefs coincided with those of the government: the way Doordarshan was funded. Like me, many officers in the Ministry of Finance and in the Planning Commission believed that Doordarshan had to be freed from dependence on state funds. Our reasons for sharing this notion were not the same, however. The financial officers saw Doordarshan's dependence as an unjustified drain on the exchequer—every year Doordarshan had to be granted funds in excess of Rs 800 crore—whereas I saw it as a means of control, a control that had to be ended if Doordarshan was indeed to become an autonomous body, not bound to carry out every direction, proper and improper, given by different ministries and politicians.

In fact, the government—and this included members of Parliament from the ruling party as well as a host of bureaucrats—had a curiously fractured view of what exactly Doordarshan was. The Planning Commission and the Ministry of Finance exhorted Doordarshan to make money, to pay its own way. At the same time, however, they would swell with indignation at the 'obscene, vulgar and shocking' entertainment programmes being shown. Show meaningful programmes that embody our glorious traditions, they would thunder, programmes that show how we have advanced, how rural India has improved, show our rural development schemes. If then I ventured that these might not fetch us any revenues, there would be a shocked silence. Revenues? We want programmes that will sensitize the masses and show them glimpses of our culture, and you talk of revenues? Are you so money-minded?

This in itself was bad enough. What was even worse was that no one was willing to debate the issue of how the two images of Doordarshan could be made to converge, how it could earn its keep and also show the kind of programmes that would present the best in our culture. Any attempt to suggest such a discussion would end up in the kind of farcical exchanges I have mentioned. The plain fact was that no one had the time or inclination to think about this medium with any seriousness. Some NGOs did, it is true. They organized seminars on the nature of broadcasting, on public service broadcasting and related subjects. I attended a number of them and never did I see anyone from the finance ministry or the Planning Commission there. They simply weren't interested.

One of the bitter criticisms made of the I & B ministry was its refusal to establish Prasar Bharati, the corporation recommended by the committee set up under the chairmanship of B.G. Verghese during the days of the Janata Party government. One of the declared missions of the Janata Party was to make AIR and its fledgling television wing autonomous, a corporation on the lines of the BBC. When the Janata Party came to power in 1977, the minister for information and broadcasting, L.K. Advani, lost no time in setting up the committee. It was originally supposed to be called Akash Bharati, but for some inexplicable reason it became Prasar Bharati. The recommendations of the committee were accepted by the government, but the government soon fell and nothing was done. Much later, the Janata Dal government came to power and P. Upendra, then I & B minister, made it a point to rush the bill setting up Prasar Bharati through Parliament. He managed this by agreeing to all the amendments suggested, whether practical or wildly impractical. The bill went through and became law, but within days the government collapsed. When the Congress formed the government again under P.V. Narasimha Rao, it was in no hurry to give effect to the new act, which had a section that said that Prasar Bharati would be set up on a day to be notified by the government. It never notified the day, and there the matter lay.

As it happened, though, as secretary I attended a meeting in the prime minister's house regarding the establishment of Prasar Bharati.

It had been demanded with a great deal of heat and noise by opposition MPs, who felt that the government was deliberately refusing to establish it on one pretext or the other. They were right, to some extent, but the act had so many patently unworkable elements built into it—the cumbersome structure of Prasar Bharati, for example, which envisaged a board on which there would be a member (radio) and a member (television) *and* the DGs of AIR and Doordarshan—that it simply had to be re-examined, which is what was being done. The meeting was to determine whether the amendments should be brought before the Cabinet and then an amendment bill moved in Parliament.

'How long has the act been in cold storage?' asked the prime minister.

I told him it had been passed four years earlier, in 1990.

'Keep it in cold storage,' he said. 'Very cold storage.'

But he agreed to the amendment bill being brought before Parliament.

In point of fact no I & B minister really wanted it. K.P. Singh Deo told me as much one day, when the amendments to the Prasar Bharati act were being discussed. He said that once Prasar Bharati came into existence, the I & B ministry ought to be abolished. According to him the rest of the work hardly justified a full-fledged ministry and could easily be farmed out to other ministries.

I was personally totally against the establishment of Prasar Bharati as it was constituted under the act. It had too many loose ends (what would happen to the staff, for example, if they opted to stay in government service) that had to be settled before we could go ahead. Most importantly, there was a basic flaw which I felt would reduce the corporation to nothing but another body dependent on, and therefore wholly under the control of, the government: there was no provision for it to raise funds to cover the deficit between what it earned from its commercial revenues and its actual yearly requirements. That gap was about Rs 800 crore, taking AIR and Doordarshan together. It would have to be given a grant from the government; in other words, we were back to square one. Nothing would really change, except that instead of being 'attached offices' AIR and Doordarshan would together become a corporation, but a corporation bound hand and foot to the Ministry of Information and Broadcasting.

I felt very strongly that, if it was to be a corporation, Prasar Bharati should be a real corporation, free of government control and with its own source of revenue. There seemed to me only one way this could be done, namely, by reviving the licence fee that used to be levied on radio and television sets at levels that reflected present-day conditions—say, Rs 100 a year for a radio set and Rs 1000 a year for a colour television set. That was, for television, not really a great deal; it was less than Rs 100 a month, and for that the owner would get to see an increasing number of channels, films and other programmes. Assuming there were then 6 crore television sets in the country, it would mean Rs 6000 crore every year from the television licence fee alone. Add the amount from radio sets—there were some 12 crore radio sets, which would mean an annual amount of Rs 1200 crore—and the new corporation wouldn't have to look anywhere else for revenues, not even to advertising. It would be wholly and completely independent, able to produce just the kind of programmes it wanted to and felt it should broadcast. It would, at last, be able to fulfil its mission as a public service broadcaster.

I took the idea to the principal secretary to the prime minister, A.N. Verma. He listened to me carefully, but then said that with elections approaching it simply would not be possible to consider introducing a measure that was bound to be unpopular, and thus give the opposition a stick with which to beat the government. I then put to him my second proposal: a small cess on the purchase of white goods like refrigerators, washing machines, air-conditioners and the like, because, I explained, any household that has these is bound to have a television set as well. Verma said he would talk to the finance secretary and get back to me. He didn't dismiss it out of hand, which I felt was a hopeful sign.

He did send for me a few weeks later, but the news was depressing. The Ministry of Finance had said it could not be done; if they put a cess on white goods for Prasar Bharati, all sorts of other agencies would demand that they, too, be financed in the same way. I asked Verma if we could levy a one-time licence fee on each new television and radio set. It would not be as much as Rs 7000 crore but would still be a substantial amount, given the number of radios and television sets being sold every year. Forget it, he said. The prime minister wasn't going to consider such measures till the elections were over.

That, then, was that. If Prasar Bharati was to come into existence, it would be as a hand-maiden of the government, autonomous only in name. It would give government bureaucrats something to pat themselves on the back about—they would be seen as furthering the cause of autonomy for the electronic media. But in actual fact both AIR and Doordarshan would remain just the same, except that there would be a board to oversee their work, which was a luxury that they could do well without. I decided that I was not going to do a thing to give birth to this sad creature. Very cold storage, Narasimha Rao had said. I would make sure it was very cold indeed.

Prasar Bharati did subsequently come into existence, thanks to the insistence of Jaipal Reddy, who was I & B minister under the short-lived government headed by I.K. Gujral. There wasn't much that needed to be done, actually; he merely needed to issue an order under the Prasar Bharati Act declaring the date on which it would come into being. I think he knew the problems that would have to be sorted out if the new corporation was to function with any kind of efficiency and autonomy. But perhaps he felt he would be able to handle all that later; he just wanted it established first. After that shaky government fell, the corporation has suffered exactly the fate I feared it would: it lives on handouts from the government. Worse, its advertising revenues are falling steadily, so its dependence on the government is even more pronounced.

It would be worthwhile at this stage to look at a survey of public service broadcasters conducted by the management consultants, McKinsey (*The McKinsey Quarterly*, Q4 1999). The survey looked closely at several public service broadcasters—including SVT in Sweden, BBC in the UK, F3 and F2 in France, ARD and ZDF in Germany, CBC in Canada, ABC in Australia, NHK in Japan and fourteen others—and assessed where they stood in relation to the other television channels in those countries. The survey found that, on the whole, public service broadcasters were not only the dominant broadcasters in their countries, but they also controlled the markets, the quality and content of programmes. McKinsey identified some of the factors responsible for this; chief among them was that these broadcasters were able to spend very large amounts of money on programmes and on their networks, but none of them were profligate. In fact, many of them were actively engaged in a more or less continuous cost-cutting exercise to keep their organizations as lean and effective as possible. The most successful public service broadcasters were dependent neither on state funds nor on advertising. Both these sources of funds, the McKinsey study stated, tended to pressure the networks in different ways, thus diverting them from their primary mission, which was to inform, educate, entertain and enlighten their audiences. Most networks received funds through licence fees, though the amount varied from 100 per cent in the case of NHK to only 18 per cent in the case of SABC (South Africa's public service network). The McKinsey report pointed out that networks which received more than 70–80 per cent of their funds through licence fees were the most dominant in their countries, as they were able to function free from any kind of pressure or obligation. In these cases the government kept scrupulously away from any kind of involvement with the running of the networks. On the other hand, the survey revealed that those public service networks that received a large proportion of their revenues from advertising—TVNZ in New Zealand, SABC in South Africa, TV2 in Denmark and RTVE in Spain—were qualitatively not in the same league as the others, since they necessarily had to make more commercially popular programmes in order to attract advertising away from the private channels.

There are two exceptions to these findings, which are unique cases that do not, on their own, prove anything except the basic attitudes towards public broadcasting in their respective countries. They are ABC in Australia and CBC in Canada, both of which are almost wholly funded by the state. In spite of this, however, there is no government interference in their operation. Indeed, the news bulletins of these networks and their current affairs programmes are often sharply critical of the government.

The McKinsey report concluded that if public service networks were to continue to hold their present overweening positions in the television market in their respective countries, they would have to continue to obtain funding from licence fees and avoid accepting both advertising revenues and government grants. In addition, the state should keep completely away from any involvement with the networks and their functioning. Only then would they be able to perform the mission they had all been given.

Contrast this to the current state of Prasar Bharati. It can hardly be said to dominate the television market, its claims to have the widest reach notwithstanding. It has set up a large number of terrestrial transmitters, true, and its signal reaches areas where the cable and satellite signals of private channels do not. But what Doordarshan does not acknowledge is that in these remote areas the population is relatively scanty and not everyone has a television set. It also does not say that where there are large concentrations of people, in cities and towns where there are cable and satellite systems, Doordarshan's share of the audience is extremely low, except for special events like a cricket match or the live telecast of the Republic Day parade. This is in spite of the ministry imposing a must-carry condition in all cable operators' licences, which makes it obligatory for operators to carry at least two Doordarshan channels on their prime bands.

In my day, Doordarshan was what is known in government jargon as an 'attached' office; in other words, it was an office of the Ministry of Information and Broadcasting where the head, the DG, had more powers than a 'subordinate' office. Yet, in a number of matters he had to seek ministry approval, even though the Doordarshan Code, duly approved by the ministry and all the other ministries concerned, including the Ministry of Finance, stated that the DG would have 'all the powers of a Central ministry'. According to the code, the DG needed to take the ministry's approval only if he wanted to create posts with a salary higher than that of an under secretary, or if he wanted to reappropriate a sum in excess of Rs 1 crore from one head to another, or if he wanted to write off things worth more than Rs 25 crore.

These sweeping powers notwithstanding, the fact is that, given the financial restrictions imposed from time to time on the creation of posts, and the limits on expenditure and virtually everything else, the Ministry of Finance in effect has transferred all these powers to either the financial adviser in the ministry or to itself. 'Adviser' is, as every bureaucrat knows, a euphemism; 'controller' is a more correct designation. And even in the ministry, the financial adviser has a rather curious position; he is subordinate to the secretary, but can disagree with him on financial matters, and if the secretary overrules him he can refer the matter to the Ministry of Finance, which can and often does uphold the view of the financial adviser. His confidential report—the one way in which control over subordinate officers is ensured in government—is written by the secretary, true, but it is also written by the secretary (expenditure) in the Ministry of Finance. No prizes for guessing whose report prevails in matters relating to final grading, promotion and all the rest, or for guessing who appoints financial advisers to different ministries.

Given the iron grip the Ministry of Finance has over the functioning of all ministries and their offices, most of the DG's powers in Doordarshan are only notional. In this kind of situation, his proposals can be blown away by the Ministry of Finance—as happened to my proposal for the Doordarshan Society—and much of what he wants done can be blocked. He can't buy the equipment he wants because the financial adviser decides just what should be bought and in what quantities. He can commission programmes, but when payments have to be made, the financial adviser and his subordinates decide whether to pay and how much.

A favourite argument of many I & B ministers, a rather tired argument at that, is that it is the minister who has to face Parliament on the working of Prasar Bharati, so if he has to take responsibility he must have a say in what the network does. None of them have bothered to look at the manner in which this issue has been dealt with in Britain. Why Britain? Well, our political leaders never cease to remind us that our parliamentary democracy is based on the 'Westminster' model, so if this is true, why not see just how Westminster has handled the issue of answerability as far as the BBC is concerned?

The House of Commons has a committee on broadcasting which meets regularly and before which the chairman of the board of governors and the DG of the BBC have to appear and answer the most detailed and searching questions. They are often criticized and that, too, sharply—I have heard friends in the BBC say that after one of the committee's sessions the DG came out 'white and trembling'. The committee prepares a report that is placed before Parliament. No questions are asked in Parliament on the BBC's functioning, or why a particular programme was shown; on the rare occasions when there are such questions, the minister of culture (earlier it used to be the home secretary) promises to get a report from the BBC and place it before the House. The minister never takes any responsibility for the functioning of the BBC and neither do the MPs expect him to.

An excellent example of how this works in the UK can be seen in the clash, in 2003, after the invasion of Iraq, between the BBC and the government over a report that the government had allegedly 'sexed up' an intelligence brief. It erupted into the prime minister calling the BBC a liar and demanding an apology, and the BBC calling the prime minister a liar and refusing to apologize. A tragic consequence of this was that the person who was apparently the source from whom the BBC correspondent had got his story was exposed and later committed suicide. A judicial enquiry was ordered and Lord Hutton, the Lord Chief Justice of Northern Ireland, was critical of the BBC's way of handling the story. As a consequence, the chairman of the board of governors, the DG and the correspondent in question, Andrew Gilligan, all resigned. Earlier the prime minister's director of communications, Alastair Campbell, who had been identified by the BBC as the key figure in the whole murky business, had also resigned. The acting chairman offered Prime Minister Tony Blair a kind of apology and the prime minister, on his part, declared publicly that it was enough and, that as far as he was concerned, the matter was closed. About a month or two later the British government appointed a new chairman of the board of governors—not a political hanger-on, but a professional broadcaster who had spent many years in the BBC before moving to Channel 4.

Would this ever have happened in India? The answer is obvious. No government is ever going to let go of the electronic media, and there will never be a dearth of servile, cunningly ambitious, petty-minded officers in the government who will be willing to head the media or the corporation and carry out their masters' commands. A genuine public service broadcasting network will never be established in India; only a government-controlled 'national' network can be, and already has been.

There is a further and more serious issue on which the government has studiously avoided taking action. This has its origins in a judgement of the supreme court delivered in 1995. Doordarshan had entered into an agreement with a firm called WorldTel to telecast the 1996 World Cup cricket matches, an agreement that was cleared by the ministry. Later the company demanded the satellite rights, which Ratikant Basu rightly said he couldn't agree to give, and this matter eventually came up before the supreme court. As secretary, I was the appellant. In the event the appeal was dismissed but the judgement itself, delivered by a division bench of the court consisting of Justice P.B. Sawant, Justice S. Mohan and Justice B.P. Jeevan Reddy, contained some directions and rulings that are not only seminal but make the working of Prasar Bharati legally rather shaky.

The majority judgement given by Justices Sawant and Mohan said, in part:

> The airwaves or frequencies are a public property. Their use has to be controlled and regulated by a public authority in the interests of the public and to prevent an invasion of their rights. Since the electronic media involve the use of the airwaves, this factor creates an in-built restriction on their use as in the case of any other public property.
>
> The right to impart or receive information is a species of the right of freedom of speech and expression guaranteed by Article 19 [1] (a) of the Constitution. A citizen has a fundamental right to use the best means of imparting and receiving information and as such to have an access to telecasting for the purpose. However, this right to have access to telecasting has limitations on account of the use of the public property, viz., the airwaves, involved in the exercise of the right and can be regulated and controlled by the public authority. This limitation imposed by the nature of the public property involved in the use of the electronic media is in addition to the restrictions imposed on the right to freedom of speech and expression under Article 19 [2] of the Constitution.
>
> The Central Government shall take immediate steps to establish an independent autonomous public authority representative of all sections and interests in the society to control and regulate the use of the airwaves.
>
> *(Civil Appeal Nos. 1429–30 of 1995 [Arising out of SLP [Civil] Nos.*

18532–33 of 1993] The Secretary, Ministry of Information & Broadcasting, Government of India and Ors. versus *Cricket Association of Bengal & Ors. With W.P. [Civil] No. 836 of 1993 Cricket Association of Bengal and Anr.* versus *Union of India & Ors.)*

By virtue of this judgement the right to use the airwaves has become a fundamental right available to any citizen of India and not necessarily the prerogative of institutions and organizations like Prasar Bharati. By the same token, Section 4 of the Telegraph Act, that ancient relic of colonial times, which asserts that the government has the 'exclusive privilege' of broadcasting in the country, obviously becomes null and void. In other words, the government no longer has a legal right to broadcast; it can only do so if it is licensed by a public authority that is independent and autonomous. However, so far no one has taken this up with the courts and drawn their attention to the fact that the government has not acted on its directions even after ten years.

I mention this because this supreme court judgement gives the government a wonderful opportunity to set up a public authority and refashion Prasar Bharati into a truly autonomous body funded publicly through a licence fee. This would represent an act of great statesmanship and give the country something it has never had before: a public service broadcasting network that over time would almost certainly produce fine programmes which would attract large audiences and set standards that private commercial channels would have to follow if they wanted a share of the audience. This is not a flight of fancy. If our space research agency, which has much more autonomy and freedom of action than other bodies of the government, can produce work of international quality, such as sophisticated satellites and long-range rockets capable of putting satellites in space, there is no reason to think something of the same kind cannot happen in television programming.

Epilogue

The Show Must Go On

I never went back to north Bengal again, to the dark, vivid green of the fields, the tangled forests and the tall mountains behind which the white tops of the higher Himalayas rose into the cold air. After I left the government, I stayed on in Delhi and found a new occupation as a columnist. I wrote only occasionally about the media, and still avoid writing too many columns on Doordarshan or Prasar Bharati. Not because of any awkwardness or imagined sense of having been wronged, but because I find I have no wish to talk about something that I no longer recognize. I watch the Doordarshan channels occasionally, as do so many others, and I have to admit they have changed a great deal.

There is, for one thing, a relatively more 'finished' look to the Doordarshan channels. The earlier erratic airing of programmes with a caption held for an interminably long time, or that famous '*Rukavat ke liye khed hai*' board which became a standing joke throughout the country, are now infrequent. Occasionally there is a new slickness, and the switchovers from programmes to advertisements or promos and back to programmes are smooth. This was started by Basu, who worked with some outfits that dealt with computer software until he was able to eliminate manual switching from programmes to advertisements and so on. But whatever its origin, it has certainly made these Doordarshan channels sometimes look as good as the private channels.

I wish I could say the same about the content. Of the few programmes I have seen, I have found the serials dull, mawkish, poorly acted and produced. This is, of course, true of many others on the private channels, but my book is not about the private channels. Some of the current affairs programmes are not bad, but again these are made by outside producers like Nalini Singh and others. There is a curious channel called DD Bharati that I watched for a time with the kind of fascination one has for something weird, like an animal with two heads. I have not been able to work out why cultural, health and children's programmes should be put together in one channel. The logic escapes me. Also why the programmes are so bad—the cultural programmes are artificial, awkward and downright mediocre and the health programmes ponderously didactic. Surely, even if this odd mix has to continue, the content can be served up better.

The newly started DD News began, as far as I am concerned, on a tragic note. It was started by shutting off DD Metro, surely one of the most foolish decisions that the makers of programme policy have ever made. DD Metro was never meant to be anything other than a channel for light entertainment, for the sort of stuff that people are expected to watch on television channels. Serials, talk shows, music and 'disco' shows that seem to be the rage, quiz programmes and so on. It was showing programmes of that sort and was making Doordarshan some money. Yes, it did bring up that old question—is this what Doordarshan is supposed to show?—but it wasn't doing too badly. To shut it down was short-sighted.

But having said that, one has to add almost immediately that DD News was initially very watchable. It was professionally presented; its reports came in from all over and were up-to-date, sometimes on-the-spot, stuff; and the discussion programmes were surprisingly lively. But this didn't last. And the reason for it having been set up at a cost of some Rs 80 or 90 crore (Rs 54 crore was given by the government to Prasar Bharati for the channel and to that one has to add the revenues which were coming in from DD Metro) was soon clear enough. The channel was set up to aid the NDA in its election campaign. It was the usual fallacy of a ruling party or coalition—television appears to them to be a sure way of getting votes, or at least, that's what their media advisers tell them. And they're always totally wrong. Television by itself never gets anyone votes. I had made this clear often enough to P.A. Sangma, not because I was an all-seeing, omniscient being but because I had had my nose rubbed into the truth of this on more than one occasion. But of course, K.S. Sarma was not going to tell his masters as much when officiating as DG during the general elections of 1996 and had worked assiduously to make little promotional programmes for Narasimha Rao.

Consequently all that DD News does is to go on and on about the government's achievements, its plans and programmes, and get people to comment on them. The trouble is that the Prasar Bharati authorities seem to have forgotten that DD News is not the only news channel that viewers have access to. And it's a channel that I, for one, have stopped watching, because the element of credibility with which it began has slipped away, and there are other, more credible channels to watch.

Stepping back a bit, then, and looking at what Doordarshan is now purveying to its viewers, one has to conclude that it is now truly a state-controlled broadcaster, a large element of whose content consists of propaganda for the ruling government's different ministries and offices. And even within this definition everyone knows that state governments that are in the hands of parties other than the ruling party at the Centre can never hope to get any of their programmes shown. One thing is certain: Doordarshan is not and cannot in its present form ever be a public service broadcaster. Its only link with public service broadcasting is the occasional documentary programme it airs made by the Public Service Broadcasting Trust, usually at 10.30 p.m. or on Sunday mornings or at any other time they find convenient.

What is truly tragic is that there are really good television people in Doordarshan—producers, engineers, editors, cameramen—all of whom have learnt that invaluable skill of making do with what they have, of doing a good job with inadequate or outdated equipment. And outside, there are fine officers in the civil service who could be taken into Doordarshan or Prasar Bharati to give it a dimension of good management. Good television people aren't always good managers; in fact real professionals are usually terrible at managing a station, let alone a giant network like Doordarshan. One can also look to corporate houses, or pick out professional managers from other agencies, if the government is prepared to pay the kind of salaries corporate houses do. The point is that there is enough talent in the country to run

Doordarshan well and make it one of the best public networks internationally.

I continue to live in hope. That hope and expectation with which I came from the rain-drenched foothills of the Himalayas to take charge of a new, exciting medium of communication hasn't really gone. There is, at the back of my mind, a hope, if not a conviction, that one day there will be a change of heart—that the government and Parliament will see the virtue of a television network that is dependent on neither state finances nor advertising and therefore is not bound to yield to pressures from either, a television network that is left free to decide what kind of programmes it will make to represent truly and further the original mission it was given. This change of heart will bring in a new determination, and the final links and controls will, like the jesses on a falcon, be removed, and the bird will finally be given the freedom to fly to its own destiny.

Acknowledgements

This is not a definitive history of Doordarshan. All I have done is recount my days there as DG and my involvement with it during my stint as secretary, I & B. To enable me to write this memoir, a large number of people helped me with material and stories which enriched my narrative, or stimulated memories that had receded into the dark, musty recesses of my mind. Among them I am particularly grateful to Mira Mozoomdar, Sadhan Mullick, Bibhas Chakravarti and Abhijit Dasgupta who took time off to tell me how Doordarshan developed, fascinating and diverting me with accounts that sometimes ranged from the droll to the farcical.

I am also grateful to Shashi Kant Kapoor, Jai Chandiram, Shiv Sharma and many others in the Doordarshan family, both engineers and programme officers, for a host of memories, and during my days as DG for advice when I was beset with the most bizarre problems and for extending a helping hand when I needed it.

I would also like to pay a special tribute to the late Madan Mohan, former engineer-in-chief, who was a mentor, colleague and friend.

I am very grateful to Diya Kar Hazra of Penguin India who not only persuaded me to write this book when I had decided I would never write a book as long as I lived, but also for always being supportive, calming me down when I threw tantrums, which I did every so often, giving me a huge amount of encouragement and actually making me believe I could write. I am also very grateful to Sumitra Srinivasan for her patience and forbearance. But for them and the team at Penguin this would have been even less of a book than it is.

Index